S0-CBA-930

Journey to Chimane Land

Dino and Elaine Kempf

This book is a true treasure trove of cultural information and inspirational stories of spiritual renewal for an unreached tribe. Readers interested in world missions and South American indigenous culture will find this book to be a true page turner. Not only do the authors keep readers engaged with stories of struggle and triumph in their forty years of missionary work in an indigenous culture, but they also collect information about the culture of the area, and recount the work of the missionaries who preceded them.

The book contains a wonderful mixture of narrative elements, from the author's own story, to the primary-source writings and letters of the missionaries who worked with the Chimane before them, to dramatizations of primitive life in the Chimane tribe prior to missionary interaction. The authors make each chapter come to life with well-crafted storytelling, making characters and scenes pop off the page, often times with a healthy dose of good humor. The many photos also help paint the picture of the book's vivid setting. Finally, the helpful subheadings within each chapter are both imaginative and informative.

Journey to Chimane Land

Journey to Chimane Land

By

Dino and Elaine Kempf

Journey to Chímane Land
by Dino and Elaine Kempf

Printed in the United States of America.

ISBN 9781498499118

www.xulonpress.com

Dino and Elaine Kempf.

Ecclesiastes, 3:1
To every thing there is a season, and a time to every purpose under the heaven:

Table of Contents

Part Three

Note from the Authors

The account we give in the beginning of this writing is an attempt to help you understand the people who lived in the rain forest long before any explorer, priest, or anyone else could have given us a record of what had been passed down to them through generations.

This is the Chimanes' story, and it is our story because, as it turns out, our story and their story became intertwined with each other.

The story is an amazing account of God's plan and His timing, and how a young couple from Washington State heard a missionary tell about his work in Bolivia, South America. He said, "God could use any life willing to serve Him, that it is not our ability or inability; it is our availability." They told God that they were available and wound up in South America living in the tropical rain forest of Bolivia.

They share how it was to live back in the time much like the early days of American history. It was a time of cowboys and horses, riding in oxcarts, and traveling in canoes on the Maniqui River. They tell about the challenge of working among a scattered group of indigenous people with an unwritten language, how the people's problems became their problems, and God's intervention for them.

Foreword

This is an important and fascinating story that needs to be told, and I am glad Dean and Elaine have taken the time and effort to put the story into print.

I first met Dean and Elaine in 1970. I was the new, young pastor of the First Presbyterian Church of Centralia, Washington, and someone had invited the Kempfs to speak at the monthly meeting of the couples' group at the church. I remember how impressed I was with them and the sacrifices they were making to live and work among the Chimanes in Bolivia. I especially remember that they were living in a hut with a dirt floor, while we were having a beautiful new home with a view built.

Some years later, I got a call from Dale Hamilton, Dean's brother-in-law, that the Kempfs were coming home quite discouraged. They had bought a large piece of property outside of San Borja with the dream of turning it into an educational center where the Chimanes could come from their small settlements up and down the rivers. There they would learn to read and write, as well as be instructed in the truths of God's Word. The whole enterprise would be self-supporting, with classes in the mornings and farm work in the afternoons. The sale of the crops and produce would cover all the expenses of the program.

Unfortunately, it didn't work out very well. The farm didn't produce like Dean hoped, and inflation and the drug traffic ruined the Bolivian economy. I called many of the pastors in Centralia and Chehalis and was able to line up speaking dates for the Kempfs and to get the project into their church mission budgets. I also helped Dale Hamilton set up the San Borja Farm and Christian Training Center Board as a non-profit corporation to raise money for the project. The board met three times a year for well over twenty years and raised substantial sums each year for the program. When Dale eventually resigned, I took over the leadership, and even after leaving the Centralia church, I came down from Seattle for the board meetings for many years.

In the early 1990s, I was able to visit San Borja with my son-in-law and see the project in action. We stayed with Wayne and Ruth Gill at La Cruz and Bruce and Jan Johnson at Horeb. The 6-week classes were in session at each grade level. Len Gill was teaching an afternoon leadership-training class. In the evening, all the Chimane families gathered for singing of Christian songs and a Bible lesson taught by one of the men in the leadership-training class. We made a run into the little hospital in town with Dean's brother, Frank, and his wife, Soledad, who had a great ministry caring for the sick and injured. All in all, it was an amazing week, and we were deeply impressed with the comprehensive education, Christian training, and care which the Chimanes were receiving under Dean and Elaine's ministry.

The crowning evidence for me was the answer to a question I directed at Jorge Añez, the young president of the Chimane Tribal Council. Our visit was not long after 1992, the 500th anniversary of Columbus landing in the Americas, when world-wide attention was focused on the rights and plight of aboriginal and tribal people in Central and South America. Jorge had represented the Chimanes at a number of major consultations and meetings with the leaders of all the other tribal peoples of Bolivia. In fact, there was one meeting where they had all been brought to the United States. Dean translated my question, "Now that you have gotten acquainted with the leaders of the other tribes of Bolivia, how would you compare the development and advancement of the Chimanes with them?"

Jorge didn't hesitate with his answer. "Oh, we are more advanced than any of the other tribes." I was amazed. The Quechuas and other highland tribes had had schools for over a century, and here was the young leader of what had been a primitive stone-age tribe only a few short years before claiming that his tribe was now the most advanced tribe in the nation. Even allowing for a little pride and prejudice, this statement was absolutely astounding, and I continue to see it as the greatest tribute I can think of to the remarkable ministry of Dean and Elaine Kempf. I count it a privilege to have had a small part in their ministry.

Dr. Ronald B. Rice – April 2016

Acknowledgments

We dedicate this book to our five children: Lori, Darrel, Randy, Dixie, and Ben who shared the journey with us, and to our eleven grandchildren: Gabe, Ines, Brittany, Brianna, Courtney, Gracie, Savanna, Dax, Kelvin, Milo, and Ethan. We want you to know that the hardest part of our missionary life has been the time apart from all of you while you were growing up. We love you all very much.

These written words will still remain when we grandparents have gone, so read this book to our great-grandkids.

We also want to give special recognition and our thanks to:

- Claire Teague, who edited this book. We appreciate her dedication and effort. We shared our information with her, and she made it possible for us to share our story with this book.
- Anne Hall, who has been involved from start to finish in helping us write this book.
- Mike Neeley, who not only said we should write a book, but actually got us started and encouraged us along the way.
- Casey Hill, for all of his help.
- Ines Gardilcic, our granddaughter, who designed the cover for this book.
- Betty Galambos, who put the finishing touches on our work.

All Scripture is from the Authorized King James Bible.

General Map of Bolivia.

Introduction

Dean writes:

I was cut out to be a preacher but sewn together wrong and instead became a missionary to a group of tribal people called Chimanes living in the tropical lowlands of Bolivia, South America.

Dean and canoes.

For years my wife, Elaine, and I canoed and camped along the Maniqui River stopping at Chimane settlements and living among them in makeshift shelters with open walls, leaf roofs, palm mats, wood fire pits, and mosquito nets. We taught the Chimanes who wanted to learn how to read.

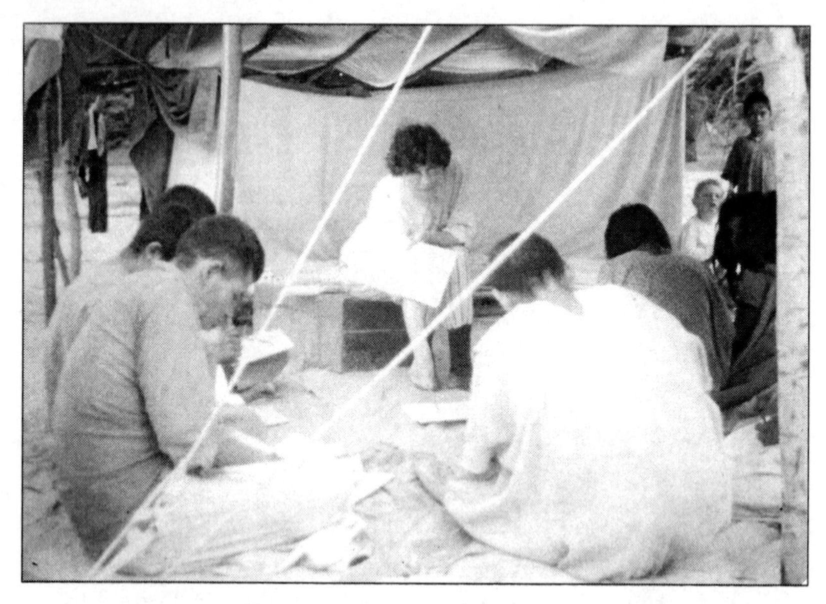

Elaine teaching a literacy class.

How did my wife, Elaine, and I get involved in missionary work anyway? Why did God choose us?

If you remember the story of Samuel, he had little choice in the matter of service to God. His mother promised him to God, and this is also what happened to me. I only learned of Mother's bargain with God after returning from the mission field on our first furlough. We were talking, and I said, "Mom, one of the greatest surprises to me has been that most of our Christian friends seem shocked that I would go to the mission field."

"I wasn't shocked or surprised," she responded. "I knew that you would go. When you were about a year-and-a-half old, you were dying of pneumonia. The doctor told us that there was no hope. In desperation, I cried out to God and promised Him that if He would spare your life, I would give you to Him as a missionary. God did spare your life, and I knew that someday He would claim the promise I made to Him."

As we look back, we can see how God brought these circumstances about. Before we went to Bolivia, we knew nothing about that country. We never dreamed that we would ever live there. Once we arrived in Bolivia, we had no idea as to what area or what people group to go to.

It was not as if those who lived in darkness were reaching out and searching for God. It was in no way man's doing.

People in darkness.

In His time, God looked down on this scattered tribe of tormented humanity and decided to have mercy on them and show them His grace.

Chimane woman

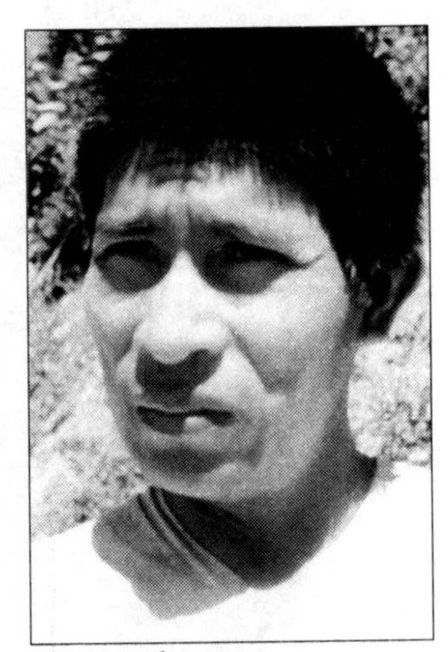

Chimane man

This book gives you an insight into how the Chimane people of the rain forest lived, and how God brought them to Jesus Christ. You may never get to visit the rain forest of Bolivia, but you can get a glimpse of it without the bugs, mosquitoes, ants, snakes, dangerous animals, or the hot, humid weather and monsoon rains of the tropics.

Man and son.

The Chimane boy is wearing clothing that has been washed in the river many times; his father is wearing new clothing that has never been washed in the brown water of the Maniqui River.

Chimane woman carrying thin bamboo to weave into mats on which to sleep.

PART ONE

Chapter 1

Life in Chimane Land Long Ago

Some of the earliest records we have were written by priests, so the story begins with a priest's account of what life was like for him many years ago, and also what it might have been like for the Chimane people who lived during that time.

The priest sat sweating in his little shelter. The mosquitoes were humming around him, diving in from time to time to settle on his hands and face. The rest of his body was wrapped in a brown robe, his feet tucked under it to keep the mosquitoes off him. The smoky fire gave some relief. This was a world foreign to him.

It was a long time ago that he had left his home and traveled by sea and then over the mountains into this jungle land. Everything here was different: the huge, towering trees, and the vines, flowers, fruits, and nuts. Animals were in abundance with varieties that he had never known existed. The rivers were teeming with fish. There was plenty to eat, but there was also so much to fear; the flesh-eating piranhas, alligators, and jaguars were always there to attack an unwary animal or person. It seemed like such a hostile place. He was keeping a record of what he saw. He wanted his people to know about this place, even though he believed he would never see his homeland again. Maybe his letters would somehow reach his people. Maybe his knowledge could be preserved for those generations still to come.

The Priest's account:

Dear Brothers, my heart is filled with sadness. This land that is so hostile to me is the home of many tribal people. Where have they come from? Why so many different languages among them? How have they survived? They know all about living in their jungle where they live in harmony with nature. The jungle provides everything for them. They've learned to make bows and arrows, and are experts in using them. They know what plants they can use for food and medicine. They even know how to put the sap of a certain tree into the water to prevent the fish from breathing so they come to the surface of the water where the people can shoot them with their arrows–yet the meat is safe for the people to eat. But now the land has been invaded by strangers, and with them have come sicknesses that have never been here before.

The Chimanes are a big tribe; thousands of them live scattered throughout the jungles along the rivers and streams. They live in small family groups with houses made of leaf roofs and bamboo walls, if they even choose to have walls.

Now they have been infected with small pox. The riverbanks are full of the dead and dying. People flee hoping to escape the sickness, but this only spreads the disease to other places. If the small pox doesn't kill them, it will be the measles or something else. I do not believe this tribe will survive past this generation...

The Big River, Early Springtime

Miro waited patiently while Sachi gathered and packed in her carrying bag what they would need to take with them. She called to her son, Mauro, to hurry and finish eating his fish and roasted banana, and smiled as she lifted the sleeping baby in her little bark-cloth sling. "Come on, Kati. We are going hunting."

Miro called to his son, "Come on, Mauro. Let's get going. The monkeys are waiting for us." He then turned and his grandmother hugged him. She said, "Bring us back lots of meat, Miro, so we won't be hungry. Take good care of those dogs; they are the best hunters in the whole area."

The rest of the family joined in to give them a good send off, and then they started out.

Dago, Naina, and their little son, Dario, were waiting for them. Mauro and Dario, about the same age and good friends, greeted each other, happy to be going hunting. They carried their little bows and arrows with them. They had been taught to use the weapons almost as soon as they could walk, and were already mighty hunters of lizards and other small animals. Everyone was happy to be on their way. The ones staying behind watched as they walked away along the trail, looking forward to their return and anticipating the feast to come.

The Hunt

They hunted for weeks during the time of year when the big black monkeys were the fattest. The best hunting was along a far-off river where the Chimanes had, on previous hunts, planted banana trees so when they hunted, there would be something besides meat for them to eat. It was the Chimane way to clear land and plant fruit trees such as papaya, bananas, and oranges wherever they went in the jungle so that there would always be food for the future.

Sachi and Naina kept a close eye on the meat roasting on the fire as Mauro and Dario played in the clearing outside of their little leaf shelter, and the baby swung peacefully in its little bark-cloth hammock.

It was getting dark. The women were getting worried because Miro and Dago hadn't yet come back, but then they heard the dogs barking and the men's voices. They smiled at each other, relieved to know that the men had returned.

On their backs, Miro and Dago carried slain monkeys. Miro called to the women, "We will have to hurry and get these roasted. We have a long trip ahead of us to get back to our home. The fresh meat will go bad before we get there, so we will have to roast it tonight. We must get an early start in the morning."

That evening everyone had plenty to eat. Even the dogs lying around the smoke of the fire, seeking some relief from the constant attacks of the mosquitoes, got a share. Miro told the women to be very careful to keep all the bones away from the dogs. "Remember that Grandfather told us that any bones left lying around would cause the game to flee the area, and this is too good of a hunting area to have something like that happen."

The Trip Back To the Big River

"Come on, everyone. Let's get going. We have a long way to go, and these bags are heavy with roasted monkey meat."

They started out through the jungle with Miro leading the way. Despite the lack of real trails, Miro seemed somehow to know where he was going. They traveled until dark, made a cold camp, slept awhile, and started again in the early morning.

One night they stopped a little earlier to start a fire and re-heat the roasted meat so that it would not spoil. They were near the Big River now and were excited about returning to their relatives who would be happy to help eat all this good monkey meat.

It rained in the night, and since there was no shelter, they were wet and cold when they set out early. Finally, it looked as if the sun was trying to come out. It was still raining, but not as hard. Suddenly, they saw a terrifying sight. The rainbow was there in the sky, right where they were going. What could it mean? Everyone knows that the rainbow is evil. It can bewitch you. Bad things happen when you see a rainbow.

As they neared the place where their relatives lived, they saw a barrier of thorns blocking the trail. They stared, and Sachi reached out her hand. "Miro, what is it? Has someone died?"

"This trail goes to the house of your parents. We can't go across the barrier. It is to keep the dead spirits from returning to harm our village."

"Can you see their hut?" she asked.

Miro answered, "It isn't there. It has been burned. Someone has died. A barrier is erected when someone dies. Come on. Let's go around to the other trail and find out what has happened."

They hurried over to the other side of the village, and, again, another barrier of thorns blocked the trail. Another hut had been burned. They called repeatedly, but no one answered. A few miserable dogs ran out and growled at them, but that was all. They could not cross the barrier of thorns, so they huddled together in their little group.

Finally, Miro said, "Let's go upriver to the next village to see if they can tell us what has happened."

"I'm really afraid," said Dago. "What has happened to our relatives? Where are they? This must have something to do with the rainbow we saw."

It took them an hour to arrive at the next village. Again, a barrier of thorns blocked the way, and one hut was still burning. Miro called, and a man came down the path. He looked ill. They stared at him. He could barely walk, and his face was covered with sores. He called out in a weak voice, "Go away. Flee from here. We are all dying. Go. Go now!"

Frantically, they ran to the river where they found a canoe. They started down river, horrified to see burned, and still burning, huts and dead bodies as they passed the places where people had lived.

Dago spoke everyone's thoughts. "Since our people always bury their dead, this could only mean that there was no one left alive to bury them."

Sachi and Naina were crying. "What can we do? Where shall we go?" The children were exhausted from the long days of walking. There seemed no safe place along the river.

Finally Miro decided, "We will go back to where we were hunting. There were bananas there, and we were not sick. We never saw the rainbow while we were there. We will go back."

They pulled over to the edge of the river and sadly started their weary way through the jungle. After several days' journey, they arrived back at the hunting camp just as the sun set. Everything was as they had left it. They were safe, at least for a season.

Although they mourned their dead family members and the happy life they left behind, they were silent in their grief. What the future held, they had no idea. They feared the sickness, and they feared the rainbow that could cause so much suffering. Tomorrow they would go hunting. They would have to be very careful not to offend the gods. As they sat around the fire, Miro said simply, "Let's get some rest. We will talk about it tomorrow."

Early the next morning, they could hear the monkeys chattering in the jungle. Miro and Dago talked together, then turned to the women, and Miro said to them, "First, we need to hunt and look for food, and then we will talk."

That night as they again sat around the fire, Sachi asked, "What are we going to do? We can't stay here much longer. When it starts to rain, the river will flood."

Dago spoke, "We must be careful not to displease the gods. The old Grandfather taught us, and we must teach the children.

"Miro, the Grandfather used to talk about a place called the Holy Hill. Do you think we could find it?" Sachi asked.

"I don't know," he answered. "The Grandfather had heard about it from another group. They believed that this was a special place that the gods had prepared for them. I don't know if Grandfather really believed that there was such a place. He said that he had hunted all over the jungle, and had never seen it. They said that there were lots of cattle, all kinds of fruit trees, and that it was a wonderful place. The Grandfather said that he never heard the cows, but sometimes he heard a bird that sounded like a cow and maybe that was it."

"We could look for it," Miro said. "We have to go somewhere. We will leave in the morning, and in the springtime, we will come back here. Then we will build a round spirit house here, and we will drink to the gods."

Journey to the River that Flows Backwards

Before daylight, Miro was already up and getting ready to leave. Sachi was worried. She turned to Miro and said, "I'm afraid. I know we can't stay here, but where will we go?"

Miro answered her. "Put some bananas on the fire to roast, and we'll talk. We can't stay here because it is too low; we have to find some place to live before the rains start. I had a dream last night. I saw the mountains. We will follow the river until we find higher ground. We will look for the Holy Hill. Maybe there is such a place. We will come back here when the monkeys are fat in the spring."

Sachi pulled the bananas from the coals of the fire, peeled them, and they ate them. She felt better. His dream was surely a good sign for them to leave here.

As the day was breaking, they were already on their way. They walked on the sandy beaches along the river, and then crossed the shallow water to the other side to walk on the next beach. The loads got heavy as they walked along. Sachi carried Kati in a carrying bag on her back. Mauro and Dario walked part of the time, and part of the time their parents took turns carrying them.

One morning Naina roasted the last of the bananas. "Dago," she said, "we have to stop to find more food. The bananas we carried are gone."

Dago said, "There are lots of fish in the river. We will stay here today."

Miro answered, "We will go hunting. You women stay here on the beach and stay together. We'll take the dogs. You keep the puppies with you. Watch them. We don't want to lose them. I don't like to leave you women and the children here alone, but I don't know what else to do. If you do go looking for food, don't go far. Break twigs as you go so you can find your way back, and so that we can find you if necessary. Be careful. I don't much like it here. I have seen a lot of jaguar tracks."

Dago and Miro had not gone far when the dogs took off running. Miro hollered, "Look, Dago! The dogs have already found something. They are digging over there by that hole."

"Acho, get over here. You are too good of a dog to lose."

"Let's take a look. There might be snakes in a hole like that."

"No, it is an armadillo, and Acho has a hold of it by its leg. Hold on there, Acho. We will get it out."

Miro grinned, "Good, there is our meal, but look, Dago. There's a broken twig. Let's look around. Here's another one. It looks like people have been through here. It has been a while ago, but I don't like it. Let's get back to the women. We can eat fish, and forget about other food for a while."

The men hurried back to camp. "Good, the women are here," said Dago. "It looks like they have found some good roots to eat. We'll roast the armadillo, and get an early start in the morning."

Sachi looked up from the fire. "Do we have to go tomorrow? We can find more food here to take with us."

"No," Dago said. "We will leave early tomorrow. We have found signs of people. Maybe they are friendly, but maybe not. We need to be careful, so we can't stay here. You know this land is low and swampy. We have to be on higher ground before the rains start. We don't know this country or how long it will take us to get to a safe place to live."

As they sat around the fire that night, Miro told Dago and Naina about his dream. "I had a dream that told me to go toward the mountains. There is a river that flows backwards. We will follow the river."

They had gathered plenty of wood to keep the fire going that night, but no one slept much. Miro got up to put more wood on the fire. "Listen." he said, "I hear something. It sounds like someone talking or laughing, but it is so dark that I cannot see anything."

"I am afraid!" cried Sachi holding Mauro tightly. "Who could it be?"

Naina drew Kati and Dario closer to the fire.

"I don't know," said Miro. "We will wait until light, and then see if we can find out who is on the other side of the river. We'll hear if they try to cross. Throw more wood on the fire. If it is an animal, it won't come near. If it is people, they already know we are here."

As the sun began to rise, Miro called softly, "Dago, let's go take a look. You women stay here. Don't wonder off."

They crossed the river, and Miro asked, "Dago, do you see any tracks?"

Dago answered, "Just tracks of the jaguar." The dogs were very nervous. The hair on their backs bristled as they sniffed around.

"I don't see any sign of people," Miro said in a nervous voice. "But it could be jaguar people. Some say that jaguars can turn into people. Let's get out of here. I don't like this place."

"I don't want to scare the women," said Dago. "We'll just say that we didn't find any sign of people. We don't know what the noise was. If they haven't thought about jaguar people, now isn't a good time to mention it."

The women were still waiting on the beach. They had roasted some edible roots in the coals for a quick meal before they gathered their things, took some of the coals from the fire with them, and started walking. That night they camped in a swamp where the mosquitoes were so terrible they had to dig holes in the ground so they could cover themselves with sand in order to sleep.

By the next day they were out of the swamp and were getting into hill country. First up one hill, then down, and then up another. They kept following the stream until they reached the River That Flows Backwards.

"It is just like your dream," said Sachi in wonder.

"Yes, this is it," replied Miro. "We will need to make a raft. Let's get a cooking fire going. Dago, you take the dogs hunting and see what you can find. Also look for some balsa to make the raft. You women get busy and find whatever you can for us to eat. We will be here a while, so I'm going to make us a shelter, and maybe I can shoot some fish."

They all spread out to do their separate tasks. It was nearly dark when the women came running, carrying a stalk of cooking bananas, some yuca, and papaya. Dago looked up in amazement.

"Look what we found!" Sachi shouted.

"What?" he asked. "Are there people?"

"No, we didn't see anyone," she answered. "We just came across a place in the jungle where there are big trees with fruit on them. Someone must have planted them a long time ago, but there is no sign of people now."

Naina smiled. "This is wonderful. We can stay here."

Dago answered, "Well, we can stay here at least for now. We will go ahead and build our raft. At least we know there is food here when we decide where we will live. Let's get back to our shelter."

As they sat around the fire that night, they decided to take turns keeping it burning. This seemed like a good place. There was food available, and they were in the hills so they wouldn't be flooded, but they were still uneasy. What had happened to the people who had planted the fruit trees? Who were they and where did they go?

Everyone else was asleep, and Miro was just throwing more wood on the fire when he heard something out in the jungle. He grabbed his bow and arrows and sat tensely, listening. The others woke and also sat listening. The dogs whined and stared out into the darkness, ears up and noses twitching.

It sounded like cattle. How could that be? Miro could hear them moving, could hear both calves and cows, and yet could not tell exactly where they were. It was impossible to tell if they were coming toward the camp or going away. He just knew there were cattle.

"Miro, remember what the Grandfather told us about the Holy Hill?" asked Sachi. "Do you think we may be near? Do you think we should go look for it?"

"Let's talk about it in the morning," Miro answered. "Dago, you keep the fire going, I'm going to sleep. Whatever we are hearing doesn't seem like it is going to harm us."

In the morning, Miro told them about the dream he had had that night. "As I slept, the voices spoke to me, 'Follow the river that flows backwards. Do not stay here. Find the woman with blue eyes. Maybe someday you will return. Many have searched for the Holy Hill and never found it. This is not the time for you to search.'"

That day they finished building the raft, and the next day they loaded it with the fruit and edible plants they had found in the jungle, and started their trip down the river.

They didn't see any sign of people. They just floated along where the current took them during the day and sleeping on the beaches at night. They were a little apprehensive. They still didn't know if there were any other people alive or if they were the only ones to survive. They had fruit and edible plants for now, and still time to clear some land to plant before the rains came.

They didn't know where they were going, but were hopeful that they were being guided.

Many times they talked about the dream of the woman with blue eyes. All of their people had dark eyes, both the men and women. They had never seen nor heard of a woman with blue eyes. Only Miro had once seen a man with blue eyes.

They traveled quite a few days on the River That Flowed Backwards until eventually they came to another river. They decided to take the raft down this river. As they floated along, they passed a number of other rivers that fed into this one. The water was no longer clear. It was a reddish color now, and they needed to be careful of log jams and sandbars.

One night they stopped early to find higher ground because it looked as if it might rain. They pulled the raft onto the shore of a little river and built a shelter. They were getting tired, their food was running low, and this seemed a good place to stay and do some hunting.

Early the next morning they heard voices, which caused the dogs to start barking. They saw a canoe with three men in it coming down the little river. Dago said, "Look. They are dressed like us. They have their bows and arrows with them, and a couple of small dogs that are barking back at our dogs. They seem to be as afraid of us as we are of them."

One of the men yelled at the dogs to be quiet. It was a miracle; they understood what he said. He was speaking their language. Miro shouted a greeting to them. "You are the first people that we have seen since leaving our village. We are relieved to know that we aren't the only ones to survive. "

Still, the men in the canoe did not come close. They were not unfriendly or threatening, but seemed afraid until Miro told them how he and his party had come to be there. He told about the sickness and the people dying, about the dreams, and about being guided here to this place. He told them about looking for the woman with blue eyes. That is when the men quit being afraid. They said to wait by the river until they returned to their people and could bring back another canoe.

When Miro, Dago and their families arrived at the village, they found the group waiting by the river bank. It was a very typical settlement much like the one where they had lived by the Big River. The Chimanes never live in big groups, always in smaller groups scattered along the river mostly with relatives that they feel they can trust. They were welcomed by the group, and then they saw her standing with a smile on her face: the woman with blue eyes. Her name was Santa.

Miro said, "We have found our people. We have come home."

The Story of the Woman with Blue Eyes:

A long time ago my relatives lived in a beautiful place. There was a small river of clear water. The land was high and fertile, and whatever we planted grew in abundance. The bananas grew for years; all we needed to do was keep them cleaned out. The other fruit trees were also loaded with fruit. There was plenty to eat and very little sickness. It was a wonderful time.

Then one day three men came to our beautiful place, and our way of life changed forever. Two of them wore brown robes; their skin was light and they had blue eyes. The other man was their guide.

We were not afraid of them. We had heard about the Brown Robes, and what we had heard was good. They spoke a language that we could not understand, but they had papers with some of our words on them. They would look at the paper and try talking to us. They told us that one of our gods, Michet, had sent them to us. Of course, we listened to them. Michet is a god that could do a lot of harm if we did not do what he said.

We built them a little house, and they lived among us. We called them Pahi Kose and Pahi Xavier. Pahi Kose was a good man; he was kind and took care of us if we were hurt. He taught us how to do many things that were new to us, and he played beautiful music with a bow that he drew across the strings of a small wooden instrument. He even taught some of us to play it.

He helped us to make our own instruments out of wood from the jungles. Of course, our instruments were not as beautiful as his, but we could make music.

Man playing a Chimane-made violin.

One of our people did learn to play by watching and listening to Pahi Kose and then he would play the same beautiful music. The Pahi was very impressed, and when he was dying, he told the man to take his violin and keep playing beautiful music. We buried Pahi Kose beside the river, and Mario played the music for him. We missed Pahi Kose. He was truly a good man. We called him Relative as he was truly one of us.

It did not take us long to see that the guide wasn't like them. His name was Reuben. He did not treat us well. He mistreated our women and beat up our men. We were afraid of him and his weapons. We were a peaceful people and tried to stay out of trouble by ignoring him. So our lives went on. We planted and harvested, hunted and fished, and, from time to time, we would celebrate our special days by making big vats of chicha. We would get together to dance, laugh, drink, and have a happy time. We would drink all night, passing the gourd from one to another.

Then Reuben started drinking with us. He would get very drunk and very mean. There would be fights, and he would grab a woman and sleep with her. He made the women make him chicha. He would have them cook it and then chew it up and spit it back into the brew. This made it very strong. He drank all the time.

Pahi Xavier was very different. He was a quiet, stern man who would often get angry. He began to change after Pahi Kose died. He seemed very bitter about things. He talked a lot to the god Michet. He told us that Michet had told him to sprinkle us with water. He then took all of our babies and sprinkled them with water, and gave them all new names.

Then he started drinking chicha with Reuben. He would get drunk, too, and once he got drunk, it was as though he could not stop drinking. He got really mean when he was drunk. He started sleeping with our daughters. He would pick out the prettiest of them that had never been with a man and tell us that Michet told him to do it. These women were set aside for Michet, and none of our men were to have them. We were afraid of Michet. He wasn't our Father God, but he was one of the brothers and had always been a troublemaker. He was a drunkard and even slept with his brother's wife, so it didn't surprise us that Michet was telling the Pahi to do these things.

One day the Pahi called us together, and told us that Michet had told him that he wanted us to build a big house so we could worship him there. The men would have to go out and bring in logs with which to build it. He told the women to go and gather the leaves to make the roof. Reuben was put in charge of the men.

We did not want to build this house for them; we had our own work to do. We didn't know how to make a big house; we had always made little houses. Reuben took his whip and beat us. He would tie some of us together so we could work, but not run away. We had to leave our own work to build the big house for him. They sent some men out to hunt for all of us, but our men no longer hunted for their own families, and the women would cook for everyone. We were kept working from early in the morning until dark. The Pahi was like a crazy man driving us on and screaming at us.

There was an old woman in our group. We never did know what had happened to make the Pahi so angry, but he hated the old woman and decided that he would punish her. He made her go naked, and when he wanted to sit down, she would have to get down on her hands and knees so he could use her as a chair. When she would get tired and fall, he would kick and beat her. Her life was a torment.

Finally, the men had the building up. It was a high building with one floor built over a lower floor. We had never seen anything like it. One day many of the men were working on the second floor when the Pahi came up. He was very angry. He said that we were lazy no-goods, and he was going to punish us for not doing a better job. He called for Reuben to bring the old woman because he needed to sit down. He ordered her to get down on her hands and knees so he could sit on her. You could tell by the way she looked at him that she hated him.

He told Reuben to start whipping us. Both of them were enjoying seeing us suffer. Finally we could take no more. We turned on Reuben, grabbed the whip, and started beating him. Then we turned on the Pahi. We were afraid of Michet, but we had been driven to more than we could stand. We jumped on the Pahi and beat him. We were like a mob of crazy people. Then the old lady that the Pahi had used as a chair grabbed him and threw him off the building, killing him. She finally had her revenge.

When Reuben saw the Pahi fall, he ran away, screaming that he would be back. He was going for help to come and punish us for our wickedness. We chased him, but could not catch him. We were so afraid that we set fire to the building and left our beautiful place and fled with our families into the jungles. Some fled so deep into the jungles that they are still out there where no other people have ever gone. They are afraid that they will be punished if someone finds them.

Our group came and settled in this place where we are now. It is a good place, but it does not compare to what we had to leave behind. Because of what happened, we can never return there. Some of our daughters had babies with blue eyes. We brought them with us. The ones of us with blue eyes are the Pahi's descendants, but we want no part of him or the god Michet."

When the blue eyed woman had finished her story, she turned to Miro. "I have heard a little of how you were guided here to us. I would like to hear your story of all that has happened to you."

Miro told them. He told them, too, how they had promised to return to the hunting place in the spring when the spider monkeys are fat, and how they would build a round house to the gods to worship them.

When he had finished, she said to him, "Miro, someday you must keep the promise you made to return there and talk to the spirits, but here you will live, plant, and hunt. This will be your new land. You have been brought here for a purpose. Now, Miro, tell us, what do you see in your dreams about this land that you have come to?"

Miro looked at her. "The voices tell me that this is a good land where we will live well for many years. But there will come a time when others will come to this land. Some will be good people; some will be bad, evil people. They will want what is ours. Many of us will leave here and find new homes. Our people will scatter throughout the jungles and along the rivers. The ones that stay will suffer. The day will come when we will not have anywhere else to go. The jungles will disappear, the animals and fish will be scarce, and our people will be hungry. This is what I see."

When Miro had finished, Santa spoke and said, "I have seen the same thing. It will happen, but not for a long time."

Back to the River That Flows Backwards

Many years later, Miro was lying on a mat with Sachi sitting beside him. He started coughing and spitting blood. He knew he had very little time left. "Sachi, call our grandchild and tell him I need to talk to Marcos. He is the one to carry the torch for us."

He watched her as she slowly walked away. He thought about all the years that had gone by and all the changes that had occurred. He remembered talking to the blue-eyed woman years ago about his dreams.

Marcos came running, "I'm here, Grandfather."

Miro looked up into the blue eyes of his great-grandson. "Sit down, Marcos. You are very young, but the voices have told me that I will soon die, and I need to tell you what you must do. You know what has been happening to our home. Even now, right where we are living, other families have moved in. They tell us that this is their land, and if we want to live here, we must work for them. We are not a people who fight back. The groups that have fought against the invasion into the jungles where they lived have been slaughtered like animals."

"The people that have taken our own living place are good people. They have papers that say it was given to them. We have no papers. They do not treat us mean, but we are still slaves to them. Others will come. All up and down the river, people are taking away our land. They come from all parts of the world which is torn by war, so the people come to our land."

"A stranger owns the beautiful land of Cara Cara. I don't know why such a man would come from a faraway country to our jungles. It is like he is hiding from someone. I don't know why a stranger can come with a paper and claim what is ours, but it is happening. The river traders that are coming are getting rich from our labor. You have heard the terrible things they are doing. You have heard how they killed Gustavo after they tortured him, doing unspeakable things to him. His son, Beto, fled after he chased down the killer and cut off his head. Then a commission came looking for Beto and found his younger brother who fought them with a machete. He was gunned down. Beto escaped to the place where I built the round house, where we go in the spring to worship the gods. Strangers have never found that place, and now I am telling you that you need to leave here. Take our people away. I have had a dream that you must go back to the River That Flows Backwards. You will find the place where we made the raft. There is a mountain with a wall of flint rock and a waterfall from a little creek."

"Do not look for the Holy Hill, even though some will tell you that they know where it is. I don't know yet if the Holy Hill is in this life or the next, but when the time is right, you will be told how to find it. I don't know if any others of our people still live. You will know where you shall settle with our people. You have been told of my dreams. Santa, the blue-eyed woman, saw it, too. Now, I tell you that not all of this will happen in your lifetime, but the time is coming."

"Now, Marcos, I am very tired and I am going to sleep. I will not wake again. After you bury me, prepare to leave. Take the old ones with you. They know the way; don't leave any behind. It isn't safe for anyone to stay."

That night a storm blew in. The next morning as the clouds cleared and the sun came out, they saw the rainbow. That put fear in their hearts. They dug a grave for Miro, poured hot peppers over him so that the one that had put the curse on him would die, and buried him. Then they burned his house and put thorns on the trails to the house. The group loaded the canoes and started the trip upriver.

They settled in the hills along the area where Miro and Dago had built the raft that had taken them down the river. They hunted, fished, and planted. They made their clothes from the bark of trees, and lived along the creeks and small rivers. From time to time, they would travel for days to buy or trade for salt, fishhooks and line, and the few things that the jungle did not provide.

As the years passed, many of the Chimanes settled along the Maniqui River in the jungle area that was separated from the grass-lands by low swampy areas. They were a timid, peaceful people who hunted and fished with bows and arrows, and raised bananas, rice, and coffee which supplied much of the food and building materials that the town of San Borja needed.

Chimane family group along the Maniqui River.

The Chimanes could neither read nor write; their language wasn't written, and they had no legal documents to claim what was theirs, so others claimed it. They became the servants, '*mozos*'. The people had a 'Patron' and they belonged to him. Under the Patron system of Bolivia, the big land owners claimed huge areas of land and the people that lived there worked for them.

In 1950, the president of Bolivia, Victor Paz Estensoro, carried out a sweeping land reform and abolished the Patron system. The people by law were freed from slavery to the big land owners, although there was still a slave mentality. For many, very little had changed, especially for the people who lived in the rain forest. Even though they planted trees and grew crops, they had no claim to the land. They were considered 'Nomads,' and the Chimanes' land was called 'No-Man's Land'.

San Borja 1950s

The town of San Borja is located in an area of natural grass-lands. It was a cattle town with cowboys, horses, longhorn cattle, and ruled by the law of the gun. It was a long trip for the Chimanes to come into town for the few things that they needed to buy, so the river merchants (*Comerciantes*) played an important part in their life. They traveled up and down the Maniqui River trading with the Indians. They would load their canoes with trade goods such as salt, cloth, fish hooks, machetes, and things that the people needed, especially cans of cane alcohol, to trade for the products found in the jungle. For the most part, the river merchants were lawless and abusive. Many of them wouldn't even bother to trade for the products; they would go in and take what they wanted at gun point. There was no law along the Maniqui River.

In the 1950s along the Maniqui River, the lives of the Chimanes, the River Merchants, and the Missionaries from North America touched one another, and none of them would ever be the same again.

San Borja early days.

Rosauro Plata, a Chimane Christian, tells in his own words about his people and when the missionaries came. It is translated from Chimane:

A testimony for you, our brothers, who live across the sea: First I, Rosauro Plata, greet all of you of the church (God's group) who follow Jesus Christ.

At the first, many years passed that our forefathers didn't know God's Word, but then afterwards, God's time arrived, and He sent the bringers of God's Word.

There wasn't even one of our relatives (fellow tribal people) who believed in God, neither man nor woman, nor did they know how to praise God, or pray to Him. Then the missionaries arrived. First they studied our language, and then they taught us God's Word. Also they taught us to read; their thoughts were so it would not be hard for us to read God's Word.

We thank you for helping the bringers of God's Word because at that time there was none of it in our language. The missionaries would read in their language and then tell us in our language. There was God's Word in Spanish, but we could not understand Spanish.

After many years passed, there were many of our relatives who believed in God, men and women; they knew how to praise God and pray to Him. After a long time our relatives believed, and then they themselves preached God's Word and helped the missionaries.

Chapter 2

How the Work Began

1950:
Gladys Callaway was one of the first missionaries to go and live among the Chimanes. She wrote the following account of the beginning of the work:

San Borja, Bolivia, South America

A small one-motor Cessna plane landed in San Borja in March of 1950 carrying the missionaries Wanda Banman and Marge Day. They were flown in by missionary pilot Mel Wyma.

Some of the townspeople met Mel at the airport saying they wanted to have a meeting with him in the school house that night. Their question was, "What power is great enough to change a man like Ramon Perez?"

Ramon Perez was an army officer who had been sent to San Borja to help keep the peace in the town. Gunfire was common there, especially at night in the plaza; however, Perez was corrupt and just added to the confusion, as well as to the cause of prostitution.

After Perez's time in San Borja, he moved to Trinidad, the capitol of the Beni Province, where he met a Christian missionary. He came to know and believe in the Lord Jesus Christ and ended up marrying the daughter of the missionary. He was a transformed person. When people from San Borja went to Trinidad on business, they saw Ramon Perez and found him completely changed. They went back to San

Borja saying that he wasn't the Ramon Perez they had known. He was a different person; hence their question to Mel Wyma.

Wanda Banman describes her first impressions of the Chimanes:

When Marge Day and I had been in San Borja only a very short time, we got our first glimpse of a group of Chimane Indians who had come into town to trade. One or two in the group spoke a few words of Spanish; the rest just jabbered in their own language. That year we spent most of our time learning Spanish and working with the Spanish-speaking people. When Marge broke her wrist, she went to Cochabamba and didn't return.

While I was there alone, an opportunity offered itself for me to go upriver with a Bolivian river merchant and his daughter to see where some of these Indians lived. We went as far as the settlement of La Cruz in a dug-out canoe and stayed overnight in their little village. It was quite exciting.

The Chimanes closer to town did not seem to be afraid of us, but the ones farther up river were. We saw the women and children fleeing into the woods as we got near. As the merchant offered his wares of beads and other needed items, some of them came back out very shyly.

Closer to town where some of them worked on the Bolivian farms, they were learning a bit of Spanish, so I tried to communicate with them and gave them a little of the gospel message of Christ. One old man seemed interested, but I don't know how much he understood. By the time I went that way again, the old man had died. Do you suppose he just might be in Heaven today? Oh, how I wish he is. He would be a kind of first-fruits of that tribe.

Gladys' record continues:

June Quick joined the work in 1951. That year Wanda and June went upriver to a place called Pupuretumsi'. They were hoping to be able to see a work come into being with the Chimane Indians. They lived with two Bolivian couples in that immediate area. They tried to spend time with the Chimanes in the day to learn some of their language, but they could see that this set-up wouldn't work out. The Bolivians were jealous when the girls would spend time with the Chimanes, and the Chimanes were jealous when they were with the Bolivians.

In January of 1952, Wanda decided to stay in the town of San Borja and do what she could to see the town work move ahead. June wanted to continue on with the Chimane work, so in January of 1952, I joined June.

June and Gladys 1951.

We settled down with an extended Chimane family known as the Guarecos. We went to their house first and asked them if we could live there with them so that we could learn their language. They had a big one-room house so they agreed, even telling us that they would put in a partition to divide it.

We decided on a date when we would go there, and told them when we would move in. Things went as planned, and we got our things out to the river on a hired oxcart. There we met a Bolivian lady, Doña Trinidad, who had just come downriver. She informed us that the Chimanes at the Guarecos had a lot of chicha (an alcoholic home brew) made up and they were planning on a big fiesta that night. We had already come that far and didn't want to turn back, so we went on, with somebody poling us upriver in a dugout canoe.

That first night gave us quite an initiation to life among the Chimanes during their fiesta. The men and women beat their drums, and other Chimanes came from far and near to drink with them. There was no sleeping that night. That was the first of many nights spent like that.

When we reached our "home," we discovered that there was no partition made in the house, but we moved our things in anyway. We both had army-surplus camp cots with the accompanying mosquito nets, which we set up. Our table was a cardboard box containing tin cans of powdered milk over which we spread some oil cloth. We sat, one of us on either side of the table which had been placed on a bamboo bench. The bamboo bench was also our seats. We had to sit sideways and turn to face our table. June's little typing

This is a typical Chimane house next to the river.

table and chair completed our furniture, but we were comfortable. We later added a stool to our accommodations.

We spent the whole year with this group of Chimanes. We became close to this family and they to us. It was an ideal place to study the language, as some of them knew quite a bit of Spanish so they could further explain their Chimane words to us.

We nursed back to health Siriaca, the old lady of the group, after she had been bitten by a poisonous snake and nearly died. She was a long time in recovering. Another time we took turns getting up every hour all night long to put mustard-plaster poultices on a little girl's chest because she had pneumonia and could hardly breathe. She lived, only to die months later when somebody spilled alcohol in the fire near her during one of their drunken fiestas.

June and I traveled to Cochabamba in January of 1953 to attend the New Tribes Mission conference. The missionaries came in from the different areas of Bolivia once a year. It was a good time for all of us to visit with one another, do our buying, and tend to medical needs. June had been having problems with her health and was unable to return to the work at this time.

Right after the conference, Gene Callaway and I were married on February 3, 1953, in Cochabamba. We went back to the same Chimane house that June and I had left. For the first few months, we continued living there with the Chimanes while Gene had a house built for us.

We later had another house built at La Cruz, but this one was built up on stilts as David, who is our oldest son, had joined our family. We didn't want him crawling on a dirt floor. We remained in the Chimane work until August of 1968, when we came back to the United States. By that time there were a few believers, and they were learning to read and write their language. Gene had made up a teaching-grammar book to help new missionaries learn the language, and he did the first translation into Chimane of Mark's gospel, as well as half of the book of Acts.

Gladys and Gene, David and John Callaway.

Chapter 3

God Can Use Any Life That Is Willing To Serve Him

June 1951:
Longview, Washington

Elaine writes:

Dean and I were married and living in Longview, Washington in 1951 when we heard a missionary from Bolivia speak at the church we were attending. We had never met a real live missionary, but the night we heard him speak changed our lives. We heard him say, "It is not your ability or inability; it is your availability." That night we told God we were available.

The next question was: how do you go about becoming a missionary? To make a long story short, it was not easy.

For one thing, the pastor wasn't happy about the decision. He asked us, "What would you be able to do on the mission field? Dean, you can't preach, and Elaine can't play the piano."

It turned out that even if I could play a piano, we wouldn't have been able to get it in the canoe, and Dean didn't need to be a preacher; he needed to learn to speak Spanish and an unwritten Indian language and just share God with the people by word and deed.

Dean and Elaine in canoe on the Maniqui River.

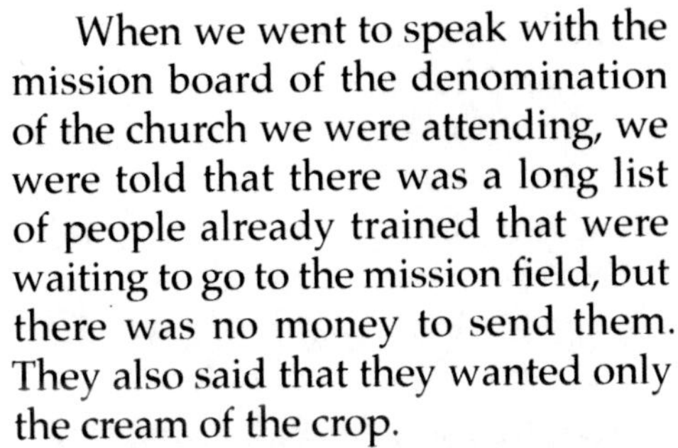

When we went to speak with the mission board of the denomination of the church we were attending, we were told that there was a long list of people already trained that were waiting to go to the mission field, but there was no money to send them. They also said that they wanted only the cream of the crop.

The missionary that we had met at church was with New Tribes Mission, which did pioneer missionary work with tribal people, so we applied and were accepted.

However, before we could begin the training, Dean received a letter, "Your friends and neighbors have chosen you, and you are ordered to report for duty in the United States Army." So Dean was drafted and went to Korea instead of missionary training.

Elaine and Dean.

We decided that I would go on ahead and take the training, with the understanding that I would have to take it over when Dean got out of the army. I entered missionary boot camp, and there I learned the reality of living for God. These were men and women who had their hearts set on serving God. New Tribes Mission's purpose is to reach the previously unreached people in the jungles and remote areas who never had a chance to hear about Jesus and how He died for them. To do that kind of work, I had to learn how to live in remote places and get along without electricity and all the other things we take for granted here in the United States and think we can't live without. I learned to depend on the Lord to provide all my needs.

At that time, New Tribes Training Center was at Fouts Springs, California. It was far back in on a winding mountain road in the Mendocino Forest near Willows, California.

In 1952, Dean was in Korea, I was in California, and the work was beginning among the Chimane Indians in Bolivia. Gladys and June had spent a whole year living with a Chimane family along the Maniqui River, learning about their culture and learning to speak their unwritten language.

Dean writes:

Elaine wrote to me and told me about the fourteen men who perished when they were called to fight a fire. The camp was in the Mendocino Forest, and during fire season the men in missionary training were asked to help fight forest fires. They were happy to do it and quite often brought a lot of food back to camp that was left over from feeding the fire fighters. But this time would be different when they got the call to go fight a fire. The fire turned, and fourteen of the men never came back. There were a few that survived, but they escaped because they didn't follow the normal procedure. It was a terribly hard time. The girls' dorm was next to the cabin of a woman whose husband had died in the fire. She had six children who had lost their dad. In the dark hours of the night, they heard her singing:

'He giveth more grace when the burdens grow greater.
He giveth more strength when the labors increase.
To added affliction, He addeth His mercy.
To multiplied trials, His multiplied peace.'

At the memorial service, one widow requested the hymn, *Am I a Soldier of the Cross?* And another's request was *Keep on Believing.*

The government people that came out to talk to the ones that had lost loved ones told how much they had dreaded coming and talking to them. But, after interviewing a few of them, they could hardly wait for the next interview as it was such a testimony of God's peace and help in times of trouble.

Korea was a hard experience, and at the time, we wondered why God allowed me to go to war when we had wanted to serve Him on the mission field. After the fire, I realized that if I had been at the mission training camp, I also might have perished.

God helped me to live for Him and endure the mocking my fellow soldiers gave me for my Christian stand in Korea. I met a Christian soldier who also lived for God, and we became close friends. He played the organ, and we often sang for hours. We also taught English to Korean orphans and learned to love them. I was sad when I was sent near the front and had to leave them.

Elaine was waiting for the day when I would come home but had no way of knowing when that would be. The Armistice had been signed while she was in California. One day her Uncle Sam called from Seattle and said that my name was listed in the newspaper as being on a troop ship due in on a certain date, so she went to Seattle to meet me. I didn't know that she knew I was coming, so when they asked who had relatives waiting for them, I didn't say anything. Since I seemed to have no one waiting, I was given the job of sweeping the ship.

Dean back from Korea, running.

When the troop ship loaded with thousands of men came in, I saw her at the dock; I had everyone wave. I had to stay on board to sweep, so she watched thousands of men come off that ship. I sent notes and even asked the second-in-command of the ship to go explain to her why I couldn't come yet. He told Elaine that he himself would have taken the broom and swept for me, but it wasn't permitted.

Finally, when the ship was almost empty, I was able to leave and came running off the ship, gave her a kiss, and ran for the buses that were ready to pull out for Fort Lewis.

The big day finally came to return home after being apart from my wife for fourteen months. Elaine had changed, and so had I. At first, it seemed like we were strangers to one another. I went back to my old job in Longview and thought about the future. One day Elaine asked me, "When are we going into missionary training?" I promised soon, but I was beginning to wonder about it now.

Dean welcomed home by Elaine.

I had little opportunity to attend church overseas and after a couple of Sundays at home, it seemed so artificial. Everything seemed to be so cut and dried. I wondered about the meaning of going to church. What benefit was it? What purpose did attendance fill? Was it just a social function? Was it a custom or habit that one feels obligated to participate in? Do we have a form of godliness, but deny the power of God in our lives?

I shared these thoughts with Elaine. "If I don't find more reality in Christianity than what I see, I don't want it."

"Dean, while you were overseas, the people I was with in missionary training were real," she assured me. "They have left all: houses, lands, family, and jobs to go and preach the Gospel of Christ. They are sold out to God," she declared. The growth I saw in her faith gave me hope. "Let's go for it!" I shouted.

Chapter 4

Missionary Training

1954:

Dean's account:

Talking about it is one thing. Doing it is another. Our first tiny step of faith seemed like a giant one for us. Meet our first saint perfecter… a car!

We called our car the Nasty Nash. It was nothing but trouble. The Nash sounded good on the car lot, but out on the road it started knocking. Before we had driven fifty miles, it threw a rod. I bought a used motor and while putting it in, the car fell off of the jack and bruised me quite badly. After that, we had continual trouble with the car, yet we were heading for California in it.

"Help us make it, Lord. Here we come." When we started out on our trip to California, we smelled something terrible. We wondered if one of Grandma's cats had gotten in the car and died.

We found out that the generator had eaten up the battery. Now we had no battery, and from there on, every time we stopped and turned off the car, we had to push it to get it started. Since it was loaded to capacity, when the car started, we had to make a flying leap over the stuff by the door to get in.

In the mountains, the Nash boiled over, killing the engine. This happened at every peak. Once I told Elaine, "When I tell you, 'Step on the gas,' then step on it." She thought I meant right then, so she stepped on the gas just as I took the radiator cap off. I got burned pretty badly, and she felt terrible. However, we somehow managed to limp into camp, but the Nasty Nash never did run for us again.

Our destination was Yuba City, California. A temporary missionary training camp was set up in a farm-labor camp for migrant workers that come in at harvest time. This would be our home for the next year. Although we were orphan missionaries, not sent out by any church, we arrived with around $250, and I felt that we could find part-time work to tide us over.

I asked one of the students where he worked. "I don't," he replied. "We have a full schedule here. We don't have time to work," he explained.

"In that case, you must have a lot of good churches to support you," I remarked.

"No, we don't," he replied. This man had a wife and four children.

"How do you live, Max?" I asked.

"We live by faith," he answered.

"Oh, so you live by faith. How does that work?" I asked.

"We just trust the Lord with our needs. God is for real. God is alive. God hears us. If we put the furtherance of His Kingdom first in our lives, priority number one, He will provide our material needs. God promises it, and He cannot lie," he answered.

Max showed me the promise in *Matthew 6:33. But seek ye first the Kingdom of God, and his righteousness; and all these things shall be added unto you.*

I had read it many times, but I had never claimed it by faith. All at once I felt like someone must feel who jumps from a plane the first time and hopes that the parachute opens. I felt that it was time to jump, and the feeling was awesome. "Lord, you said it. I believe it. That settles it." I asked for reality. I wanted to experience God up front. "Lord, like Peter, I'm stepping out of the boat. I'm going to walk on the seas of faith. Lord, if I set my eyes on the waves and begin to sink, hold me up."

"Hey, these guys are nuts! They are fanatics. They have gone off the deep end."

"I heard you, Devil. I either step off of the boat at this point and walk by faith, or we pack up and leave camp. There's no in-between. Living by faith is par for the course here." (Remember we were orphans. No home church was praying for us or supporting us.)

We lived in a little tin house. Moisture condensed inside on the ceiling and kept up a constant drip. We hoarded our money as much as we could, but one day it ran out. That's usually the way it happens when you walk by faith. I kept looking for miracles, but nothing happened until eventually, the $250 was gone.

We had taken that first step of faith, but now I was scared. I began to search madly through the dresser drawers. I searched through our clothing. I looked anywhere and everywhere I could think of where I might find money. God often gives reprieves to beginners. In a footlocker, I found a fifty-dollar traveler's check. I was encouraged by this first provision, and it challenged me to trust more when that money was gone.

All of us students were really hard up. When company came to visit the camp, we would gather together and have a potluck to feed them. We used to go to a butcher shop that gave dog bones away free. We would ask for bones "to feed our dog," but we used them to make a soup first. Our potlucks were dog-bone soup and biscuits. That was with everyone sharing.

Living in a fruit-labor camp meant we were in the heart of orchards. We went out to the fields where the owners let us have as many tomatoes and peaches as we could pick. They also had a place where we could can food, so we canned them, too. How good God is! To this day, we still like to eat tomatoes and peaches. We were very thankful, too, when we had some beans to go along with them.

Once we took care of a little boy whose mother was sick. His name was Rene. He would always ask what we had to eat. We'd tell him tomatoes. "Oh boy, tomatoes!" He would be really happy about whatever it was. It was good for us to have him so enthusiastic about our tomatoes, peaches, and pancakes with no eggs or milk, not to mention the dog-bone soup.

In all the years that have passed since we took those first little steps of faith, God has always met our needs. He hardly ever supplies like we think he will, but he always answers our prayers and supplies our needs. Often he does it better than we could ask or think.

Specific Answers to Prayers

Does God really answer our prayers? One example among many would be the miracle of the razor blade. Remember, we had no money and no job. No support was coming in, but my face didn't know that, and my whiskers continued to grow. Beards weren't in fashion in those days, so I had to shave daily. My blades became dull, and I learned a trick from a fellow missionary. Take a water glass and rub the blade inside the glass, and the blade will give another shave. Having done this many times and now failing to get a dull blade to operate, I came to the conclusion that I needed a new razor blade. "Elaine, do you think it would be all right to pray and ask God for something as small as a razor blade?"

"Why not?" she answered.

My prayer was short. It was specific. It was also sincere. "Lord, I ask you to provide me with a razor blade sharp enough to shave with. In Jesus' name, Amen."

Since we had no money, we had no food. I also asked God to supply for us. We thought of others in need, and so we asked God to give us enough food to have company. In less than two hours, these two separate prayers were answered. Actually before we even prayed, the answer was on its way. Ike and Mary Lou Christen, a couple who had stepped out by faith to follow the Lord the same night we did from the same church, rolled into camp. We hadn't seen them for two years, so it was quite a surprise to see them again. They had finished training and were on their way to their field of labor in Panama. They had not been delayed by the Korean War, as we were, so they were full-fledged missionaries already.

The first thing Ike asked me was, "Do you have a razor? I forgot mine."

I confessed, "I have one, but no blades."

"I have blades," he assured me, "just no razor." When he returned from the car, he brought in two bags of groceries. The Lord had provided food and company. Ike shaved and said, "Here are two blades I have left over." Then, he went to the car and returned with an electric razor. "I can't plug this into a palm tree in Panama," he exclaimed. "You can have it."

Another proof of God's care about small things is an incident we had with a 35mm camera. One day this camera quit working. A fellow missionary candidate offered to take the camera to a repair shop for us. "It will cost too much," I said.

"Let me take it and see," he said, "It may be something small." Doug took the camera and when he returned, he said that the repairman would fix it for sixteen dollars. "I'll take it Saturday," he offered.

"No way," I protested. "Even if I had sixteen dollars, I wouldn't spend it for camera repair. I would buy food with it."

"Dean, where is your faith in the Lord?" he scolded. "It is simple. Just pray and ask the Lord to provide exactly sixteen dollars, no more and no less. If he supplies that money, you will know it is for getting the camera repaired." Doug was adamant.

I felt at liberty to pray if the prayer was that specific. "Lord, send me exactly sixteen dollars, not a penny more and not a penny less," I prayed. "Do this by Saturday, and I will send the camera with Doug. Amen."

Seldom did we receive money in the mail; however, that week a ten dollar bill arrived in a letter. Someone else gave me two dollars. Late on Friday night, someone slipped a manila envelope under the door with some coins in it, mostly pennies. I can't even remember the fourth source, but I do remember that the money came from four different places, and when we counted the last penny, it totaled exactly sixteen dollars.

I felt like how the disciples must have felt when they saw Jesus walking on the water. It was an awesome experience. I ran across to Doug's apartment and gave him the money. The camera got repaired, and some of the pictures in this book were taken with that camera.

Part of our training program was to go door to door in the afternoons and present Christ. When there was interest, we went in the evenings and held a Bible study. In one home where we had a study, the man of the house asked us if we liked fish. I told him we did. He said, "I have a deep freezer full of salmon. I like to catch them, but don't like to eat them." He gave us several big salmon and several loaves of bread. It was God's provision, and Jesus once again provided "loaves and fishes."

We also had a Bible study with a woman and her two small daughters. She was amazed when we shared stories of God's provision. At that time we only had tomatoes and peaches, but we invited her to come to our Sunday meeting and have lunch with us. She accepted, and on Saturday we received a package in the mail with chocolate chip cookies. A neighbor gave Elaine lettuce, but what we lacked now was meat. At 9:00 a.m. I reminded the Lord that we needed meat and our guests would arrive at 10 o'clock. Suddenly there was a knock on the door. I opened it, and two one-dollar bills floated down and landed at my feet. I quickly ran around the house to catch the donor, but there was no one there. I concluded that it was an angel unaware. I bought a nice roast, and we dined well that day with our guests.

Finally, the day arrived that we were told we could go to Wisconsin and continue our training. We went with another family but left the Nasty Nash behind, as it wasn't running anyway.

New Tribes had just bought the Wisconsin property, which had previously been a dancehall and bar. We went with the group that was going to get it ready for the language and linguistic training part of the work. We worked on making apartments out of the dancehall.

The next story Elaine doesn't like for me to tell; she says it sounds too bizarre. I don't give it as an example for receiving guidance from the Lord, but it happened, and we were convinced it was divine guidance for us. We had to choose a foreign language to learn which depended on which country we were going to. I hadn't even thought about going anywhere but Bolivia, since the missionaries that challenged us were from there. Elaine had heard about the many tribes in New Guinea, so she wanted to go there. If we went to Bolivia, our language would be Spanish, the official language of the country. There are thirty-four known languages spoken there, but Spanish is the trade language. New Guinea has over 700 languages; the trade language is Pidgin English, so I prayed, "Lord, you know about our problem. Elaine wants to go to New Guinea, and I feel that we should go to Bolivia. Please show us, Lord, in a vision or a dream, which place we should go. Amen."

The following morning Elaine asked me if I had experienced a vision. I told her no. Then she asked, "Did you have a dream?" "No," I responded. Actually, I had forgotten about the problem.

Elaine said, "I had a dream that I was sitting at a table. I held three large white cards in my hands. I turned the first card over, and it was blank. I turned the second card over, and it was also blank. I turned the third card over, and it had BOLIVIA written in capital letters. I'm ready to go to Bolivia."

Elaine continues:

We liked the literacy part of the training and decided that when we got to Bolivia, we would like to work in that field.

When we were almost finished with our training, we owed quite a bit of money. Our food had come from the garden and various sources, but money was still needed to pay other bills. The veterans from Washington State who had served in Korea were given a bonus, so Dean received a check in the mail, which paid what we owed up to that time, but we were still in training, so we still had more bills. We were praying that we would be able to pay them. Someone made a generous donation to pay the bills of the three people who owed the most. We were one of the three, so we left not owing anything.

Dean continues:

Sometimes Elaine would come up with something that I couldn't see. We had been married four years and had no children. We wanted children and prayed about it, but no baby yet. One day, she came into the living room excited. "Honey, guess what. I'm going to have a baby!"

"You mean you are pregnant?" I asked.

"No", she said, "but I will be. Look at this verse. I was reading the Bible, and God showed this verse just for me. *Isaiah 43:19, "Behold, I will do a new thing; now it shall spring forth; shall ye not know it?"...*

"That's great, honey." I did not have the heart to tell her that I felt she was taking the verse out of context. And I am glad I did not, because nine months later, baby Lori was born. I still wasn't one hundred percent convinced that it was a miracle in answer to prayer, but later, after we had arrived in Bolivia, Elaine had to have surgery. The doctor told her after the operation that it should have been impossible for her to have had her first child in her condition.

"I know that," she told the doctor. "Lori was given to me in answer to a prayer."

"Well, now you can have more children," he assured her. Baby Darrel was born and after that Randy, Dixie and Ben.

Since we had left the Nasty Nash in California, some people decided to fix it up and drive it to Wisconsin. They had all kinds of problems on their trip, just like we did with the Nasty Nash. After they got to Wisconsin, the car never ran again while it was there. Then another family that was leaving prayed for a car. God kept saying to us, "Give them the Nash." We did not want to give them something so obviously worthless, but God kept prompting us to do it, so we offered the car. We told them we didn't know if it would be a curse or a blessing, but it was theirs if they wanted it. They were happy and got a couple of mechanics on it. It only cost 75 cents to fix it, and they took off in the middle of a Wisconsin winter on icy roads. They putted along, passing cars that couldn't drive on the icy roads, and they were warm because of the stopped-up radiator. They arrived in Florida still driving the Nasty Nash. It never did give them any trouble, and to them it was a blessing. As it turned out, we traveled to Bolivia with that family on the same ship.

Chapter 5

Faith Trip in a Fifty-Dollar Ford

December 1955:

Now it was time for Elaine and me to leave camp. We had finished the course, so now we needed a car to go back to Washington State. On Thursday nights, we always had meetings and on this particular night, a man from Sheboygan Falls, twenty-five miles away, came to the meeting. One of my jobs at school was to put coal in the boiler that steam-heated our buildings. When the meeting ended, I went down into the basement to shovel in more coal. Our visitor followed me down the steps and stuck a check in my pocket. After my chore, I looked at it and saw that it was for fifty dollars. The following day, as I walked past the office, I happened to overhear a phone conversation from a local farmer to one of the missionaries offering him a car. I heard the missionary tell him that he didn't need one, but that he would announce the offer. I talked to Ray and asked about the car. He said this man has a good Ford for sale for fifty dollars. Little bells began to go off in my head, and I felt that this was meant to be.

Ray offered to take me over to see the car, so we went and looked it over. The body looked okay, but the tires were bald, and the battery was dead as the car had not run in months. I thought it was a good buy for fifty dollars, so I bought it, charged up the battery, and we were ready to travel in the winter to the west coast in our fifty-dollar Ford.

Two single missionaries asked to travel with us and said that we could pool our resources. Between the four of us, we had lots of baggage. How in the world would we ever fit it all?

The day before we left, since a new family would be occupying our apartment, our things sat in the hall.

Then a family arrived from California asking, "Does anyone here need a trailer who's heading for the west coast?"

"Do we ever!" we shouted. The four of us got together, prayed, and planned our trip as there were several people that we wanted to stop and visit along the way.

Then came the time to face reality; we had only twenty dollars between the four of us. The trailer was loaded, and we bid our friends goodbye. Several pushed what was probably their last dollars through the window as we started to pull away. The snow was several inches thick on the road, it was still snowing, and all four tires were bald, but our journey had begun, and now there was no turning back.

Near nightfall, we rolled into Davenport, Iowa. One of our passengers, Dick, had a friend living there who he wanted to visit. Dick had led him to the Lord when they worked together in Washington, D.C. We were well received by Dick's friend, who seemed to be really glad to see him. The house was large, and I thought to myself that we would probably spend the night there. I noticed, however, that the man's wife seemed somewhat nervous.

Around nine o'clock that evening, we felt that we should go and look for a place to stay the night. We bid them goodbye and left the house. Dick's friend followed us and looked at the old Ford and our trailer. "Will you make it?" he inquired.

"Yes," we assured him.

"Do you have a tire pump?" he asked.

We confessed we did not, and he insisted we take his. Then he told us to follow him into town. I wondered what was up. He parked us by the best hotel in town, went in, and paid for our rooms. "No one visits me without me putting them up for the night," he affirmed. He then insisted that we take twenty dollars for our breakfast, and then he returned home. I remember walking barefoot on those thick rugs. We would have never taken rooms this nice on our own. The next morning, after a good ham and egg breakfast, we moved on.

It was really cold outside, just a few degrees above zero. A few miles outside of Lincoln, Nebraska, we blew out a tire. We put on the spare, which had a big bulge on it. That took us a few more miles before it also blew out. We now had two ruined tires and no spare. What do we do now?

"I know," Don said, "Let's have a praise meeting. Let's thank the Lord for this problem." This sounded as good as anything else we could think of, so we began to sing and praise the Lord. We were making a joyful noise and shivering at the same time when a pickup stopped. The driver, who worked in a tire shop, had been out on a call and was returning to Lincoln. He had a big lift jack with him, so he took off our wheel and put it in the back of his pickup. We threw in the spare, and Don and I accompanied him back to his shop. Think of that: us with no jack and a tire-shop worker who is out on a call comes along as we are having a praise meeting. We talked about our Lord on the way in, and the man admitted he was a Christian. He gave us a really good deal on a used tire and tube and threw in a spare as well.

While we were getting the spare mounted, Don said, "Hey, the Buttermores live here." John and Edith had been in missionary training with us back in Yuba City, California. We called them, and they were thrilled to hear from us. They insisted that we spend the night with them, which we did, and after a hearty breakfast the next morning, we continued our journey.

John gave us forty dollars, and Edith packed us a lunch of fried chicken with all the trimmings for the road. This came just in time because buying the used tire had depleted our resources.

Dick was home when we reached Los Angeles. We had arrived with one traveler safe and sound. When we arrived in Washington State, we took Don to relatives in Seattle. After we delivered him, we drove south a hundred miles to Elaine's parents' home in Onalaska. Our records showed that we had been four weeks and one day on the road. We had made the journey in a fifty-dollar Ford with bald tires. We either stayed with friends and ate with them, or stayed at a hotel or motel and ate in restaurants. Apart from what was paid for by others, we paid out $345 for gasoline, rooms, and food. We arrived at our destination with fifteen dollars in our pockets. God went before us and prepared our way. God gave us a Faithful Ford in exchange for the Nasty Nash.

Chapter 6

Bolivia Bound

Early 1956:

We finished our training in 1956, and then spent some time back in Washington State where our daughter, Lori, was born. We bought clothing, dishes, and other equipment that we felt were necessary, and packed them in 55-gallon steel drums with lockable lids.

We needed to ship the barrels to Florida, but the shipping costs could run several hundred dollars because we had a lot of them. I happened to mention this dilemma to a friend who had been a cook at the high school we went to. I had been a dishwasher at the school where she cooked during my senior year, and we had gotten to know each other fairly well. She phoned her son in Oregon, who was planning to drive to Florida in an empty pickup truck. He was going within thirty miles of our missionary-training camp, and when she told him of our need, he was more than happy to take the freight. When I tried to pay him, he refused to take any money. This is another example of God's provisions as He blessed us; a man with an empty pickup truck was traveling from one end of the United States to the other and leaving just in time to get the supplies there when we needed them.

We were going to travel by ferry from Florida to the Bahamas and then travel on a cruise ship through the Panama Canal to Chile where we would then travel by train over the Andes Mountains to Bolivia.

Our daughter, Lori, was four-and-a-half months old when we left Washington. We traveled by train to Florida where fellow missionaries picked us up. At the mission camp, Rolf and Irene Fostervald arrived, still driving the Nasty Nash. We hugged them with joy as they climbed out of the car that had faithfully carried them on their long journey.

They were going to be traveling on the same ship as we were. Elaine and I had our tickets and around two-hundred and fifty dollars cash, so we felt we had sufficient funds to get us safely to Bolivia. Then we learned that we also had to buy tickets for the ferry boat that would take us to our ship, which was docked in the Bahamas. Rolf and Irene had given their last dollars to the owners of the guest house where we stayed in Miami. The tickets were twenty-eight dollars each; Elaine and I felt that we should buy their ferry tickets for them.

The man who ran the guest house for missionaries told us that he had sixteen barrels and crates for other missionaries in Bolivia and asked us if we would be willing to take them along with our baggage. He said that he wasn't given any money for shipping; we were to charge the missionaries when we arrived. Like dummies, we accepted the freight and paid a truck to haul it to the ferry. We were each allowed four-hundred pounds of baggage, so we weighed up everything with the checker and discounted our sixteen-hundred pounds for the four of us. I took the bill to the desk to pay it, and kept looking for some mysterious person to rush up and help us pay for the shipping expense. No one came. The clerk looked over the bill and said, "You are each allowed four-hundred pounds of baggage allowance. Your two young daughters don't have a ticket, but we are also going to give them four-hundred pounds allowance."

I confessed that we had already taken off the sixteen-hundred pounds that were allowed. "That's okay," he quipped. "Let's do it again, just for kicks." Two thousand pounds more at four cents a pound was subtracted. It came to eighty dollars. I had heard stories about missionaries in line to buy a ticket with not enough money, and someone would walk up and hand them the needed amount. This time, that person was the clerk, and he was there waiting for us the whole time.

As we started to board the ferry, Rolf was anxiously wrestling with a red-cap baggage handler over his hand luggage.

"Let him take it," I said.

"I can't. I don't have money for a tip," he whispered. I gave him a bill, and we boarded in style. Dinner was a fancy chicken supper, but Elaine got seasick and couldn't enjoy it. We docked that night and had to find a hotel as the ship wouldn't leave until the following day. The hotel for four and our meals left our meager funds standing at $15.17.

We attended a church that night and made friends with a Christian brother who was very friendly. He drove us all over the island in his new Oldsmobile. This man was in charge of shipping and would be the one to help us get our cargo on board the following morning.

He told us that he would do all he could to cut costs on our shipping fees the following day, and I'm sure he did. Isn't that something that he would be the one we got acquainted with and he was the shipping controller?

I was somewhat concerned about all of the cargo, but since the Lord had already saved us money on shipping once and this man was in charge of the freight handling, I felt it would turn out all right. The next morning the phone rang at the hotel. It was our friend from the night before. "If you will come down to the office and take care of the bill, we will load your freight."

I asked him how much the bill was. "Only $165," he said cheerfully. I gulped and said, "We'll be right down."

I told Rolf the news, and we felt sick. Here we were in the Bahamas, without a place to wire for money, and besides, we didn't have any place to wire to. What do we do now? We prayed, of course, and asked the Lord what we should do next.

Wanda Banman was returning to Bolivia for her second term as a missionary with New Tribes. This is the same woman who flew into San Borja on the little plane in 1950. We had just met her moments before and had learned that she would be traveling on the same ship. She overheard our prayers as we cried out to God and humbly came over to us. "I happen to have an extra $150," she informed us. "I will loan you the money until we get to Bolivia where we can get the money owed to us from the missionaries for their freight." With our $15 and her $150, we were able to pay the shipping costs, and no one but us and the Lord knew that we had only seventeen cents left in our pockets.

Through the years I have often prayed, "Lord, let me not be ashamed. I'm the provider, and responsible for my wife and children." As I have trusted Him, I have never had to be ashamed. It took us three weeks to arrive in Antofagasta, Chile. We were traveling on a Princess Line cruise ship, and stopped at many exotic places. Most of the passengers hailed a taxi or took a bus and went into town to sightsee, but we never got far from the ship because we had our three meals a day included in our passage, and we had no money for taxis or restaurants. The same waiter attended our table the entire trip; he had to be there every meal, because we never missed one. We were concerned that he should be given a good tip for his service, so we made it a matter of prayer. We mingled with other people on the boat, and talked to people about the Lord. We made friends with a Christian doctor who worked in Jamaica. When he arrived at his destination, he came to our cabin and announced that he had some English pounds left over. He could not use them in Jamaica and wondered if we had a use for them. "Yes," we assured him, and those English pounds were the answer to our prayer for a tip for our faithful English waiter.

When we docked in Panama, we were surprised to see some New Tribes missionaries waiting for us. We had a good visit with them, and they passed along letters to Rolf and to us. Inside was a note from mission headquarters that said, "We felt that you would have a need for this money." Even in the middle of our journey, the Lord had provided.

We arrived at Antofagasta, Chile, on a Sunday morning. The longshoremen wanted to overcharge us for unloading the cargo, but we quickly learned to haggle through Wanda as our interpreter. Wanda spoke excellent Spanish; her skill was invaluable to us since no one there spoke English, and our Spanish was a little thin.

The weekly train to Bolivia left every Saturday night, so we, along with all of our freight, had to stay in a hotel for a week. Back in those days, prices were so cheap that we were able to stay right beside the ocean and have a restful week in Chile.

Then, we had to put ourselves and our cargo on the train for the eighteen-hour ride to Cochabamba, Bolivia, our mission headquarters.

The train trip through the mountains was at night so we booked a sleeper car. The customs officials boarded the train at the Chilean-Bolivian border. As soon as we awoke, they started talking, but, of course, we didn't understand Spanish, so there was some confusion for a while. Finally, we were on our way again, to Oruro, Bolivia, where we were to change trains. However, our train arrived late so we had to run to catch the other train, and we had a lot of baggage to transfer. Rolf and Irene Fostervald had their little girl, and we had Lori. Oruro, Bolivia, is up high on the Altiplano, a high plateau, in the Andes Mountains, and it is very flat. Picture us running, and panting from the lack of oxygen, carrying all the baggage, and hearing loud voices all around in both English and Spanish. We did catch the train, but we had to actually hand the two babies through the train window in order to do it. We finally arrived in Cochabamba, Bolivia, with twenty-five cents in our pocket.

Sometimes it is scary living on the edge, but I would not trade that experience for any amount of money in the world.

Chapter 7

Cochabamba, Bolivia

November 1956:

Dean to Dino, Elaine to Elena

The first hurdle for us was learning Spanish. Our names Dean and Elaine didn't sound the same in Spanish, so from then on we were called Dino and Elena. Lori didn't need to change her name as it was pronounced the same way it was spelled.

Dean, Elaine, and Lori in Cochabamba, Bolivia.

Our first year was a struggle of intense Spanish language study even though we still didn't know where in Bolivia we would be working.

In May, the missionaries came in for the yearly conference. During this time, each of the missionaries gave a report of their work at their stations. We listened carefully to each one.

Gene Callaway told us about his and Gladys' work among the Chimane Indians. They both suffered health problems, but they had been working in Bolivia nine years without a furlough because they didn't have anyone to help them.

Gene needed help with a literacy program and since we had liked the literacy part of missionary training, we decided that when we got to Bolivia, we would like to work in that field. This time, Elaine and I had no need to pray for dreams or visions; we both knew that the Lord wanted us to go to the Chimanes.

Gene Callaway at a Chimane village along the Maniqui River.

By May of 1958, we were ready to make the move to San Borja. Our son, Darrel, who was born in March, was two-months old, and our daughter, Lori, was two-years old when we left the city of Cochabamba to live in the tropical lowlands of Bolivia.

We were prepared to live in the steaming tropics, but no one had mentioned that in Bolivia, when a south wind starts blowing from the South Pole, the steaming tropics can get really cold. We learned quickly to have some warm sweaters, coats, quilts, and blankets ready. At least the cold usually only lasted for a few days at a time.

There was no easy way to travel to San Borja. First was the nightmare ride from Cochabamba to La Paz over a narrow, winding road through the Andes Mountains. The road wasn't wide enough for two vehicles to pass, so when two vehicles met, one had to back up. Often the drivers would engage in a shouting match, and we would all sit and wait until one or the other gave in and moved. La Paz is at 12,000 feet. The airport is 14,000 feet and is the highest commercial airport in the world. (Elaine always had a hard time because of the altitude.) The hotels we stayed in didn't have any heat, and it was cold in the mountains. Often we would go to the airport early in the morning, get flight-delay notices every hour only to have the flight canceled about five in the afternoon. It then took another hour to get back to the city. We would then repeat the same routine the next day.

Back then, there were no roads connecting La Paz with the town of San Borja. Our choices were to fly in on the weekly Bolivian airline, Lloyd Aereo Boliviano, which seldom made their flights on schedule, or take our chances on an unscheduled cargo plane that flew cargo from the city of La Paz to San Borja.

Rain was usually the excuse given for the delay as the airstrip in San Borja was dirt, and when it rained, the planes could not land until the runway was completely dry. In the rainy season, this could go on for days. However, San Borja is a cattle-producing area, so if we had the nerve, there were old Douglas DC3 airplanes that had been used in the Second World War that flew over the Andes Mountains from La Paz to San Borja and back hauling beef to market. These pilots were willing to take more risks than the commercial pilots. For years this was the way we traveled because the commercial-airline schedule was not dependable.

I can remember very vividly one trip out of San Borja on a meat plane. Elaine was several months along with baby number three, and they put her up front next to another passenger. I was in the back with the other two kids and a pile of quartered steers that had just been butchered. We had flown for only about five minutes before I felt the plane turn around. Elaine said that she looked at the passenger sitting beside her. He was hanging on and sweating profusely. She asked him what was wrong, and he said, "We are turning around; the plane is going in for a landing."

She asked where we were, and he told her, "San Borja." We hit the ground with a wallop. When they opened the door, I found out that a long weld on one of the motors had broken loose, and this had somehow caught the motor on fire. Nevertheless, the plane was repaired, and we flew out that afternoon with Elaine in the back with me, the same meat, and the flies that had been added while the plane was being repaired.

The Town of San Borja

San Borja is an old town with a vast jungle area on one side and huge grasslands on the other. Guns were common, and there were lots of feuds and shootings. This was the kind of place where writers of cowboy stories would have found plenty of material to work with. However, this town was strategic to our work among the Chimanes because it was a central location for the tribe. The Chimanes came to trade and sell, and brought down rafts loaded with cargo to the port outside of town for the Bolivian river merchants.

Elaine writes:

When we got off the plane, the first thing we felt was a blast of hot, humid, tropical heat. San Borja was mostly mud houses with leaf roofs, and many houses had bamboo walls. There was no electricity, no plumbing, and no telephones. Cows and pigs ran freely in the streets.

Gene and Gladys Callaway, along with their two sons, David and John, who were just a little bit older than our two children, were there to meet the plane.

San Borja was the cattle center of Bolivia, and there was meat in abundance. In order to buy meat, we would walk around town until we saw some lungs hanging on a pole. Lungs on display showed who butchered a beef that day. The next day it would be someone else at a different location. Since we were not able to buy the choicest cuts of meat, they would chop off a piece and some bones, and whatever we got is what we cooked. Our diet was mainly rice and meat; we also ate all kinds of cooking plantains, bananas, and papaya.

We stayed with the Callaways where living conditions were primitive at best. Red fire ants were a really big problem. Their sting was really painful, especially to someone who was allergic. They would invade everywhere. If any food got on the floor, they would swarm on it, and they would get into the sugar, too, so we kept the table legs in cans of kerosene to keep the ants off of the table. The crib had to sit in cans of kerosene, too, because if the baby spit up, the ants would climb up the crib legs and bite the baby.

Because we got our water from a water hole, it had to be boiled for drinking. We would pour it into clay water pots to cool, but since it had been boiled over an open fire, the drinking water tasted like smoke. We caught rain water off of the roof into our water barrels when we could. We didn't have to boil rainwater, and it tasted a lot better.

Of course, we did not have a refrigerator or a clothes washer. We washed clothes by hand or, at times, we would get someone to wash them for us. For lights, we had a bottle filled with kerosene with a little strip of cotton rag in it for a wick. The mosquitoes came out at night, so we really did not stay up late. We got under our mosquito nets and hoped we did not have to get out again.

We seldom got a letter or were able to send one. It was like living back in the days of the Old West. Needless to say, things have changed a lot since then. It was a challenge, but we did it.

Chapter 8

Gene and Gladys

July 1958:

Gladys Callaway started working with the Chimanes in 1952. She and June Quick lived with a Chimane family in their village for a year studying the Chimane language and learning it fairly well.

Gene had a talent for learning languages. He had spent some time in Brazil and had picked up Portuguese quickly, and when he came to Bolivia, he learned to speak Spanish well.

He also had a good sense of humor. Someone would say, "Hey, Gene, what are you up to?" And he would answer, "Oh, about 5′8″." or "Do you think it's going to rain?" and he would answer, "Well, I don't have my degree in divining the weather."

He and Gladys had married on February 3, 1953, in Cochabamba, and then returned to that same Chimane settlement where Gladys had been living. For the first few months, they continued to live with the same Chimane family until Gene built a house for them.

Getting supplies upriver was a problem. Getting meat was a real problem, too, and Gene had to spend time hunting that he would have liked to have used in language work. His children were sick, and so was Gladys. Gene felt that it was taking most of his time just to live.

Euwert Sadler and his wife, Jean, were also missionaries with New Tribes Mission and were working in another area of Bolivia.

Dino, Gene, and Euwert.

Elaine tells this part of our story:

Dino and Gene talked it over, and they decided that they would make trips among the Chimanes who lived along the Maniqui River, and the women and children would live in the town of San Borja.

Dino focused on learning to speak Chimane. I focused on taking care of Lori and Darrel. Lori, Dave, and Johnny focused on managing to be in trouble most of the time.

Darrel was still a young baby when he started having problems with projectile vomiting. Everything he ate came up again; he needed medical attention quickly. Dino was gone, and I had no way to contact him. I didn't have any money, and neither did Gladys. I was a stranger in town and spoke limited Spanish. Gladys talked to a man that owned a store in town, and he gave me the money for a plane ticket to La Paz.

I got on the plane with my baby boy and flew out from the lowland steaming tropics over the Andes Mountains to the cold, barren high altitude of the city of La Paz without knowing a single person who lived there. When God says He will never leave you nor forsake you, believe me, it is true. The plane landed, and I met some missionaries who spoke English. They helped me get to the Methodist Hospital where Darrel was treated; I was even able to stay with him until he recovered and we were able to go back to San Borja again.

During that time, the words to a song kept going through my mind. You may never have heard it, but the name of it is, *I Walk with the King, Hallelujah!* Believe me, I knew that as I walked through that whole experience, God the King, was there taking care of us.

Dino writes:

Gene, the senior missionary, felt that it was too hard for a family to try to live among the Indians. Elaine was not very happy about this arrangement because we had come to reach these people, and she wanted to live among them. She would beg to be able to be with me among the Chimane people. It was not easy to leave her and the children behind. After returning from Korea, I had vowed never to leave her again, but I had done it for my country, and we could do it for the Lord.

Darrel and Lori in a small cart.

I must admit that I learned the Chimane language a lot faster being alone and not having to do a lot of family chores. I had grammar classes with Gene each day, and, while he worked on translation, I walked the beaches memorizing phrases in the Chimane language. At night I would sit around the campfires with the Indians and listen to them speak. I would try to write down words to help me remember them.

Strangely enough, in Chimane, *you* is *me* and *me* is *you*. Once I was going to the river to take a bath and met an Indian returning from taking a bath. I thought I said; I'm going to take a bath, but I got *you* and *me* mixed up and said; "*You* are going to take a bath." He looked disgusted and headed back to the river.

Then, too, we had been told to listen to the more-experienced missionaries, and there was a certain fear in taking my wife and two children up among a group of alcoholic Indians where there were no stores, no doctors, and no law enforcement.

After seven months of separation except for monthly visits, Elaine would take no more. "You said I would hold you up on the language study," she argued. "I'll carry the water from the river,

I'll chop the wood, and I'll sleep under a tree. As far as food is concerned, the Lord will provide," she stated. "Those Chimanes eat something."

I guess my biggest problem was a fear that our co-workers wouldn't approve of us moving up among the Indians because of their own bad experiences. Gene and Gladys felt it would be too hard for us. The people in San Borja told us that the bugs would eat us alive, that food was going to be a problem, etc.

Nevertheless, we decided to build a house at La Cruz, which was a little Chimane settlement of about twenty families on the Maniqui River. If life was too difficult, we could move back to San Borja.

I only had fifty dollars to spend for building a house. Wages were only a dollar a day, so I hired some men and began to chop down trees to build a one-room house. We used bamboo leaves for the roof and bamboo for the walls. Our house had no nails in it; we tied everything together with vines. We made crude furniture, and the floor was just packed-down dirt.

Chapter 9

Our Move to Chimane Land

October 1958:

Now, my wife is a queen and I would have loved to have built her a palace out there, but our love for God and our desire to do His will caused us to live in a one-room house.

Leaving San Borja, we loaded an oxcart with supplies such as flour, sugar, powdered milk, kerosene, lard, medicine, and things a family would need in order to live in the remote area where the Chimanes lived. The first night we were there as a family, a welcoming committee of drunken men surrounded our house. They beat their drums, played their flutes, and danced about wildly. Since our walls were just bamboo poles, we could look out at them and they could stare in at us.

Typical oxcart.

The Chimanes lived in small family clan groups, and drinking parties were planned between the members of the clan. It was the only social function among them. While the men went out to hunt, the women made the beer. Every home within the clan felt great social pressure to make a huge vat of drink. When the men returned from hunting, the drinking began and did not end until the last vat of beer was consumed at the last house in the clan.

Our kitchen was built separately from the main house with a fire-box of adobe blocks that had a piece of barrel across the top to cook on. The oven was a barrel that the heat from the fire went around before going out of the stove pipe. The Chimanes were very impressed with the stove. They cooked on logs pushed together that could hold a cooking pot.

Of course, there was no indoor plumbing. The first day the family arrived at our new jungle home, I began making an outhouse. The Indians asked what that little house was for. When I told them, they laughed and said, "You are building a house for that?"

We used a kerosene lamp for light at night, but it attracted mosquitoes. We and the children escaped mosquitoes, bats, and whatever else was out there by climbing inside the mosquito net; however, some mosquitoes usually got inside before we did, so our first challenge was to get rid of them. The jungle offers a wide variety of ants and spiders, in addition to mosquitoes. Fighting bugs was a never-ending task.

We got up with the chickens, but by that time, the Indians were already up and around and usually looking through the spaces in the bamboo walls to see what we were doing. The bamboo walls had cracks between them, so there really was no privacy; the people would come and look through the cracks to see how these strange foreigners lived.

Water was carried from the river unless we could catch rain water in a barrel. Clothes were washed in the river; the water was usually a reddish brown color, so most of the clothes took on the same color in just a couple washings. If you asked a Chimane what color water was, they would have said brown because they had never seen blue water.

Finally, we got an old James washer with a handle that swung back and forth and a hand-crank wringer. Just daily living was time consuming, but this washer was a real blessing and time saver for us.

[See Appendix (A) for more on the James washer.]

We learned to eat what the Chimanes ate. They would take sap from a certain tree, fence off an area of the river, and put the sap in the water, which caused the fish to come to the surface for air. Then the Chimanes would shoot them with arrows. There was always plenty of fish to eat. They raised rice, corn, yuca, and all kinds of bananas. Plantains were their basic food. When we sang the song, "Where He leads me, I will follow", we just added another line, "What He feeds me, I will swallow."

Dino continued to learn to speak Chimane; however, I had been struggling to learn Spanish, and now I was here where people didn't speak Spanish or English. I told Dino one morning that we needed wood to cook with. He told me to ask the Indians to bring some. He told me the words to say, so I started speaking Chimane out of necessity.

The Chimanes really liked our children, Lori and Darrel. Our son's first words were in Chimane. He heard us tell the Chimane dogs to get out of the open part of our house so often that he would speak up *"Taij mi acho."* (Get out of here, dog.)

Chapter 10

Miracle of the Meat

May 1959:

Truly God prepared a table for us in the midst of our enemies. He loved us even when we were enemies of His, and with His help we can love the unlovable. *Luke 6:27-28 But I say unto you which hear, Love your enemies, do good to them which hate you, Bless them that curse you, and pray for them which despitefully use you.*

Dino writes:

We lived in a Chimane settlement along the Maniqui River called La Cruz. We had our home built among the Chimanes. Enrique, a Bolivian farmer, and his family, who lived a half mile upriver from us, hated everything we stood for, and told the Indians lies about us.

We were a threat to their livelihood because they made their living farming by the "slash and burn" method. They first cut the smaller plants with machetes, and then felled the trees on top of them. They let this dry for a month or more and then set fire to it. They had to pile the unburned brush up and plant in between the logs. They could use the Chimanes as slave labor, because they knew that the Chimanes were addicted to alcohol.

Enrique would come with a five-gallon can of cane alcohol and insist that the Chimane take a "free" drink. Once weakened, the Indians wanted more. Thus, indebted to Enrique, the Chimanes were marched over in the early morning to pay for the alcohol by hard labor.

The fights and misery that went on among the drunken Chimanes were terrible to watch.

Enrique said things like, "The gringo is not your boss. You can drink if you want to." There would be times when we would go to Cochabamba and not return as planned. Some of the Chimanes asked Enrique why we had not returned. His answer would be, "When Dino is here, he does not drink, but when he goes to the city, he gets drunk and gets into fights and is in jail."

In my Bible it said: Love your enemies. Of course, God zeroed in on me to love this particular family, especially the dad who was the head rattlesnake. I went back and forth, but finally I said, "Lord, I can't love this man in my own strength. If you want me to love him, please give me the fortitude to do so." I prayed that God would open the way for me to show love to this family.

It was not many days later when the opportunity came to show love. Alfonso, the oldest son, came one evening and said, "My little sister is very sick with a fever, and Dad wants you to come to give her a shot of antibiotic." I thanked the Lord for answering my prayer. I went and gave the shot and did so each evening for two more days. The girl got well. The father, Enrique, also got sick, and I went over three consecutive nights to give him a shot. After that, there was peace with this family that had been my enemies.

The family was very grateful, and they gave me a hind leg of deer they had shot that day. Enrique and his two grown sons were all good hunters. I am terrible at hunting. God planted an idea in my mind. I told Enrique that I had a repeating .22 rifle and a shot gun. I would let him use them if he would give us some of the meat he killed. I also told him that I would furnish the ammunition, as it was expensive for them. They always got close to their prey when they hunted, so they wasted very little ammunition.

Enrique accepted my offer, and for the next few years while we were there, we never lacked for meat. He had a lagoon behind his house which he called the "miracle lagoon." He would only be gone a few minutes before he would find a deer, wild pig, big black ducks, or something else to bring back. On one occasion he said, "I believe that God is giving us this meat, because when you aren't here, we go hunting and find nothing."

When God stirred my heart to love this family and do good for them, I never dreamed that God would use my former enemy to supply our meat. Do you have an enemy–someone who hates you? Pray for him/her and ask God for the opportunity to show love.

We were really happy as a family and never felt that what we were doing was a sacrifice; people praying for you make a big difference. One dear lady wrote that she felt our diet was lacking and said that she was praying that we would have a better diet. From that time on, the Indians brought us tomatoes, onions, peanuts, and fruit of all kind. We did have a good diet, and we feel that her specific prayers had a major part in it.

Elaine writes:

Our third child, Randy, was born in December of 1959. Dino was still spending hours each day on learning the Chimane language. I was spending most of my time on day-to-day living and trying to keep him free to study. It took a lot of time preparing meals over a wood fire, carrying water, washing clothes, and taking care of three small children, not to mention entertaining the steady stream of visitors.

The Indians were constantly there, and the river merchants dropped in to visit on their way up or down river. In the Spanish culture, hospitality is a must. You drop everything and invite people in. You need to serve them at least a glass of water or a cup of coffee, and you usually invite them to stay for a meal. I would also work on literacy, making the primers and trying to pick up as much of the Chimane language as I could manage.

Lori, Randy, and Darrel in our home at La Cruz (The Cross).

Chapter 11

Literacy and Culture in Chimane Land

The many years that Gene and Gladys spent working with the Chimanes made it easier for us. Gene was to the place where we could establish the Chimane alphabet; we needed to decide what letters we would use for their sounds and symbols. In case you are wondering, there are phonetic symbols for the sounds, but when you decide to teach literacy, you need to use letters to represent the sounds. The Bolivian government at that time didn't pay much attention to the Chimanes, but did want the alphabet to be as close to Spanish as possible because Spanish is the official language of the country. The next logical choice was to find letters that occurred on a typewriter in order to be able to print the books. The Chimane language has extra letters, so we had to decide which symbol to use to represent the sound for that letter.

We had a Chimane man check out the primer and were told that men wore clothing with a 'V' neck, and the women wore clothing with a round neck. After correcting our pictures, we never forgot it again. We had learned quite a bit about culture, even if we hadn´t noticed the difference between the men and women´s dress.

Some things we had observed, however. We had certainly learned a lot about their drinking habits. That was a very negative part of their culture. We also knew about their fear of the rainbow; they blamed the rainbow for many of the bad things that happened.

We knew that they lived in small family groups because they feared being bewitched. When someone dies, they put thorns in the trail to the house, burn the house, and pour hot peppers on the body, so that whoever bewitched them would die. They chant, "Let the rainbow die, let the rainbow die." They believed sickness was caused by witchcraft. The wind can bring sickness. The big trees have spirits. There are spirits that live in the lagoons and control the fish. They will not let their dogs have the bones from the animals that they hunt, because they believe if they do, the game will leave the area.

See Appendix (B) for more information on how the Chimanes view the rainbow as a bewitching force and the particular challenges in tribal ministry, in an article by Wayne Gill.

July 1960:

Spiritual Vocabulary

Another year had gone by, and we were still struggling to find a spiritual vocabulary. What is their word for God? This was a puzzler. The Chimanes actually had three words for God. God was three brothers, Dojich, Jen', and Michet. Dojich lives where the sun rises, Michet lives where the sun sets, Jen' lives where the sun is directly above at midday. *Jen'* is also the Chimane word for father. He has two wives, one which he stole from his brother. The brothers get together from time to time and get drunk; that is when you hear the thunder and lightning. They tell about the gods' mother, the moon, making up the starchy root drink I described earlier, and Jen' drinking with her. They felt that if Jen' could get drunk and sleep with women and even steal his brother's wife, then it must be okay for them to do it, too.

"What is wrong with drinking?" a Chimane once asked me. "After all, Jen' gets drunk," he argued. The Chimanes never realized that these were the very things which held them in slavery.

The Bible teaches that God is Holy. The Chimanes were told that God is immoral. The Bible teaches that the rainbow is a promise from God. The Chimanes were told that it is an evil spirit who causes sickness and death. So which of those words would you choose for God? Maybe you would not choose any of them. Why not use the Spanish word *Dios*? Would that change their belief? Probably not; they would likely transfer what they knew about God to that word. We opted to use their word for father, "Jen'," and then we taught them about the true God.

In one of the first villages where we presented the story of Noah, they openly cheered in the meeting when we told them why God put the rainbow in the clouds. "The rainbow is not dangerous," they cried. I felt real triumph over the lesson. Now we were getting somewhere, I mused.

A few days later in that same village, a sixteen-year-old boy died. As his body lay on the ground near the grave they were digging, I heard one of them ask what caused his death. The father replied that the rainbow bewitched him.

Some anthropologists fault missionaries for destroying culture. "Missionaries are culture killers," they cry. "Get them out of the tribes."

Culture is not sacred. Not all culture is good. Alcoholism that dominates a culture brings grief, sorrow, and frustration to its victims. Many were looking for a way out of a life of drunkenness. God's Word offers an alternative through faith in Jesus Christ. We do not apologize for telling them how they can be free from the slavery of alcohol.

Because it appeared so awful to us, I started preaching the wrong message: "The Bad News about Drinking." It didn't change one life to tell them that drunkenness was wrong. They would hear us coming and quit the party until we left. They would hide the alcoholic drink from us, but as we headed down the trail away from them, we would hear the flutes and drums start up again.

The next step that we needed to take was to teach them to read and write. We prepared basic primers in the Chimane language and told the people that we would come to their village and start literacy classes on Monday. When we arrived on Sunday, we learned that part of the village had left. They left houses and fields and moved about twenty miles downriver to escape the school.

"We don't want schools," the remaining ones declared. "Schools will separate us from our children," they argued. The river merchants were no help to us in this either. Realizing the potential of what learning could do for the Chimanes, they warned them to not allow us to teach their children.

We were working with a face-to-face culture where everyone did the same things. There was no generation gap between the parents and children. We concluded that we would have to teach parents and children together.

But, how will we ever reach all of this tribe when they live scattered over a vast lowland jungle area? Once I made a survey and walked for nineteen days through the jungles visiting small groups.

My tennis shoes fell apart, and my feet were so covered with blisters I could hardly walk. Through all this effort I had probably only visited between two and three hundred people. Even if I could visit them all, what good is just a visit? They must learn to read, and they must be able to understand what they read. We decided to start out by spending ten days in each village before moving on so the people would not get tired of us. Our main desire above all was to get God's Word to as many as we could.

When we arrived at a village, everyone would come to the river to see what was happening. "Did you bring any trade goods?" they asked.

"We only brought a few things to trade for food," we answered. "We didn't come as traders; we came to tell you about God and teach you to read."

No one got excited or jumped for joy over this announcement. They always asked if we brought medicine so we always tried to bring along some basic medical supplies. Each village was taking us further from civilization, so we needed some medical supplies for our own needs, too.

They had little interest in money, but trading with fish hooks, needles, matches, thread, flashlights and batteries, and the many other items they wanted, kept us well supplied with meat, fish, and other basic foods.

When we first arrived in Bolivia, over fifty percent of the Chimane children died before they were two-years old. As long as they nursed their mothers, they were fat and healthy, but once the milk dried up, they faced a harsh meat and banana diet, and the lack of hygiene and contact with disease took their lives. We learned that the way to be accepted by the Indians was to aid them when they were sick or injured, and have trade goods to swap with them.

The children had big tummies caused by malnutrition and intestinal parasites. There was also a lot of pink eye. We had had a course in field medicine and studied a lot of medical books, as we knew we may need to attend to the sick and injured. Medicine could be bought in Bolivia without a prescription by anyone. Many had a skin disease that left big black splotches on them. Tuberculosis was rampant among them. Their habit of everyone drinking their home brew from the same gourd didn't help.

Some of them suffered from a tropical ulcer caused by an insect infected with *leishmaniasis,* which causes huge, painful sores. The sores finally heal, but it remains in the blood. Years later it appears inside the nose or mouth and eats away at the tissue until it kills the victim. There was a cure for this, but it was expensive and at least sixty shots were required. Strangely enough, there was no problem with malaria in that area of Bolivia. There was an abundance of mosquitoes of all varieties and all kinds of biting insects, but no malaria.

The Chimanes sleep on the ground, and since the ground is hard and uncomfortable, they are early risers. We had to be ready for them at daybreak. "Let's learn to read," we urged.

"It is too hard," they argued. "We can't learn."

"Yes, you can," we countered.

We finally got them seated on grass mats and began school. Everything was a big joke to them. I became a clown. They tried as long as it was fun and then informed us that they were leaving. "It is hard," they reasoned. They would sometimes be out of food and so would go hunting for a couple days or longer. When they returned with the meat, the wives would have vats of home brew waiting for them. We tried to have meetings, but they would often be drunk as they slurred the choruses that spoke of God's love.

We wrestled with this. "Is it right to have them sing praises to the Lord when they are drunk? But when aren't they drunk? Maybe something will stick in their minds," we speculated.

However, we seemed to be getting nowhere with our literacy program. We would return to a village where we had taught before and find that they had forgotten everything from our previous visit. Their brains were so numb from alcohol that they could not grasp reading.

It seemed impossible that we would ever see churches planted among the scattered, drunken Chimanes, and I became discouraged. Although I believed that somehow God would show us the way to reach these people, it was very hard to wait on His timing when there were so many Spanish-speaking Bolivians we could reach by just taking our Spanish Bibles and sharing the Word with them.

When Casiano Ramirez, a Bolivian farmer, came and asked us to teach him and his family God's Word, we accepted. We warned him from the beginning that we could only spend a few months teaching them, because our task was to evangelize the Chimanes.

We did not worry about a building as the weather was hot, and all we needed was shade. This man, along with his wife and children, believed when we told them about Jesus' life, death, and resurrection.

Neighbors began coming, and, in a few months, we had a group of forty believers gathered together. This farmer began to show leadership ability, and I spent a lot of time teaching him. After a year, this man and others like him were able to give messages and minister to the people.

Spanish-speaking neighbors at Sunday meeting.

On Sunday morning the Spanish-speaking neighbors that lived along the Maniqui River would walk along the trails throughout the jungle and gather together for a meeting. Some of our children are included in the picture. Our dog, Happy, is in the front.

Chapter 12

The Spirit House

Early 1961:

Wayne Gill, one of the mission leaders and, later on, the translator of the Chimane Bible, came with his wife, Ruth, to visit us. One of the first questions he asked me was, "When are you going to get back to reaching the Chimanes?"

"Wayne, I don't know how to reach them. How do I begin? Where do I start?"

Wayne answered, "I have no idea, but let's spend some time in prayer and let the Lord show us what to do."

So we spent the next two days in prayer, seeking God's will and His plan for reaching the Chimanes. Shortly after we had prayed, we received a visit from Salvador, a Chimane who lived far upriver from us. During our conversation, he told about his visit to a spirit house at a village called Yocumo.

He said, "I went inside the round spirit house where we sat on low benches. The Witch Doctor's wife had prepared vats of homemade beer to drink. He dipped a gourd into the beer vat and passed it around. The Witch Doctor had a small drum which he began to beat. As he played, he began to chant for the spirits to come join us; then, all at once, people from the other world descended from the roof. They weren't Chimanes; they were dressed like you and wore shoes and they drank beer with us."

Salvador tried to pronounce a few words in English, which I knew he could not have heard anywhere else except in that spirit house.

He said one of the women said her name was Alice. Strangely enough that was Elaine's middle name; only I, and a very few others, called her Alice. I shuddered when he told me this because this is not a name they use, and this man had not been around any other people who spoke English. The Spanish name for Alice is Alicia. He spoke a couple more English words that he said he had heard in the spirit house. Salvador went on with his story; he said that the spirits told them that someone was going to come and bring a book that was written in the Chimane language that would tell us about God.

Wayne and I looked at one another and agreed that God, through this man, was showing us where to start. So we took our wives and the gospel of Mark (which was the only book of the Bible translated into Chimane at this time) and prepared to head upriver.

We loaded a dugout canoe with supplies and bedding and started off upriver to where the group lived who had heard the message in the spirit house. We had no motor, so we hired Chimanes to "pole" us upriver. This is done by shoving a long bamboo pole into the sand and pushing off on it. Going upriver against the current is faster and easier using this method than using a paddle. It was a three-day journey.

When we arrived at the village, we asked the people if the story we heard from Salvador was true. They all said that they had heard the message. "Look," I cried, "I have God's Word. I have come to tell you about the true God." I waved the book of Mark in the air to show them I had it.

That evening grass mats were brought out, and everyone sat down on them. There were around forty people present. I began, in my still limited Chimane, to tell them about Jesus. Chimanes are different from a regular group of listeners. If they are listening, they would repeat the words out loud. I started teaching about Jesus from the book of Mark.

Someone interrupted me and asked, "Where does this Jesus live? Does he live upriver or downriver?" The man asking the question wasn't trying to be funny; he just had no idea who I was talking about. Jesus is a common name in Spanish, and the Indians often take Spanish names. I recognized that this was not working; I had to somehow teach them how Jesus fit into the story. I would have to start from square one with them.

The following evening, I started from the beginning teaching about God and the creation given to us in Genesis. For several nights I laid the foundation for their understanding, but I realized how much I missed the mark because I did not have the Scriptures written in their language. We only had the book of Mark to teach from.

The Chimanes of Yocumo who were the breakthrough we needed.

The last night we were there, I talked about the two roads: the broad road that they were on, and then the Jesus road that God wants them to take. I told them that they must choose which road they are going to travel. Will you continue on the devil's road, or will you choose to switch over to Jesus' road?

They did not respond for several minutes. Then they began to talk very loudly and excitedly between themselves, as they sat on their grass mats on the ground. I remember there was one woman who had a small grey monkey on her head.

I didn't push them. I just told them that if they wanted to leave the devil's road and walk Jesus' Road, they should get up off of the mats and come forward.

I admit I was elated when, after talking it over for about five minutes, the entire group arose from the mats and came forward, indicating that they wanted to follow Jesus' road.

This story will always remain a mystery to me. Did God give a message in the spirit house? How does one explain the strange spirits who Salvador thought were Americans? Regardless, this was the breakthrough we needed, and this was the beginning of our travels on the Maniqui River.

While we were with Wayne and Ruth, we took advantage to work more on the dictionary and primers. The word for mother-in-law was "kiss"; to modify it to say "your mother-in-law," one said, "kiss me." Pascual, the Chimane man helping us with translation was a funny-looking fellow who wore a long dress and had splotchy blue, black, and white skin from a disease. He had two wives and a flock of kids. He was amazed that there were so many words in the Chimane language.

When we found this combination of words that said "kiss me" in English, we decided to have some fun with Elaine. I called her and said, "Elaine, you have a real good ear. Put your ear up close to Pascual, and see if you can hear exactly what he is saying.

Wayne urged, "Get closer so you can hear him." So she bent closer. They asked Pascual to say "your mother-in-law" so she could hear it. So he got close to her and said, "Kiss me." We got quite a kick out of that one. Pascual laughed along with us but had no idea as to why we were laughing. I am sad to say that a few weeks afterward, as Pascual was weaving some leaves for use as roofing, a river merchant came along and told him to get his bed because he was taking him downriver with a load of cargo. Pascual told him that he owed the leaves to another merchant who would be angry if he came to get them and they were not ready.

The merchant put his rifle up to Pascual's head and said, "Come with me, or I will kill you." Pascual refused, so the merchant shot him in the head. There was never anything done to the merchant for this murder. We were not there when this happened, and how our hearts ached for the two wives and small children left behind. The memory of 'your mother-in-law' in the Chimane language will always linger in our minds. What a gentle, simple man Pascual was. He loved his family, but his life was snuffed out like a candle before its time.

The people still did not want us to teach their children; they were afraid it would cause division if they learned to read. The only alternative we were left with was to also teach adults to read. Anyone will tell you that teaching adults to read is not easy. And it was very challenging to teach adults who lived in small groups scattered along the jungle rivers, especially when there were no books except a few hand-written primers. Their daily lives consisted of hunting, fishing, and working. For entertainment, they made their own alcoholic drink so they could gather around vats of it to get drunk on weekends and all known fiesta days.

Our first efforts to get the Chimanes to sing were pathetic. They had never sung before. The old men chanted about birds and animals when they were drunk, but no one could carry a tune. Elaine was overcome with laughter when a woman got up close to her mouth and tried to sing a half line behind her. Finally, when we sang the chorus, "Be careful little feet where you go" with the motions, one old grandmother got excited. "Hey! This is like dancing," she exclaimed and took off. She danced clear around the house before we could restore order again. Today they sing songs of praise to Christ. Now there are songs in the rain forest being sung by Chimanes who had never sung until they knew Jesus.

More questions: How does one get a church planted among a tribe of people who are steeped in witchcraft, abused by many of the Bolivian people, are alcoholics, and are living scattered over such a vast area that is in many parts inaccessible? Besides that, clans seldom mix because they believe that sickness and death is a result of being cursed by another clan.

We were given two precious promises from God's Word that assured us of victory when it once looked so hopeless. The first promise that the Holy Spirit quickened to our hearts was *Matthew 16:18 …and upon this rock I will build my church; and the gates of hell shall not prevail against it.* The devil and all his angels could not prevail against it. God's message came right out in the Witch Doctor's round house.

The next promise God made real to us was *Rev 7:9 After this I beheld, and, lo, a great multitude, which no man could number, of all nations, and kindreds, and people, and tongues, stood before the throne, and before the Lamb, clothed with white robes, and palms in their hands.*

We knew from that promise that there will be Chimanes standing there in white robes, praising and worshipping God. God is building His church among the Chimanes. In His time, God will have His way, and no power can prevent it.

Chapter 13

Back in the United States

In March of 1961, we had another little girl we named Dixie. The four children seemed to thrive in and love the jungle. When Dixie was six-months old, we felt that it was time to return to the States on furlough. We had arrived in Bolivia in 1956.

Looking back, it seems that our first five years in the field were spent just in preparation to start the work.

Baby Dixie.

August 1961:

We were two adults and four children, so we needed the price of four tickets home. We had not laid money aside to pay for the passage, so we wondered just how the Lord would supply our fare.

In our small hometown, there is a Presbyterian church. One of the members felt compelled to raise money to bring us back to the States, so he put a box at the back of the church and announced that if anyone wanted to donate to help the Kempfs return from Bolivia, they could put their contributions in the box. They raised $1100, and we soon returned to Washington.

Ben, our fifth child, was born while we were home in the States, and now we were seven. I was concerned about going back to the mission field with five children because we were still orphan missionaries, and our home church had no interest in missions. I talked with one of the New Tribes Mission leaders about my concern and the problem I had of traveling to meetings because I was working a job to support us.

The director advised me to get involved in a local church and help out; then they would probably help support us when we returned to the field. The church that had brought us home was without a pastor, so it seemed like a good place to start. I was asked to preach there several times, and I taught the adult Bible class. Then the youth group was turned over to us, and we were bringing some of them to the Lord.

The Kempf Family with Baby Ben.

I felt sure that this church would help support us when we returned to Bolivia because we had done as the director said and became really involved. However, a few months before we returned to Bolivia, a new pastor came to the church. He seemed like a very good man, but he was a one-man show. He immediately took over the classes that I had been teaching. When we left, we didn't even get a farewell send off. The Lord had closed that door.

It seemed foolish and risky to move out to the field again with no promised support. Nevertheless, we had seen God take care of us in Bolivia with four children, so how could we conclude that the Lord could provide for a couple with four children, but He could not provide for a family with five? I felt ashamed at my lack of faith. I thought of the manna in the wilderness that fed over two-and-a-half million people for forty years, and I realized that nothing is too hard for the Lord.

I prayed, "Lord, don't let me be ashamed. I will go back to Bolivia, but I feel responsible for my family, and I feel that it would be wrong if I let them go hungry. If I have to work for an oil company, in construction, or whatever, I will do it, Lord. We really want to continue in missionary work to the Chimanes and will trust in You to provide for us."

Having made that speech to the Lord, I asked Him when He wanted us to return to Bolivia. I waited and listened, and I heard one word very clearly. The word was "June." That was it, just one word, "June." I told Elaine, and she was content and ready to go. She has always had more faith than I have.

During the last part of May, we paid all of our bills, bought and shipped supplies, and found that we were left with twenty dollars. I told God that we would go as far as we could toward Bolivia. "It may take a year to get there, but we will head out, Lord."

We got one big encouragement through the mail; a turkey farmer who had heard us speak months before sent us a check for four hundred dollars with a note that said: "This is to help you return to Bolivia."

The night before we left on our trip, some friends with whom we had been in Bible study came over and gave us their gas card. "Use this along the way," Alex instructed. "If you need something like a tire, buy it on the card. When you get to Miami, cut it up."

Just before we pulled out, an old couple drove in and handed us twenty dollars.

Elaine had found a song that was first written in Chinese during the Communist occupation and which had been later translated into English. Its title was, *I Will Not Be Afraid*. The words to the song say:

"I will not be afraid;
I will not be afraid.
He goes before me,
His banner 'ore me,
So I'm not afraid."

There are several more verses, and we kept the song sheet up on the sun visor the entire trip. As we travelled, Elaine would often take it down, and we would sing it at the top of our voices.

With the help of the gas card, we made it to Modesto, California. The mission had closed down the camp there, but still maintained some apartments that missionaries could use. After we bought groceries, we had one dollar left. I asked the Lord if this was where I should look for a job.

All at once, my mother's words flashed into my mind: "Brother Damon wrote to me that if you ever get to California, you should look him up."

Reverend Damon Matlock had been my pastor in New Mexico when I was a boy. Mother had kept in contact with him through the years. I made the call to him with my last dollar, and he was anxious to see me. He said that usually the meetings were scheduled weeks ahead, but he had an opening for Sunday night for me to speak. He lived 105 miles away in Stockton. In that service, I showed slides and talked about our work. They took in an offering of forty dollars. One man even took off his watch and put it in the plate. The people had no idea about our situation. After all, who would head out to a mission field without adequate funding?

When I returned, Elaine was planning a further leap of faith. She needed dental work done and suggested that we go to Old Mexico to have it done at a dental school for missionaries. "It will be cheaper to have dental work done there," she said.

"I don't know how God will do it, but if you feel strongly about it, I'm ready to give it a try," I conceded.

We planned to leave for Mexico early the next morning. That evening we stayed up talking instead of going to bed. Around 11 o'clock, another missionary family rolled in who were on their way to New Guinea. When Tuss Tucelli, the missionary, heard that we were going to Mexico, he asked why.

"We are going to get dental work done," we replied.

"Stay here," he said. "I'm a dentist and have all of the equipment needed in the trailer. I'll do it for free." We stayed, and he did a good job. From there we traveled on to New Mexico. I was born and raised in Clovis, and still have a lot of relatives there. We arrived on a Saturday night around 10 o'clock. We drove to my grandparents' home and found them already asleep. Not wanting to wake them, we drove across town to my Uncle John's house. They put us up for the night, and the next morning, we went to church with them.

When Uncle John introduced us to the pastor, he asked me to come and share about our work with the congregation that evening. I showed our slides and started to preach, but the preacher stopped me. "The Lord has spoken to us, brothers. Let's make a victory march for these missionaries." He took a large Bible, put it on the table and told the people to march up and put money in the Bible for our work. They put several hundred dollars in that Bible.

The very next morning, our tickets arrived for Bolivia. I had asked that they be sent to my uncle's address in Clovis. When we had received the four hundred dollars from the turkey farmer, we sent it to the mission and told them we felt that the Lord would supply the rest, so would they please send the tickets we ordered? We counted the money we had been given; we had enough to pay for the tickets with eight dollars left over.

Then, *Operation Aunt Power* took over. Some of my aunts spoke to pastors about having us speak in their churches, and soon we had meetings all over town. When we left Clovis, we had several hundred dollars, so we cut up the gas card so as not to cause any more expense to our friends who had given it to us.

We arrived at our mission headquarters in Cochabamba, Bolivia, with two hundred and thirty-seven dollars left. God raised up support as we were on our way to the field. Friends we had met in Bible studies while at home began sending to us. One church adopted us as their missionaries, and, for the first time since we began this journey, we were not orphans.

It was God Who had given us the word "June," and God Who made our journey possible. God wanted the Chimane Indians to learn of His love, and we had been chosen as ambassadors for Him.

Chapter 14

Return to Bolivia

Dino continues:

"In June 1963, our family returned to Bolivia. We now had school-aged children. Because the Indians lived in such small, scattered groups, there was no way to reach them but to travel among them. This meant traveling in the blazing sun and sleeping in crude shacks on beaches. We could see no way to educate our children under those conditions. Our children did not choose to be born and raised in the jungles of Bolivia, but they were happy to be there with Mom and Dad. We would have loved to be able to keep them at home and teach them. We would have welcomed a teacher to come and say, "I would be happy to come live in the jungles to help you and teach your children." Maybe all of the other difficulties involved could have been resolved.

"What would happen when the children were older and had no proof that they had ever been to school? What about the isolated life they were living? What about their future?" We did not have the answers to any of these questions. In all fairness to them, they needed an education. This has been the most painful part of our missionary life: separation from our children.

New Tribes Mission, the mission we were working with, had established a missionary-boarding school, and we saw no other alternative but to send our children to the mission school.

The school was hundreds of miles away from us and very hard to get to. As I mentioned earlier, we could only travel to our area by plane because of the lack of roads. The planes' schedules were very irregular and undependable. After we finally did arrive via plane to the capitol city, we had a day's bus ride to Cochabamba and another eight-hour trip to the school. The school had a two-week vacation at Christmas and a three-month vacation in the summer. One by one, as they reached six years old, we had to leave them at the school. Most of the staff were wonderful Christians and very dedicated to being second daddy or mommy to the children. However, we learned, years later, about some that weren't the best, and mental scars are still appearing from actions that, out of fear, were not reported.

Sometimes late at night, I would wake up and hear Elaine crying. "What's wrong, honey?" I'd ask.

"I just miss the kids so badly," she would sob, and some nights she cried herself to sleep as I held her in my arms.

At Christmas, the kids came home, but this was a big expense to us. The schooling took over half of our allowance. What was more traumatic was that, during December, the heavy rains came, and sometimes we would lose precious days of vacation waiting for a flight to come in or go out. The dirt airstrip in San Borja became a quagmire when it rained, canceling flights for days.

One year, a teacher offered to bring the kids down to us at Christmas. They went to La Paz by bus and tried to make the flight, but it was canceled for several days. The day the flight did get out, they overslept and missed it. Elaine could not stand it and went out on a meat plane to be with them. Since we had already spent a lot on hotel bills in La Paz, I decided to stay home. To put it more accurately, I couldn't afford to go out, or I surely would have.

I went back upriver and plunged into language study to drown my disappointment at not being with my family. After some days, I decided to go upriver and spend some time with my language informant, Hilario. He and his wife lived about three miles on the other side of the river from us. Hilario was blind, but he was amazing; his family had to eat, and he could not go hunting, but he was strong, and he could work. He had a farm where he cleared land by the slash-and-burn method. His wife would lead him to a tree, hand him the ax, and he would chop it down. With his wife's help, he could walk to town. Hilario never let his blindness stop him. He was also bilingual, and his being able to work with me was a mutual blessing.

It was a muddy three-mile journey on a vague trail that I could barely follow. When I finally arrived, I found Hilario leaving to attend a drinking party downriver, so he bid me good-by and left.

There I sat, in that little shack with no walls. The temperature was in the nineties, and it started to rain. I suddenly realized that it was Christmas Day. Then I heard the drums coming from the drinking party where my blind informant had gone.

I thought of Christmas in the States with the trees, toys, and family get-togethers. I thought of my own family in Cochabamba, and I longed for them. It was past noon, and I was hungry. I spied the leg portion of a huge rodent called a capybara. When I took it down to cut a piece off, I noticed that it was green and spoiled so I didn't eat it.

I didn't hear Him come. I saw nothing, but His presence was suddenly there. Jesus, whose birthday we celebrate on December 25th, was there with me. His presence flooded my soul, and I could hardly contain the joy and fullness that I felt. Time had no essence for me, and I don't know how long His strong presence accompanied me. I only knew that it was Him. It wasn't something that I had conjured up. It was completely unexpected. I knew that God is like that. He comes in our times of greatest sorrow. He comes in times of deep trial. He comes to comfort the lonely.

Elaine writes:

Due to the unpredictable Maniqui River, we spent a lot of time building houses. When the river rose and started eroding the bank, we could see we were going to lose another house. There are no rocks in this part of the river; rocks are so treasured that people from upriver would bring rocks with them to sharpen their knives and machetes. We didn't want to build another house at La Cruz, so we bought a piece of land a little downriver. Strangely enough it was called "America," not because we gave it that name; that was already it. It had a beautiful sandy beach, and then one tier of land sloped up from the river and then another gentle slope to the top. It had a lot of fruit trees, and the river was not cutting there. We felt we could build a more permanent house there. Even if it was not immediately among the Chimanes, it was still close.

Lori had gone to first grade in the States, and then, when we got back to Bolivia, she went to Tambo, the mission's school. The next year Darrel went to school, and then Randy and Dixie, We got to keep Ben with us a little longer. When the children were in school, we made literacy trips among the Chimanes and took Ben along with us. When the children were home from school, we would take them along, too.

Chapter 15

Journal of the Kempf Family River Trip

July 1968:

Our five children on the river trip.

This is a journal of one of our river trips in 1968 with our five children. We traveled by canoe and had to carry all of our supplies with us.

Two Chimanes came along and poled us upriver. We made these trips to visit the Chimane families, to talk about God, and teach literacy to those that were interested.

Monday, the 15th: We were quite calm about getting ready, and then, at the last minute, the canoe took off in a hurry. It was loaded with a lot of provisions, and our three younger children had neither their hats nor their life jackets on, which caused a few minutes of excitement. Dino, and I and our two older children were going to walk as the canoe was well loaded with our supplies. On the way, a man gave us a leg of wild pig. We arrived first where we were to meet the canoe, borrowed a kettle, and cooked the pig leg. When the canoe arrived, we added rice and roasted some bananas. We were able to beat the canoe because sometimes walking the trails through the jungle is much faster than going up or downriver in a canoe. The Maniqui River has many curves as displayed on our book's cover. You can see that walking on land and crossing the narrow part of the river is much faster than poling a canoe that has to follow all the bends and curves.

After eating, we continued on for a couple more hours that day and slept on the beach. We warned all the children to get undressed and to shake out all their clothes before getting under the mosquito net and into bed. Only one forgot, and that was enough to have a bed full of sand. We had one big mosquito net for all of us and five mattresses under it.

Tuesday, the 16th: Early start today. Got a couple of hours in and then cooked breakfast. The kids had fun finding frogs and lizards. They caught one lizard that ran up Dino's pant leg while he was trying to light the fire. We stopped for lunch in a shady place and discovered, from Benny's screams, that it was thickly inhabited with ants. We cooked and ate anyway, evading them by throwing water on them when they got too close.

It looked like rain, so we put up a little shelter and used the canvas tarp for a roof. This time the children remembered about shaking out their clothes before getting in bed; only Dino forgot as he was fixing the net, and he got more sand in the bed.

Wednesday, the 17th: Even though this is the dry season, this morning it started raining and we all got soaked. Whenever we could, we walked along the bank to lighten the load in the canoe. We had an awful time getting a fire started that night as it had continued raining on and off all day. At least we had enough dry blankets to sleep comfortably until about 5 a.m. when we awoke. We all huddled together under the tarp as it was still dark. As soon as we could, we loaded the canoe and got going.

As we drew near to Maraca, we saw little houses on the beach. These are used in the dry season when the river is low. There are fewer mosquitos near the river, and the sand is softer to sleep on.

Beach houses along Maniqui River.

We ate breakfast on the beach and arrived at Maraca where we had a house. The sun came out, and we dried out somewhat. Now we had a roof over our heads. We even got a stand built for the kids to sleep on. We put two wooden suitcases on a stand for a table and are now more or less settled.

Friday, the 19th: Today one of the men who brought us upriver shot a turkey, Dino and the boys went to Yocumo, where Dino fell in the river, and they even killed a snake. We were sad to hear that José, Pascual's son and one of our students, had been killed by a jaguar the day before our arrival. The people said that it jumped him from behind, and now they were out trying to find it. They were getting ready to move their houses closer to our house. Pascual told them, "Dino speaks good words, and it is good for us to hear them."

The house at Maraca.

We spent the day getting settled. We decided to start classes Monday and give the people a little time to gather food and get their work done. We needed a little time to get rested up and to finally get dried out after our wet trip. One fellow came over early with his books anyway; he already knew the first book completely and that was encouraging!

Saturday, the 20th: Andre's wife died. They burned the little house in which she died as is the custom.

The people came over last night. A big tarantula dropped down in our midst and caused some excitement before Dino killed it.

Sunday, the 21st: Another turkey this morning. (These are small birds weighing 2 to 3 pounds.) We had a quiet day and a meeting at night. The people listened, and we were pleased that they had remembered quite a bit from before.

After we got to sleep, we were awakened by the man next door talking excitedly about a jaguar. He had been at a house not far from here, when a jaguar jumped out and bit a roll of leaves that were there to make roofs. The people all ran for the beach. It was quite upsetting since Pascual's son, José, had just been killed by a jaguar a few days ago. I got up and put our gun within easy reach just in case the jaguar should decide to come back. There is really very little protection to be had in an open house with no walls: just a roof over our heads and a mosquito net.

The people wondered if it wasn't the dead woman coming around instead of a jaguar.

Monday, the 22nd: Our day started at daybreak. The men showed up early to class.

River-trip literacy class.

We didn't teach very long because the people here are in debt to a river merchant, and we felt it would not be good to keep them away from their work too long. They are doing well in their reading. Our children got their little fishhooks out and tried their hand at fishing, but they didn't catch anything.

Emilio went to see the folks at Yocumo. Pascual is still out hunting the jaguar that killed his son. News on the radio is not good: Bolivia is in a state of siege.

The bugs are thick, so in the afternoon the kids lie around in the mosquito net and read. We've added a cedar-chest bench to our suitcase table and also hung up a hammock, which is where I'm writing now. Almost all the people showed up to the meeting. We put grass mats on the ground for them to sit on, used a couple of barn lanterns for light, and used a folded flannel sheet when we have a flannel-graph lesson. So far not too many sick people but we did have to give a shot to a small baby. Most of the people have pinkeye and come for medicine. A man brought us a wild duck.

Tuesday, the 23rd: Another early start. The men all showed up for classes. One brought a wild turkey ready for the kettle, but before it was cooked, we were given a piece of wild pig and a little later a piece of tapir. The dinner menu that night was pig and tapir steaks, rice and gravy, green papaya salad, and bananas roasted in the coals, topped off by a cup of instant coffee followed by ripe papaya if anybody was still hungry. I have a daily job of washing clothes, and since we each brought only three changes, I don't dare let the dirty laundry pile up. We have another turkey to add to all the other meat. We are really eating a lot of meat lately. God has always been faithful in sending us plenty to eat.

We have a meeting every night, and just last night, another tarantula showed up over our heads. Randy pointed at it and yelled, "Look there!" Emilio grabbed a knife and thus ended the second tarantula that had come to a meeting.

A little old grandmother comes every night and listens so carefully. She really seems thrilled to be able to hear these words.

Wednesday, the 24th: Breakfast today was fried yeast bread and roasted smoked tapir. Delicious. Our daughter is learning to cook the hard way: over a campfire with plenty of smoky wood to keep us all in tears. They finally decided it wasn't a jaguar that killed José; it might have been lightning or something else, because he had no marks on him other than a little blood from his ear, and he hadn't moved from where he was struck down.

Some of the people think that it was "jaguar people" or something like that. We got another turkey for the kettle. There was a good crowd for the meeting this night. Each night a few more show up.

Thursday, the 25th: They brought the poles needed to make a second little house for the school. Ours is about full with us and five children in it. Carlos came to visit. He is quite a character; he chanted for us and told about the Chimanes who are still so wild that they don't eat salt. He also said that he had seen savages and that one of the Chimanes is a killer who is hiding out with the savages and knows their language. You can't believe much of what Carlos says. Carlos keeps threatening to kill the Bolivian merchant. The Bolivian is pretty scared and wants to get out of here.

Friday, the 26th: No turkey today. This was the first time in quite a while. So we opened up a can of corned beef and had gravy over instant mashed potatoes, a treat that came down in the barrels. We did have a piece of deer meat roasted over the open fire for supper.

Emilio and the Bolivian went downriver today. Emilio will be back in a few days. The men are still pretty enthused about studying and show up pretty well. There are always a lot that show up at night. Pascual came by today; they are really afraid of jaguars now. People are seeing them all over the place. They are claiming that there are five jaguars walking around together and that the people are being attacked in their houses.

Many from here have moved out and are living on the beaches for fear of jaguars. Pascual told us that all of the village of Yocumo was moving out to the mouth of the Yocumo River where it enters the Maniqui River. This will save us at least two days going in and out of the Yocumo River, but it will also mean putting up another shelter to live in.

They are moving for fear of the jaguar. They say the jaguars want to get their children. They believe that jaguars can turn into people, so this isn't a fear of just an animal, but of something supernatural. The other day I noticed one of the trails had a vine with leaves hanging down stretched across the trail. I mentioned it to Dino, and he said they had their house like that, too. The dead woman's husband was staying there and that was to keep her away.

Jesus and Manuel, Bolivian river merchants, stopped by today. Manuel was the one we had asked to bring our mail, but he didn't have any for us.

We all took a walk back into the jungle. The trail went up a hill, and we are starting to get into the foothills. We got to the top and, by looking through the branches, we could see quite a way over to another hill. Would it be possible to make a landing strip between these two hills? Being able to fly in and then return downriver, stopping in the villages and teaching the Chimanes along the way would be a lot easier and would save a lot of time. Tortillas and beans for supper. Boy, can the kids ever put away a lot of food.

Sunday, the 28th: No school this morning so we slept in a little later. Hot biscuits baked in a frying pan over the coals for breakfast and, for a special treat, I made up a package of jelly we had with us. The days have been beautiful. No cold weather so far. The bugs in the afternoon are dense, but that makes the mornings and the evenings seem especially nice. The people were drinking today. Some of them got pretty drunk but showed up to the meeting anyway. Another tarantula came out during the meeting.

Monday, the 29th: Classes went pretty well. Some that got too much drink were pretty dense, but that made the slower ones look good. The days have been beautiful, very few mosquitoes here. Just a few people out to the meeting; they're probably sleepy from staying up so late into the night during the weekend.

Tuesday, the 30th: Not too many for class this morning. Some were fishing; they're probably out of food. The ones that came have gotten through the study book, so from here on everything will be review to be sure they know it. A good group turned out and listened very closely to the crucifixion story.

Two turkeys today, so we're back onto our meat diet. Randy had a fever and a sore leg. He had cut his foot on a clam shell, and we were concerned it might be a quick infection setting in. The kids had a good time digging clams today; they had enough to eat a few and even had the Indians helping them. The Chimanes don't eat clams, but they use the shells for spoons.

Wednesday, the 31st: A woman brought us roasted fish for breakfast. Emilio is back and is doing really well on the review. He got us some palmheart and that, with the turkey, makes a nice meal. We heard a strange sound during class today. It sounded like thunder, but the sky was clear as a bell. All the people were excited and wondered what it was, but they couldn't explain it. They weren't alone; we couldn't explain it either.

Dino went to see Pascual, who is the father of the young man who died. He has moved out to this river now and says the whole group is moving; they're all afraid. So many things are happening since his son's strange death. They wonder if there are savages in there. They hear groups of people talking, and it gets louder and closer, but they never see them. They see strange lights flash in their house, then disappear. They claim a jaguar ran right through the house where they live. He also heard the same strange noise that we heard today, two or three different times. I don't try to explain it, I'm just writing what we were told.

We have been working on primer number four, but haven't made too much progress so far; hope we can squeeze it in as we need it printed before our next trip. Pascual also told us about them seeing three people close by one night. He told them to come in, but they did not. He said, "Don't be afraid," but they took off through the jungle even though there were thorns. They could hear them running away.

When he went out to look for his son who died, he saw a man with a white shirt coming toward him. He raised his gun to shoot and then felt it would be wrong to shoot someone, so he waited, and the man disappeared. Another man had his gun up against a tree, and it went off by itself; that really scared him. He said, "That could have killed me!"

Also, five others went out to hunt the jaguar that they thought had killed the boy, (we doubt it was a jaguar). They reasoned that this jaguar person traveled at night so they would need to have a good flashlight with which to spot him. The men were very nervous and a bit scared as they fanned out in the area where Jose died. After hours of searching for the jaguar person, the hunters came to the conclusion that he would not allow them to see him. "We heard him and when we tried to shine our flashlights on him, the bulbs would go out." When they wanted to use their flashlights to shine on the jaguars, they would not work, but otherwise they had no trouble with the flashlights, so they gave up on finding the jaguar person.

Thursday, the 1st: Another turkey today. Emilio went to clear a place for our house up river. The people have not moved yet. Little by little we worked on the primers. Ben has pink eye, and his asthma is bothering him. You can tell when the people have just about reached their limit of studying for awhile. Dino gave a message on how we don't need to fear, and all of a sudden, a light flashed. Probably lightening in the distance, but it disturbed the meeting.

Friday, the 2nd: Class today; this is supposed to be the last class here for this time. Dino went to check on our house. The plans were for us to move today, but we might not because there is no house yet. It was so good to hear that the Wymas had gotten a letter from Dino's dad and sent the news on the radio. We're glad he is better. It has been quite a while since we've had any mail. Dino went up to where we will be moving and helped clear the jungle.

Saturday, the 3rd: Moving day. Emilio is working on the house. He was supposed to take the leaves for the roof with him, but he left without them. We got everything in the canoe. The heat was bad, and no one else was there to help, so the kids did most of the carrying except for the heavy things. No one was around to take the things up river, so we prayed about it, and soon Jose came.

House being built.

We walked up. The poles were up for the house, but no roof. We strung the canvas up on the kids' side and went to bed. We did not sleep very well; we were in a small cleared-out place in the jungle without a roof over our heads, and all the night noises kept waking us up.

Sunday, the 4th: We got up early and got the leaves on for the roof, but Emilio didn't measure the length right, so we don't have enough leaves. We have half a roof over our heads. It is enough so we can at least be dry when we sleep, but the sun shines in. The day is terribly hot, and we are dragging around just getting the necessary stands built and settled. I had a pile of clothes to wash. It's thundering now, and a cool wind is blowing in. It looks like bad weather coming. The others haven't moved out from Yocumo yet, but they are supposed to be moving and bringing us leaves when they come for the rest of the roof. Turned into bed early.

Monday, the 5th: It rained during the night, but half a roof kept us dry. Pascual and the boys are going right through the new third book. The group across the river came, so Dino taught from the second book. The women wanted me to teach them, too, so I started from the beginning with them. Leoncio moved over for classes. No meeting last night, and Dino announced that there would be no meeting for tonight, and they all seemed glad about it. We now have three quarters of a roof over us. The children really seem to be enjoying themselves by playing in the river, fishing, and being with the people.

Tuesday, the 6th: Early start today, and I have been dragging my feet ever since we moved here. It is sure a problem of how to keep the people off our bedding. I gave up trying to make the beds in the daytime. I'm leery of the people sitting on them. We tried folding bedding in a pile, but they lay across them anyhow. We finally decided to leave one net up and put all the things inside it. I did not think that most of them would get inside it, although one little girl did one morning, muddy feet and all. These people are spotted from a skin disease, and we don't know how it spreads. When they lay their heads on our pillows, I keep thinking about the little inhabitants in their hair, and it bothers me. Maybe it should not, but it does. Two turkeys today. A good meeting, the people are interested. Pascual wanted the meetings at his house so that his three wives and all his children could listen, so that makes a big group. They had the children gathered together singing, too.

Wednesday, the 7th: Another turkey today plus fish. Randy and Darrel had a good time catching the fish. We cooked them for supper. The people continue to be fearful of the strange things going on in Yocumo. They feel that there must be savages, although they have not seen footprints, just jaguar prints. A fellow claims that two jaguars jumped out at his wives today. It is doubful there really are jaguars, but now the people are so afraid that they are seeing jaguars everywhere.

But something did happen that sounds like people: one of the Indians had a bag in his house tied up on a pole. It had clothes and new material in it, and someone came in and burned the bag. Nothing else was touched. We heard Emilio, who is far more advanced in civilization than the other Indians, say, "It was probably the dead boy. He must have gotten mad and burned the bag."

Tonight at the meeting Emilio all of a sudden started jumping and, since he gets epileptic siezures sometimes, I was afraid that maybe he was going into one, but then Dixie screamed and a big tarantula jumped on Lori's leg. She brushed it off quickly, and Emilio came over and stomped on it. It had jumped on him first and scared him. Things got settled down, and we finished the chorus. The rest of the meeting went okay.

Thursday, the 8th: We now have a whole roof over our heads. We had another turkey for dinner. Some came early for class, so Lori cooked breakfast and got the children fed, then Dino came from his class and ate, then he took my place as I ate. Pascual went to Yocumo today to get his things which he had left there lest something should happen to them. He got to drinking chicha and got real sad about his dead son. When he got back here, he was talking again about all that had happened. There sure is a mystery about Jose's death. They say that his upper body was broken up pretty badly, and they feel there are savages there who must have done it. It does not seem like a jaguar as first thought. If it was lightening, why was not the tree next to where he was standing split or anything else to indicate lightning, but if not that, what? Pascual also says that they have missed bananas, yuca, and corn from their farms. The meeting got started late, but all from around here came.

Friday, the 9th: We got mixed up on the days and thought that today was Saturday. We did not realize it was not until we turned on the radio to a children's program that only comes on Saturday, and it was not on. Come to find it out, it was only Friday. We had already told the people that tomorrow is Sunday, and there won't be any classes on Sunday so we are taking Saturday off. Now we have an extra day we didn't know about. The rain that has been threatening for days finally hit along with a cold south wind. It sure is nice to have a whole roof over our heads. Most of the people from here weren't around for the meeting, but the ones from across the river came, and they usually do not.

Saturday, the 10th: This is the day we lost, and the people all still think it is Sunday. We have not told them differently because they might stay home two days from classes instead of one. It is a cold, drizzly day. A man who is called a brother stopped in; he is not a priest, but has some office in the church. He was very friendly. We worked on primers for most of the day. Turtle eggs for supper. No meeting as the people weren't around.

Sunday, the 11th: Since yesterday was supposed to be Sunday, we had classes today. They are all doing well; they have a good attitude. They say, "By this time next year we will know how to read it all." Got a turkey, a leg of wild pig, and also, for a treat, some sweet watermelon. They claim a couple of trappers have caught two jaguars in the Yocumo. It is so hard to know the truth from fiction. All the people from across the river were here for the meeting, all from the group here, and three more people that were on their way up river. They live at Cosincho, the place where we hope to go on the next trip. There were over fifty adults in attendance. The ones from Cosincho said, "We are waiting for you up there." We gave them one of the first little charts, and after studying it for a while, they all wanted one.

Monday, the 12th: Two turkeys today. I'm sure feeling tired; a trip like this sure exhausts one. Classes in the morning. Another good meeting with the ones from the other side of the river attending. It sure is a thrill to be among them and see their interest. They listen so intently. I went to bed right after the meeting, but Dino stayed up. The people wanted to listen to the radio, and he had two turkeys to clean.

Tuesday, the 13th: Feeling a little more rested today. Had to figure out a new recipe as we are almost out of cooking oil and never have eggs. So I made up a thin yeast dough last night and let it rise. This morning we spread it thinly in an almost greaseless skillet and after that first light greasing, never added more. They turned out pretty good. It was something the kids could cook while I had classes. Today they brought us a little oil they got from a fruit that grows around here, so that will last us until we get to our home at America in a few days. Dino preached on baptism, and Randy wants to be baptized, so we plan on baptizing him here before we leave. The people sure show up faithfully to the meetings and classes, too.

Wednesday, the 14th: Another turkey today. The kids played almost all afternoon at the river. A woman brought us thirteen watermelons, most of them sweet. Forgot about baptizing Randy after classes, so we had an evening service. It was a real blessing. Dino spoke in Chimane and explained baptism. We sang a Chimane chorus, "I have decided to follow Jesus." Then Randy said a few words in Spanish.

Friday, the 16th: Rained during the night, but had stopped by morning; this has been a wet dry season. People came early for classes. We taught for a little while, then quit to get ready to go. There must have been fifty people crowded in our house while we were trying to get breakfast and get packed. Things were pretty hectic. We ate an early lunch and got off at noon. Dino shot a couple of birds for supper. Emilio shot another one. They look something like a black duck and are pretty good eating. Pulled onto a beach at evening and gathered up some wood to cook with. Got our net hung up, then went and visited a Bolivian family who lived close by. Then got into bed; the sand really made pretty soft sleeping.

Saturday, the 17th: Up early, got the canoe loaded and took off. Cooked breakfast around 10 a.m. and got to America about 3 p.m. Tired, but praising God for the way He had worked in hearts and taken care of us.

Elaine Kempf.

Chapter 16

Rumored Dead

October 1968

The Chimanes were really bad about spreading false rumors. Since they had no police, they controlled their society by gossip. If someone got out of line, others would just talk bad about him/her and the wrongdoer would usually straighten up.

On one occasion, Elaine and I were up river at Yocumo, teaching literacy. The people there were very friendly, and we were enjoying our time there; however, unbeknownst to us, two Chimane men were taking a raft down river.

Two men in a Balsa raft transporting woven 'jatata' leaves used for roofs.

As they passed by the port of La Cruz, a man standing on the bank shouted out to one of the Chimanes piloting the raft, "What's new upriver?" The man, Julio, answered, "What happened is that the people at Yocumo killed the American missionary, his wife, and their son."

Before more inquiry could be made, the raft was out of hearing distance, but the listener of the rumor began to proclaim the news to everyone he met. In just a couple of days, the news had reached the town of San Borja, and people there were in shock.

The church in town sent one of the believers to La Cruz where the rumor originated. Meanwhile, the Chimanes had embellished the story with vivid details about how we were killed. San Borja went into mourning. When we found out about this, we were greatly surprised to hear of the concern the townspeople had for us, even the non-believers. Some started burning candles for us.

The chief of police went to our fellow missionary, Gene Callaway, who owned a launch, and ordered him to take a commission up river to the suspected crime scene. Body bags and lots of disinfectant were sent along to bring back our corpses.

A day or two later, we were out on the river bank and heard the launch coming. We recognized it as Gene's boat because there were no others on the river like it.

When they docked, we greeted them, and I asked where they were going. "We have come to take your bodies back to town," they answered. The officer in charge questioned us as to any threats or danger we encountered. I assured him that there had been none and that we were about ready to head back to San Borja. He had come with armed soldiers to exterminate the people had the rumor been true.

The people at Yocumo marveled at the false rumor and said, "Julio is a big liar."

It was amusing once we got into town. People began to shout, "Look! The dead man." Many of them came and hugged us and told us they were happy that it was only a rumor. For Elaine and me, the entire ordeal was a real blessing. We had no idea that the people cared so much about us. How often we fail to show that we appreciate someone until after they are gone.

What was interesting was that the people who lived at La Cruz added on and amplified the rumor, making it sound more credible. Since unbelievers are slaves to Satan, the father of lies, it should not be surprising to hear such lies, but it was a shock to hear of our own deaths.

Chapter 17

Down River without a Canoe

December 1968:

Dugout canoes are made by felling a tree and then hollowing out the log with an ax and a small tool called a froe. These canoes are long and narrow and can easily tip over if they are not steered by experienced pilots. Mahogany is the best wood for these canoes, but very few mahogany trees are left because of the demand for the wood on the world market.

To the Chimanes, the rivers of the rain forest are their "highways," and the canoe is their means of transportation. Most of their needs they find in the jungle, but there are a few things like salt, fishhooks, fishing line, and cloth that they have to buy. They have very little money, so they trade food like rice and bananas that they grow on their little farms. They also weave a certain kind of a leaf to roof houses.

I wondered if we could find a better market for the Chimanes' products because the river merchants greatly exploited them. Downriver from where we lived was a town called Santa Ana. I wondered if it might be feasible for the Chimanes to take their products there to get a better price. The Chimanes might even return with products they could sell in our area. The town was a little over sixty miles away, as the crow flies.

We had a good Indian guide, Jose, who had made a number of trips down river with some of the river merchants. He had felled a palm tree that was covered with thorns, one of which entered his leg and penetrated to the bone. Jose had tried to remove the thorn but could not get it out because it had broken off and was deep in the calf muscle of his leg.

He came to us to get help because the leg had festered and swelled, and he could hardly walk. "This happens every time I go hunting," he complained. I took him to a doctor, but the doctor cut and pressed and only hurt his leg more; the thorn didn't come out.

On one of his trips downriver, Jose and his boss set up camp along the river as night approached. Jose decided to take a bath but didn't realize that the water was teeming with man-eating piranhas. Suddenly, dozens of piranhas were biting his leg. He left the water quickly but discovered that his leg was bleeding, and the fish had eaten a good-sized chunk of flesh from his leg, right where the thorn had been.

By the time that Jose returned from the trip down river, his leg had healed. He could go hunting and walk a long way without his leg hurting. He was cured; the thorn was gone. It had been tormenting him for more than ten years. Jose laughed when he told us about the piranhas biting his leg. "They were better doctors than the doctors," he said.

Woman weaving *jatata* leaves.

The Indians who live upriver pick a certain leaf called *jatata* which they weave onto a long strip of bamboo. It is in demand for roofing houses downriver because it is long lasting and durable. The pieces, when woven, are about two-and-a-half feet wide and eight feet long. They are fastened to rafters and make a good roof that will last for years. We were sure we could sell all the leaves we could take with us. We also went to our neighbors who made two-pound squares of brown sugar and loaded a big box of it. We took other things, but these were the two main trade items.

We had an outboard motor that would speed the trip considerably, and we would pack both guns and fishing line to use to get meat and fish along the way. There would be plenty of fish to catch down among the log jams. A gung-ho missionary kid of eighteen wanted to be our pilot. A retired minister had come down to accompany us, and, with Jose and me, there were four of us to make the journey.

Shortly before Christmas, we loaded our canoe with leaves for roofing houses, cubes of brown sugar, and bananas. We were looking for a route downriver to open up trade and also to visit the Chimane family groups that lived there.

The river was swift and full of log jams and sand bars, but once it reached the flat grasslands, it spread out into a series of lagoons and lakes. Without a guide who knew the area, one could easily get lost.

On the first day of our journey we got through the log jams, but the following day we had quite a time finding our way through the lakes.

Our first stop was at a small ranch where we sold some brown sugar. This man was an Indian from another tribe. He had a small ranch with about fifty head of cattle. He had earned the money to start his cattle business by hunting alligators at night and selling their hides in Santa Ana.

Traveling on downriver, we arrived at a big ranch where they wanted all of the leaves we had brought. The ranchers in that area made huge molds of cheese of a good quality, which they sold cheaply. We bought around three-hundred and fifty pounds of it and knew that we could double our money if we took it back to San Borja to sell.

By the time we reached our destination, we had sold everything we had and had bought jerky and other things. The town of Santa Ana was only a few miles downriver from where we were. The river had a deep, clear channel, and from there, it emptied into a larger river which eventually emptied into the Amazon.

Our goal was to be home by Christmas Eve, and we had only a few days left, so we decided to turn around and go back home. Our return upriver was against the current, but we made it fine the first day even though we had some trouble getting through the lakes.

Once as we neared the riverbank, we spied a huge anaconda snake. It just lay there on the bank, and we wondered if it was dead. Suddenly, it made a swift movement and hit the water. Brian, our pilot, began frantically to shoot it in the head as it came towards us. After thirteen shots, it finally lay dead. Upon closer observation, we could see the tip of two hooves sticking just outside the snake's mouth. The anaconda had unhinged its jaws and swallowed a full-grown deer which weighed over a hundred pounds. The anaconda was in the process of digesting his dinner when we found him.

At one place, a log jam had caused a small waterfall. Brian, our young motorist, tried to climb it instead of trying to avoid it. Our boat quickly turned crossways and flipped upside down. Brian grabbed a tree limb and held on, but the canoe was torn from him. The rest of us were near the middle of the boat. Jose dived in for our bedding. I grabbed onto the canoe. The river shot the canoe and me a few hundred feet down river where we slammed up against a log jam.

Brian came swimming toward us and when he reached the upturned canoe, he climbed on and began to walk the length of it. His weight caused the water to suck it in underneath the log jam. The canoe disappeared and stuck fast under tons of pressure from the rushing water. We were alone, miles from home, with no canoe.

Jose came into view. He had managed to save our mosquito nets. Our guns, cheese, dishes, food, and clothing were all gone. The river had risen several feet because of rain in the mountains. Where there would have normally been sandy beaches to walk on, there was just muddy silt. There was nothing more to do. We had to leave the canoe wedged under the log jam and try to walk out.

We had no dry place to lay our bed during the night, only a log lying up out of the water. All four of us huddled on that log. None of us slept because we had to balance ourselves on the log. I do not know what we would have done if Jose had not rescued our mosquito nets. Even so, it was difficult to keep the nets tucked under us and not get bitten by the black hordes of mosquitoes that stabbed us through the net or got in underneath it. So, besides balancing ourselves on the log all night, we were slapping mosquitoes. Pastor George suffered the most. When it was light, and the mosquitoes left, he clapped his hands at the many still inside his net. Both of his hands were dripping with his own blood. I felt so sorry for him, but he never complained.

Early the next morning, we realized that we could not stay there in the swamps. We must try to get help. There had been a flood, but now the river was dropping. We found no dry ground, only mud that ranged from ankle to knee deep. To complicate matters, all of the bushes were filled with fire ants that had climbed up to escape the flood. As we brushed against the bushes, these ants crawled on us and stung us.

We had not eaten the previous day, and our food supplies were now food for the river fish. We started walking, but soon the jungle sun was too hot. Because we were weak from lack of sleep and food, it was a real effort to keep walking through the mud mile after mile, but we had no choice.

Finally Jose said, "There are people up ahead."

"How do you know?" we inquired.

"I heard a monkey," he answered.

"But what has that to do with people?" we asked.

In just a few minutes, however, we saw several men coming out of the jungle pulling a newly-made canoe. Because of the flood, they could bring it out through the jungle. One of them carried a pet monkey, the one our Chimane guide had heard.

They agreed to pole their canoe carrying us to their village about twenty minutes away. Once there, we pounced on some half-cooked fish and bananas that were roasting over the coals. Our first meal in two days!

We decided that Pastor George should stay in camp while Jose and Brian, with two more of the Indians, returned by canoe to the log jam to chop the canoe loose. They would try to dive under and at least retrieve the motor. By the time they arrived, the water level had dropped enough that they could see how to get the canoe out. They did have to chop a piece out of the canoe to free it. (The owner we had borrowed it from was not happy when he saw the notch, but we compensated him for the damage.)

While they were freeing the canoe, I walked to a nearby ranch where I rented a horse with tack so I could cross the grasslands to San Borja to find someone to help us bring the canoe to the port.

As I rode to San Borja, a huge buck mule deer, the biggest deer I have ever seen, came charging straight for my horse. All I could do was to shout at him at the top of my voice, and he finally trotted away. I could imagine having to pay for a horse, too.

When I arrived in town, it was already three days after Christmas. I found a friend who owned a boat which he let me borrow, and I took it down river to help retrieve our canoe. I met him at the Indian village, after returning the rented horse, and, a few miles down river, we met Brian coming upriver with the boat and motor. He had fished the motor out, dried it out and got it running.

So, we arrived back at San Borja shortly before dark and our adventure ended.

We did locate some previously unreached Chimane villages that were later reached with the gospel, and we had found a market for their products, but the trip was such a nightmare, I don't ever have a desire to return. You have heard the saying, "I'm up a creek without a paddle," but we were literally down the river without a canoe!

Dangerous River Debris

Chapter 18

Our Final Literacy Trip (Kids at Tambo)

Elaine Writes:

We made our final literacy trip up the Maniqui River in October, 1969. Some of the Chimanes had learned to read, and we were able to start teaching them to be the teachers.

We set out to travel on what was usually a day's journey upriver to Napolis where our co-workers, Harold and Nora Rainey, lived. It started to rain and kept on raining. We finally made it to Harold and Nora's, where we stayed the night. The rain stopped, but the river rose so high that it was almost too full and swift to travel.

We got up early and cooked breakfast, knowing that it would be a blistering hot day. We got to Puchuya where Harold and Nora had been teaching literacy, and the people there were very interested in the gospel.

As we unloaded the canoe, Dino tossed our mattress up the river bank to one of the men helping us, but he wasn't able to catch it, and it fell back into the water. The protective plastic bag had a hole in it, so it got soaked. About that time, I was so tired that I already felt like crying. The wet mattress seemed too much. It took a while to feel happy again, but I was grateful to the people who had cleaned out and given us their best house to sleep in. I made our bed, hung up the mosquito netting, and then went to the meeting.

After the meeting as I went to get in bed, I found that a chicken had climbed inside our mosquito net. I hauled the chicken out, but sure enough, it had made a mess, and I accidentally stuck my hand right in it. After I cleaned my hand and the chicken's mess up with a wash cloth, Dino and I fell into bed.

In the morning we decided to leave without breakfast and wait to cook until later on when the sun was hotter. An earlier start would be cooler for the men poling the canoe.

As we passed a house, some people came out very happy to see us. One of the men had fallen while chasing a monkey and ran a stick into his head. It was a terrible gash, and they had no medicine to treat it. We stopped the canoe, took out some hydrogen peroxide to clean it and our syringe so we could give him an injection of long-acting penicillin. I tried to cut away the matted hair with some dull scissors I had borrowed, but the cut was still oozing, and my stomach felt pretty queasy. I prayed and asked God to help. He did; suddenly I felt fine and doctored the man as best I could. We left the hydrogen peroxide and some aspirin with him.

On the sixth day of our trip, we arrived at Maraca. It was a thrill to see the way they had retained so much of what had been taught. This group was reading and all they needed now was lots of practice.

One young fellow named Julian, who had seemed so dense that we could not get him to learn even the six vowels, surprised us by reading the first two primers. It was such a nice surprise. He was reading, and he could even write well, too. Another Chimane boy named Victor had taught him to read.

At Yocumo we had a number of fellows in their early teens attend class, and they did quite well. They struggled sometimes, but, for the most part, did really well. If we could just stop another couple of times and stay a few days to help them read, they will be reading completely on their own. What thrills us more is that they have been teaching others!

From Dino's Journal:

We left Yocumo on November 18th to go up river. The goal of our trip was the headwaters of the Maniqui to look at the possibility of making an airstrip. If it is feasible, we would be able to fly in and then float down the river, saving a lot of time and energy.

We were now on our second day of our trip up river. It was cloudy, and it thundered, but we decided to take off anyway. I bought a leg of wild pig, so we would have some meat for our journey, but it turned out to be rotten. For the next three weeks our meat will be just what the two Chimanes with us are able to find.

It was still raining by the third day of the trip; we were soaked to the skin; and, for a change, it was cold. One fellow decided to just get down in the warm river water, clothes and all. We found a crude shelter and huddled under it for protection from the rain. Some traveler before us had left a fire, so we made tea and then set off in the rain to reach a shelter of which the men knew. When we got there, we found that the house had fallen down sometime before. We all were wet and cold and it was still raining, so we made camp for the night without the promised shelter.

We arose at five a.m. and by five thirty we were on our way up river. We decided to stop and cook breakfast about nine a.m. Turkey and rice sounded delicious.

We stopped as the two fellows saw some turkeys out in the bush. They shot at a turkey and wounded it, but it got away. Ignacio shot a big fish. (I never understood how they saw them in the murky waters.) The fish snapped off the arrow and would no doubt die down river. Missed a turkey, missed a fish, and we wondered just what the Lord had for us. Then suddenly, several wild pigs came out of the jungle right at our canoe. Two of them dived in the river and started swimming. We were sure of meat this time. The Chimane in the front of the canoe shot, and one went down. The Chimane in the back of the canoe shot, and the other went down but the swift current carried the bodies off. The Chimanes were so sad. "Let's go downriver and look for them," they said. "Later on they will float."

Elaine and I got out onto the beach and began cooking breakfast. The Indians left. It was so beautiful there on the beach. How we felt for those at home who would just love a spot like this with no people around. About three hours later the Chimanes returned with one of the pigs, so we had meat.

Elaine and Dino cooking on the river beach.

That night we stayed at a place where some Chimanes were living. We knew one of the men who had been in our classes down river. He was making a canoe, and we were able to trade our heavier mahogany canoe for his cedar one. Elaine and I were out of bed by five and ready to travel, but it was near seven a.m. before the two men came back after hunting down river. We got on our way and stopped to cook breakfast in a banana patch at nine a.m. Elaine was the last one getting off the canoe; I was carrying water and the cooking pot up the bank when, to our horror, the canoe came untied. The swift current caught the point of the boat and swung it around. Suddenly, Elaine was on her way down river. If the canoe flipped over, she (and all our supplies) would be thrown into the river. Thankfully, she did have a life belt on. I jumped in the river, fully clothed, and barely managed to grab the back of the canoe. I yelled for help, and the fellows came running. We soon had the boat tied up and Elaine safely on shore.

The sun was beating down, and the heat was terrible. The Chimanes wanted to stop and rest in the shade. Finally, we saw a place on a high bank. They pulled in the canoe and we climbed up the bank. As we rested there, we roasted a *jochi pintado,* a rodent- like animal that weighs about thirty pounds and looks like a giant guinea pig. This meat was another gift from God. It was swimming right down the middle of the river when Ignacio put an arrow through it and dragged it into the canoe.

We spent the night on the beach, threw our tarp over an old shelter we found, and made dinner which consisted of roasted pig and parrot and rice soup. Can those guys eat! They ate almost the entire leg of pig, a big kettle of parrot soup and lots of roasted bananas, and tea. On this trip we only stopped to eat twice a day so we could make better time.

We passed the Cosincho River where it ran into the Maniqui River. We planned to spend a week in the village of Cosincho on our way back downriver. We still have three-and-a-half days going up river to the headwaters.

The sun was terribly hot, so we stopped for about three hours. A big snake came out of the bushes as we pulled onto the bank. The man poling the canoe hit him. The snake tried to bite him but was too far away. Yesterday we had killed another snake along the bank.

We stopped for a rest because the young fellow poling the canoe up front was exhausted. I saw a fish flop up on the bank, and the boys soon had it. After our break, we traveled until dark and stopped on another beach. It looked like rain, so we put up the tarp. By the time we got the tarp up and the bed ready, we were too tired to eat.

It didn't rain that night and by five a.m. we were up and starting out again; however, by six-thirty it was raining, so we found some shelter and cooked breakfast. Luckily, we still had plenty of meat to eat.

We passed the Chimane River where a priest had a big ranch and where a lot of Chimanes lived.

We stopped to talk to a one-legged fellow, and he told us of two empty shelters. By the time we got settled in to them, it was dark. Elaine had lost her hat, and, in these circumstances, it is a big deal to lose your hat.

While I roasted some meat, the fellows went to visit the man who had told us about the empty houses. They came back with lots of stories about jaguars. Needless to say, we did not sleep well that night.

The next morning we finally got underway at seven forty-five. The guys had been goofing around, probably because they were just tired out and knew we had to push up a lot of rapids that day. The water was clear, and Ignacio shot a fish. We stopped for a breakfast of turkey and rice. The fellows shot six more fish, and we planned to eat fish and green bananas for supper. The fish was delicious, but it was sure full of bones.

We got into Ocuña about six in the evening. This was our destination. It is a beautiful area with mountains on both sides of the crystal clear river. Elaine and I went for a bath at the river, but people began to appear from all over. There we were in the water with just our underclothes on, and they kept coming over to us and shaking our hands.

We sang with the people that night, and a neighbor joined in. We had a good bunch out for singing. Miro, one of the men that came with us, told them quite a bit about what we had taught him about God and demonstrated his reading ability.

On November 25th, we explored the area looking for a place to build an airstrip. It looked like it would be possible. There had been fields there before but had grown up since, so the vegetation would need to be hacked down with machetes and the ground leveled. Traveling by river, it is a hard nine-day's journey from the town of San Borja to this place. An airstrip would be wonderful to have.

Once again, we were out of meat; we had eaten the last turkey for breakfast. The fellows planned to go hunting.

That night, we stayed up late talking to a river merchant. The fellows brought us two big fish for supper. They had also found two small stone axes. The river merchant gave us some meat and sold us some jerky, so we were in good shape for meat again. How we marveled at the way food just keeps coming in.

We expected the downriver trip to be a thriller. The first day we encountered a lot of rapids, but after that, we just floated along with the current and did some hunting. The fellows shot fish with both the guns and the bows and arrows. I shot with a shotgun at what I thought was a fish, but it turned out to be a log. The fellows got a big laugh at that.

When we reached the Donai River, we had the men make a shade over the canoe while we stopped to cook lunch. Miro had forgotten his machete and had to return by trail for it.

A river merchant and another canoe came by going upriver. They had found Elaine's hat, which had rotted a little but was still usable.

The men heard some howler monkeys and took off for the woods. They never caught up with the monkeys, but they came back with a turkey. We had planned to sleep in a while, but the men said it looked like rain, so before six a.m. we were on our way again. Then we waited three hours while they chased monkeys. We cooked breakfast on the hot beach. The jerky was very salty.

We arrived at the mouth of the Cosincho River about one thirty, the hottest part of the day. The Cosincho River is so shallow that at times we had to drag the canoe. The sun was almost unbearable. We finally got to where the people lived. They were really friendly, and there was a large house where they let us stay.

That evening, we had a meeting. A large group came out for it. They entered into the singing and seemed to accept all we said. When they left, we headed for bed. This was our fifth week of traveling, and we were very tired and ached all over.

The next day, we had about ten men in class. They really tried hard; our co-workers, Len and Elsie Gill, had done a good job of teaching them.

We had many come out for the meeting again. I spoke on Noah and there was a lot of interest. Yesterday some men that had studied downriver came, and, as usual, the sick came from all over when they heard we were there.

We had another good group for evening service, and I talked about the two roads. Several prayed and told God they wanted to leave the road of sin and follow His road. One old man was too sick to come, but I went to talk to him the next day. He was all swollen up, showing signs of heart trouble. His old one-legged wife came crawling in on hands and knees.

After raining all night and nearly all day, the river had risen ten to fifteen feet. We planned to leave the day after tomorrow if the weather permitted. Literacy class went well that morning; the people stayed until almost noon.

Nevertheless, not everyone was friendly. There were three groups in the area. The leader of the unfriendly group told the people he did not want us there, but a woman from that group came with a sick baby anyway.

A river merchant sent a note asking to borrow my canoe. He took Robert, the leader of the Chimanes in that area; Robert did not want to go. It was quite a ticklish situation trying to be friends with the river merchants and helping the Chimanes. The Chimanes and the river merchants thought of each other as a necessary evil.

We had to make a lot of adjustments to teach literacy. They had their own work to do: hunting and fishing for themselves plus working for the river merchants. In spite of it all, little by little they learned to read.

We had about forty people out the final night. Even Pascual, the one who had talked against us, came. As I presented Christ and gave opportunity to accept Him, I felt that most of them did, praying out loud as a group.

We left to go down river with two fellows from here. One fellow traded us a chicken, and we bought a big basket of avocados. We had the chicken for supper. Some river merchants came and spent the night. That night the Chimanes didn´t come for a meeting. They thought we were going to stay and teach them, but we had to move on.

We rose at dawn to load the canoe to go down river. Elaine had a sore foot and could hardly walk. Ignacio did not show up, so we had to go down river with just one of the fellows, Miro. It was more dangerous that way, but it could be done. We ate lunch where we had tended the man with the head injury when we were coming up river and saw that he was fine now.

Miro had been up drinking the night before and kept dozing off. We had to keep shouting at him so the canoe would not get stuck in a log jam or hit something else in the water. Drifting downriver with the current can be really tricky; the current can get you in trouble in a hurry. It takes both skill and alertness to travel the river safely.

Our supplies would just last the return trip. We gave a turkey away where we stayed because we still had some dried meat left over. The fish were coming up river, and our man could not resist it. He shot an arrow into the muddy water at about forty feet and got a two-pound bass for his supper.

Elaine writes:

As I think back over all that happened on that river trip, I think about one incident in particular. We mentioned before about the old man and his wife. They were such a pitiful sight. An old, one-eyed man with blue lips and so swollen he could hardly walk, looked at us with pleading…"Can't you help me?"

His wife hobbled in beside him. She had only one leg and used a stick to walk with. She finally gave up on the stick and came crawling into the house.

They were so hopeful, so sure we could do something. We gave him some medicine that might possibly relieve some of the suffering.

Dino told him, "Old one, God alone can help you. You are old and haven't much longer to live. God has made a way that we can go and be with Him. Up there, in heaven, there is no more suffering, no more tears and no more pain."

The old man with one eye.

As Dino talked, the old woman turned happily to me. "Just think, he won't be like that up there"

I thought back to a few days before. We were coming down river after the long hard up-river trip on our way home. We were so tired, and it would have been so easy to not struggle into this little shallow river, to not spend hours dragging and pushing the canoe to get in, to just hurry on by and forget these people; yet we knew in our hearts God wanted us to stay. We had promised them we would stay a week. As Dino spoke about heaven, the old woman asked, "Will there be any bananas there?"

It was such a wonderful week. They were so happy to receive us, and now the old man was sitting and listening, along with all the others. It was his one and only opportunity to hear about God's love and how He sent His Son to us. The old man's hope in this life was so small, yet his hope in heaven so great. They stayed a few days, and we took them in our canoe when we left to go downriver. We left them on the river bank, a sick old man and the old one-legged woman struggling up the bank. To think we might have hurried by, and they might never have heard the Gospel of Christ.

Chapter 19

Volunteers Needed

The Second Furlough

1968:

We spent a year back in the States. Lori was now twelve years old, and all of our children would be in school.

Dino Kempf Family in 1968

It was always so good to get to spend time with our children. The Lord had gone before us and prepared a house for us. Our brother-in-law, Dale Hamilton, tried to rent a house for us and could not find one, so he bought a house where we lived while we were home, rent free. He then sold it after we left. Dino worked for him on his dairy farm cleaning barns and feeding calves for a few weeks until he was hired on at the brick yard again.

From that time on, Dale and Edna, Dino's sister, continued to help us shoulder the work. They had made many trips to Bolivia, helped us out with the book work on this end, and created interest in the work. They have also invested thousands of dollars to the cause.

It meant a lot to be able to spend time with our friends and relatives. Dino was able to spend a month alone with his dad in New Mexico, who had gone there for a visit. He became so sick while there that he could not return to Washington. It was a very precious time that Dino will always treasure because he knew it would be their last goodbye when he left the States and returned to Bolivia. He cried many times on the way to Bolivia knowing that he would not see his father again until they met in heaven.

December 1971:

A Christmas Family Vacation:

When we returned to Bolivia, our five children went to the boarding school at Tambo. That year when the school had a break for Christmas vacation, we decided that instead of flying the children in, we would use the money to travel as a family. We all boarded the train and made a circle through part of Brazil, Paraguay, and Argentina and from there back to Bolivia. It was a great trip that we will never forget.

We had quite an adventure at Iguasu Falls, Argentina. We had boarded the train and settled down for the trip, but after the train started, we did not see our son, Randy. We looked up and down the train, but no Randy. We talked to the conductor, who called back to the station. Randy had fallen asleep after boarding the last car of the train, but before the train pulled out of the station, they had disconnected it. When Randy woke up, he found out the train had left him behind. At our next stop, Dino caught a bus back to Iguasu Falls and found Randy. The rest of the family continued on and waited for them at the border between Argentina and Bolivia. The trip had to eventually end; the children returned to school, and we went back to the jungle.

Volunteers needed to cook for the school:

On some occasions, we did get extra time with our children. At one point, the mission school needed somebody to cook for them because a missionary who was on furlough could not get back in time for the start of school, so we volunteered to stay for three months to do the cooking. It was a lot of work, but our kids were really happy. We said we would not dare embarrass them by not doing a good job, and we knew all the things they did not like about the food at school, so we did our best not to serve those things. The children loved being able to come to the kitchen with their friends to see us and get little snacks.

Volunteers needed in San Borja:

We were asked to work with the church in San Borja while the regular missionaries that worked there were on furlough. Our co-workers, the Callaways, had just returned from their own furlough. Because they were not able to live as a family among the Chimanes, they felt that a houseboat might solve their problems.

A friend took on this project and invested his time and finances in making a fiber-glass houseboat for the Chimane work. They shipped the hull of this boat from the States, but the rest of the construction was to be done in the field.

Gene had his boat-building project in full swing a couple miles from town and was unable to abandon the activity because if he did, the boat would be vulnerable to vandals. Because of this dilemma, no one was able to shepherd the church, and the sheep began to scatter.

I was completely surprised when the mission director told me that he thought I should come into town and take over the work until the missionaries on furlough returned.

We finally had things in good shape at our home on the river. We had decided to start school at our house instead of traveling, so we had built a better home and planted fruit trees. We had also planted a large garden with plenty of vegetables. We had around forty head of hogs and over one-hundred chickens and had just planted five acres of corn to have feed for them, but now we had to leave it all for a year.

So, we hired a Christian man to take care of our worldly goods and moved into town. Unfortunately, this man was lazy. The hogs got sick and died. The corn was not hoed and produced no grain.

We thought of the verse that says, "*...and took joyfully, the spoiling of your goods, knowing in yourselves that ye have in heaven a better and an enduring substance." (Hebrews 10:34)*, so we said, "All right, Lord."

We did take our milk cow to town with us. Her calf had died, but we continued to milk her. That was a big novelty to the people in San Borja. Dino would chop up some bananas for her, put some salt on them and at milking time she would come running for her treat. People would gather around just to watch something they had not seen before. When they milk a cow, they let the calf start suckling first, and then when the cow lets down her milk, they pull the calf away, so they can start milking. That was the only way they had seen it done.

Gene and Gladys Callaway and the Launch:

Gene continued doing a good job on the launch, but the Maniqui River is a terrible river to travel. In dry season, it is too shallow, so Gene's boat would get hung up on sand bars and submerged logs. In rainy season, the river could raise several feet in only an hour's time, and trees would come crashing down as the soil became saturated. Travel was very dangerous. Once a huge tree hit the boat and tore it from its mooring chain. Luckily, some men saw it drifting, dived in, and saved it from the log jams down river.

Gene and Gladys were able to travel in the launch and have a place to cook and eat, which made life easier for them. They were able to use it for a while, but eventually, because of health reasons they could not continue to work in Bolivia, so they returned to the States. They had certainly poured themselves into the work year after year and did their part in planting the seeds that eventually led to the harvest.

Gladys and Gene Callaway at their home in Seattle, Washington.

We will always be thankful to them for all those years of laying the ground work for us to follow.

The San Borja Church

When we arrived in town, we found that the believers were not meeting together any more. The congregation had disappeared. "Lord, what do we do next?" we prayed.

A birthday party or a fiesta will bring people because of the food, so we decided to host a dinner for the men who had attended church but were no longer coming. We bought a side of beef and prepared a meal. We sent out invitations to all the former members of the church; they all came. After the meal, I asked them what could be done to best serve them. We informed them that Elaine and I would be there to serve them for the next year. Almost as one, they told me that they wanted a decent church building. The place where they met was a "bamboo shack that looked like a chicken coop." We asked them if there were any funds that they could put towards a building. They gave me the figures in pesos, and I quickly calculated it in my head. The sum was around four hundred dollars. They stressed that they had been collecting for the building for six years. I told them that if they had enough faith, God would help them build the church.

"Do you want to start right away or wait for more money?" I inquired.

"We want to start," they answered. "If we start, we will give more money."

The following day, we invited all the former women members to our house for cake and tea. We asked them the same question, and their answer was the same: a decent building. Now we had no doubt about where they itched. Just how we could best scratch it, with such limited funds, was the question.

We hired a brick layer and began construction on the foundation. Some believers donated materials and money, so we did manage to quickly finish the foundation.

At the boarding school in Tambo, we had made several large buildings out of cement and gravel blocks, which had proved to be cheap material. A hand-operated ram for making these blocks was only two-hundred and fifty dollars, so I offered to pay half of it. The members agreed on the purchase, and we got our block-making ram. What I had not taken into consideration was that the cement had to be flown in by plane as there were no roads. Even though we used only one part cement to ten parts gravel, the cost was still too high for us to consider going further with the project.

I was feeling terrible, and I prayed, "Lord, somehow get me out of this mess. I stepped into this as a leader, and now I don't know what to do, and the believers will become discouraged."

The Lord gave me the idea of making giant bricks out of clay with the machine. I put a wooden block in the center of the mold to make the bricks hollow so they could be baked. We started making raw bricks. I went to the owner of a brick kiln and asked him how much he would charge to bake the bricks. He said that since the bricks would be used for a church building, he would only charge us for the wood needed to fire the bricks. The Lord sent Dennis, a college student on summer vacation from Wheaton, to help me.

Ambrosio dug the clay for us. When we first met Ambrosio, he was dying of tuberculosis. He could not walk or talk, and he was skin and bones. We doubted that we could save him; we thought he was too far gone, but now, a year later, this man was strong and healthy, and able to work all day in hundred degree heat.

Dennis and I pressed all the bricks for the church, and, after the first firing, we began to lay the first row. Dennis had worked for a bricklayer as a helper, so he had a general idea of how to lay bricks. We slowly and carefully raised the wall up to window height, but by then Dennis had to return to the States and college.

By that time, I was somewhat disgusted with the believers. They itched for a church, but they wanted me to do all the scratching. We knew that they would not appreciate the church if they did not take part in its construction. It had to be their church, not the gringos'. I told the people that they would have to hire someone to finish the building. Most of the believers were dirt poor. There were two families, however, who owned several large ranches.

One day the wife of one of these ranchers asked me when the Americans would send the dollars to finish the church. I told her that no Americans would be sending money because most of the ones who helped us in Bolivia were much poorer than she was. The stalemate continued for several weeks. Nothing moved. Then, one rancher told the other one that he would pay half if the other rancher paid the other half. The challenge was accepted, and, in a few weeks, the church was finished. It had happened!

When the missionaries returned from furlough, we had a membership of around one hundred believers attending the new church.

Problems

A big problem we had in the Hispanic culture was dealing with sin in the life of the believers. At first, we missionaries would explain the sin problem. The offenders got angry at "the foreigner," but continued to visit with the believers. "The gringo is mad at me," they would say. We realized that it had to be the church-body of believers that judged the sin, or nothing would change.

A member of the church came to us with a problem. Her husband had left her for a fourteen-year-old girl, she complained. I went to this man and talked to him. He admitted that he was wrong and promised to return to his wife. After two weeks of no change, I went back with two other believers. They talked to him, and again he cried and said that he knew he was wrong and would return. He did say that he suspected that his wife had also cheated on him. He had no proof of that, but stuck with the story. After another month of no change, I felt that the matter was serious enough to bring it before the church body.

The man and wife arrived. I didn't know exactly how to begin, but I had the woman swear on the Bible to tell the truth, and she told her story. I did the same with the husband, and he told his story. I then asked the congregation, the meeting being open, "What do you say should be done? How can we correct this problem?"

Seven different people rose one by one and told the man that he should return to his wife. He became very angry and said, "You people don't understand." With that, he stormed out of the church. The church, not the gringo, had judged the matter, and the man chose to refuse council.

He sold the hide and got the bride

In another Hispanic church up river where we ministered, several of the members were not married–just living together. In the same church, we had a problem with gossip on the part of one lady in particular. I taught extensively on these two subjects, but seemed to get nowhere. Finally, I decided that if we were just going to be hearers of the word and not doers, it might be better to just quit meeting altogether.

I expressed my frustration in the morning meeting. "Brothers, I am perplexed. I don't know where to go from here or what to preach. I feel that marriage and gossip are two valid issues, but no one does anything about obeying God's word. Do you want to just quit meeting and live as you please?" I inquired.

The leader of the group said, "I want to pray." He prayed, "Dear Lord, You know that I have known that I should get married. I don't have the money, Lord, to do it. I will go hunting for an alligator tonight, Lord, and if you allow me to kill a big one, I will sell the hide and get married. Amen." The gossip lady also prayed and asked the Lord to forgive her and help her control her tongue.

Sure enough, that night, Casiano, the leader, went downriver in a dugout canoe. He shined his flashlight, and soon found a pair of eyes that shone like coals of fire. His son paddled close, and just before the barrel touched the critter's head, Casiano fired. He reached out with his big hook, and felt the death thrash of one of the largest gators he had ever seen. He sold the hide and wed his bride. He had ten children; each one was registered as legitimate, and they were a big, happy family.

Wayne and Ruth Gill join the work

With the Callaway's leaving, we were left alone in the work. However, Wayne and Ruth Gill, who had made the trip with us to the spirit house, came for a visit. Wayne was a field leader, and a few years later came into the Chimane work and did the Bible translation into the Chimane language.

He and his wife, Ruth, seemed always to show up when we were floundering and somewhat discouraged. They had a great ministry of encouragement. I was trying to continue the translation and was having some problems with the language.

Wayne & Ruth Gill.

Wayne told us his brother, Len, might not be coming back to Bolivia; they did not need him in the Araona tribe where he and his wife, Elsie, had worked before. One of the main problems was that Len had not been able to learn the language. "I think they could help us teach the Chimanes to read," I exclaimed. "If you want, I'll talk to them," he promised.

Len and Elsie Gill come into the work

Talk about troopers and great people to work with; they were world class. Len was an incredible example of determination. He never gave up on the language. He studied it daily and learned to speak it well.

Len and Elsie Gill with their son, Loren.

Len and Elsie continued using the launch that Gene and Gladys had been using. It traveled up and down the Maniqui River for years and suffered many near disasters because it could only travel in the rainy season when the river was full and, therefore, very dangerous to navigate.

Harold and Nora Rainey join the team

Another world-class couple came from Canada. Harold Rainey had worked for several years helping to make friendly contact with two different savage tribes, but after the contacts were made, he was no longer needed. Harold had a cleft palate, so speaking was never very easy for him; nevertheless, he was another determined man, and ministered in both Spanish and Chimane. When he was home during one of his furloughs, he met the one woman he had been seeking for fifty-one years. She was a single school teacher, and they met on a church bus.

Nora was in her forties when she first went to Chimane land. She landed on her feet and never quit marching beside Harold until the day they tearfully left Bolivia because of Harold's health. He was seventy-five at the time.

Harold and Nora Rainey at their home along the Maniqui River.

Gene and Gladys, Wayne and Ruth, and Harold and Nora have finished their time here on earth, and I know that God is telling them, "Well done, my good and faithful servants."

Words are not capable of expressing our deep feelings and admiration for these people who faced the heat, bugs, mud, loneliness, and loss without complaint. Len and Elsie are retired and living in Florida, and we are in Washington State.

Chapter 20

Change of Strategy

As I mentioned earlier, we were now ready to make a change in our strategy for reaching the Chimane people.

An offer from the Wycliffe Mission shaped this change. They notified us that they were starting a Bilingual Teacher's Training program at their base at Tumichuqua, and we could take any candidates for teachers that we had available for this course.

We looked our people over and found two young fellows that we felt were qualified to attend the school, but there was still one problem. Since Chimanes take a wife at an early age, both of these fellows were married. We would need to take their wives with us because the course would be three-months long.

The day we were to leave one of the young wives was afraid to get in the small single-engine plane for the two-hour flight to the Wycliffe mission. We waited, but she would not budge. Finally, I picked her up, carried her to the plane, and stuffed her in. She hid her face the whole trip, afraid to look out the window. "Lord, please don't let us crash. I made this poor woman come against her will."

On the return flight three months later, she enjoyed the trip, and she was not afraid to look out the window. You have to realize that this flight to her was like a flight to Mars for us. And, in one way, the trip had been dangerous. We didn't know that our people had been exposed to measles, and soon after we arrived at the Wycliffe base, the whole camp of one hundred fifty students plus their families, were infected.

Dionicio Roca, one of the first Chimane school teachers,
in his class room at La Cruz.

Nevertheless, they received excellent training, and when they returned to Chimane land, the two fellows started schools in their villages. When the Chimanes realized that the teacher would be a Chimane, one of their own, they finally consented to send their children to school. The teaching would also be in Chimane, and the children would not have to lose their language.

It had been a long, hard road to get to this place in the work, but the Chimanes had finally accepted the idea of school and from these students, we could train other teachers and spread the word of God through the schools. We now had helpers to carry on the work while we went home on furlough.

By this time, our own children hated life at the boarding school. They begged and pleaded with us to not leave them there. The situation was bad, and we requested to be able to move to the small town across from the school so that we could have our children at home with us until school was out. We were at a place with the Chimane work that we could have used the time for language and lessons, etc., and still make trips to the Chimanes when necessary, but our request was denied.

Darrel was so insistent that we took him home with us and left the others there. Seven weeks before Lori was to graduate from high school, she ran away from the school and pleaded with us to allow her to return home. We told her to come ahead. We didn't know until years later what the exact problems were.

After vacation, none of the children wanted to return to the boarding school, so we kept them with us. We were able to borrow some school books from a family that had home-schooled their children, so our children were able to keep up with their studies, and when we went back to the States, they were accepted at their grade level.

The kids were always outgoing, and they had a lot of Bolivian friends. That was both good and bad. This place had a wild culture, and was often like a shoot 'em up cow town; we were very concerned about the whole situation.

With pressures of the growing work, the problems with part of the field leadership, and five teenagers who needed their parents, it was time for a break. For years things had gone really well, but it just seemed that at this time the enemy came in like a flood, and we were overcome. I felt like I did not qualify for missionary service because my own house was not in order.

Vision of a Center

It took a while to work everything out in order to leave Bolivia. Before we left, I had this vision of a training center. We needed a place out on the grass lands, far enough in so the river would not erode the banks and destroy our buildings, far enough from town to not cause problems, but close so getting supplies would not be a problem.

I went to every rancher around and asked them to sell me a piece of their property to build a center. No one was willing to do it, but, I was informed by supposedly reliable sources that there was a place three miles from the city of San Borja, which was a center for the Indians to do their trading. We hired a surveyor and measured off 100 hectares of land. (A hectare is 2.2 acres, which would be a total of 220 acres.) He asked us what the name of the land would be. We looked at one another, and Don Osbaldo, one of the believers from the church in town, said, "Horeb is a good name."

We all agreed that Horeb would be a good name; we just didn't realize at the time how appropriate a name it was.

I fenced it and put up a lean-to. A few nights later a woman came and told me to get my fence and lean-to off of her land. I was shocked. I explained to her about the work we were doing among the Chimanes, and that I needed a place for a center where they could come and further their studies. We were told that we should solicit that piece of land, and that is how it came about that I measured the land.

She said, "I don't blame you. They misinformed you." She showed me the title and I was embarrassed. I asked her if she would sell the land to us. Even though she was a card-carrying Communist, she needed money to pay a bill, so when I asked her to sell me the property, she consented. However, she needed the money in just a few days.

I didn't have the money to pay her the approximate $5,000 she asked for the property. I had $1,000 and an outboard motor I could sell for $900. The owner of the property told me that unless I had the money by the following Friday, there would be no deal. I told her that I would pray and ask God to supply the money.

When I went into town, I dropped into a shop run by one of the believers from our local Spanish-speaking church. I casually told her about the land, never dreaming she would help me. She asked me, "How much do you need, Brother?" I told her in pesos and she reached under the counter and pulled out a stack of bills the size of a shoe box. It was the exact amount, to the peso, that I needed. That had to be the Holy Spirit's leading because she had no idea about the land or the price of it before I talked to her.

I asked her how much interest she would charge me, and she said none. I asked her when the money needed to be paid back. She replied, "When you get it." That was the miracle God performed in order for us to have a training center.

Chapter 21

A Time to Wait

God is faithful. He already had prepared a home for us in the States; however, we had used the money that we had saved for our passage back, so we had no idea how the Lord would get us home this time.

One day we received a letter from the Buttermores, a family we had known when we were in missionary training in California. We had visited them after we had finished our training when we were on our way back to Washington, and we had kept in touch with them through the years via letters. In their letter, they commented on how much they enjoyed hearing from us about the work among the Chimanes. They went on to say that they wanted to pay our passage home from the field.

"Elaine!" I shouted. "Read this. The Buttermores want to pay our way home."

"Surely they don't mean all of it," she corrected.

"Read the letter," I urged.

I wrote and told them how the Wycliffe mission was going to fly us home in their own DC-3 airplane and how we could all go on it to Miami for $900. We could save $700 by not going commercial. Sure enough, next month's voucher contained $900 from the Buttermores for passage.

We made plans to travel, and the next month, another $500 came from the Buttermores. We got to Miami, and there was another $500 from them. We looked for a car in the $500 range. The chances of finding a good one were very limited for that price, even back then.

However, a Christian car dealer took us under his wing and found us a one-owner Pontiac with power brakes, power steering, and air conditioning with very low mileage for only $400.

Here we were: God's servants, traveling across the States for a month in a comfortable car, and we even had several hundred dollars in our pockets to make the trip.

Since it was summer, we could camp along the way, so we bought a big used tent for fifty dollars. We stopped in famous places like Carlsbad Caverns in New Mexico, and had a great trip across the country from Florida to Washington State.

When we got to Washington, we walked into a completely furnished house supplied with everything we needed: sheets, blankets, towels, etc. The kitchen was ready for cooking, including food. We felt overwhelmed with the goodness of God and all the love shown to us.

I had four sisters and two brothers. When Dad died, instead of selling the home place and dividing the proceeds up into seven parts, they decided to give the home place to us. We had no idea that this had happened until we returned home. It is a beautiful place with huge fir trees in front along a crystal clear river. We built a large living room onto the house, dug a deep well, and settled into the American system of living once more.

We stayed there five years because we needed the time with our family. We had five teenage children, and we had been absent for a good part of their lives. We were tired and needed encouragement. I had also suffered a mental meltdown and needed rest.

Can you imagine what it was like for our children to be raised in Bolivia and then to be transplanted in the United States? They all got drivers' licenses, and, from that time on, whenever the phone rang, we would wonder, "Which one is it this time?"

There were a number of car wrecks, but, most of the time it was someone else's fault, like other people running red lights. That is not all, however. One of our sons survived being shot by a crazy man. Three of our children signed up for military service. While we were hoping to have some time as a family, they were ready to spread their wings and move onward.

God kept telling us, "You haven't finished the job; you need to go back to Bolivia."

This was going to be difficult for us. We had been out of the mission work for five years, working at jobs like the ones most people do in the States. New Tribes had kept us on the active list because we were needed in Bolivia, but they wanted us to go back to one of their training centers for a while. We still had the vision of the training center in Bolivia, and we already had the land to build it on, but we were back to the dilemma of support. So we did a lot of praying.

In September, 1978, I wrote the following letter to the mission in Bolivia: "Several weeks ago we received a letter from you, inquiring about our plans and status of the mission. I have put off replying because I don't know how to answer you. I still don't, but I will attempt to get my thoughts down so that you can see where I am.

As to your inquiry concerning our attempt at re-entry into the program, in 1976 the following occurred: We came home from Bolivia in 1974, because we felt we needed to be together as a family and work out problems that had arisen with the children.

Some of this improved after we were home, and Elaine and I felt we would like to attempt to get back into the fellowship by moving into the missionary camp at Baker, Oregon. We shared this with the director of the camp, and he said that there was no place at present to have a teaching ministry. I asked if he felt we should go in as students. I don't remember the answer, but there was no encouragement from him. In view of this, I said we would just like to come to be a part of the fellowship but take a job in the area. He said that if we came, we would have to live by faith like the students. This posed a problem, because I didn't feel I could ask folks to support us if we weren't there in a definite ministry or in preparation for one. I don't know whether we appeared like a hopeless case or not, but we weren't encouraged in any way to be at Baker. So we felt that door was closed for the time. No one told us that we couldn't return to Bolivia, but we felt that the fellowship would be good.

I went back to Bolivia in May and was there for two months. I enjoyed the fellowship and was at both the New Tribes Mission conference and also the national conference and took part in teaching at the latter. I spent some time in several of the churches and among the Chimane Indians where we had spent fifteen years of our life. The whole trip was a blessing, and it stirred my heart anew to get back down there.

Family-wise, I feel there is nothing holding us from returning. We have one son still with us, and he is taking extra classes at the college here in order to finish high school before we leave. We have a goal to return to Bolivia next summer, sometime after school is out in June. At present we are getting equipment together and fixing up our home to rent out while we are gone.

We would like to return under the auspices of New Tribes if we can work it out, but there are many questions in our minds that need answering before we can make the decision. At the same time, we have felt no liberty to resign from New Tribes.

For a number of years, God has been speaking to us to concentrate on training leaders among the Bolivians and Chimanes. There are so many areas where we babysat for years and must continue to do so as there are no mature leaders to carry on with the work. My burden is to concentrate on teaching to see men grounded and able to carry on this work. We purchased two hundred twenty acres of land, and we have a home in the area and some cattle. Our plan is to build several simple houses on the property, bring in key men and their families to teach, and then send them back to their areas to put this teaching into practice. We would also have them work part-time to help defray expenses of the room and board. We will teach various trades and try to equip the brothers so that they might be able to make a living and preach God's Word. This has been a number-one problem for some of our best fellows that are either hooked up with a group that gives them some financial help, or they are struggling to make a living. Now, I'm not talking about a three to four-year Bible school; I am thinking of one to three months per year and getting them right back to their areas. They would be brought back twice a year or whenever possible for further teaching.

This has really worked out well for the Indian teachers among the Chimanes. Some have been getting teacher-training for three months a year at the Wycliffe bilingual school, and then they go back to teach their people.

Wycliffe will soon be phasing out this school; consequently, we will need to have our own teacher-training school. So, the leadership-training school will teach teachers to teach, teach trades, and teach short-term Bible schools. This is an important need I see for the work there.

At the conference in May for the nationals, there were thirty-five churches represented; of those thirty-five, only about five had leadership grounded enough to really teach the Word. We have been losing many churches because of this lack.

You might ask: why not go teach where the people are instead of bringing them out to a base? I realize that some have been discipled on a one-to-one basis, and this is good. Most groups in our area are very scattered, and the disadvantages I see are that when these fellows are in their own home, they have to be out a lot hunting for meat, plus the Bolivians often have them tied up in work, often involuntarily. If I go to them, I cannot reach as many since they live in little clan groups, and there are usually only a few there who attend the class.

Over the years we have seen God provide the land and other necessities in a miraculous way for this project. We have a church here in the States that is ready to help us get a tractor, sawmill, and other necessities for this project.

While in Bolivia, I talked with the field committee about this, and they see the need for teaching. The one area they weren't sure about my ideas was that Elaine and I plan to go down with what capital we can scrape together to put in a business and work with our hands among the people.

So you see why the problem is so complex. We feel God has shown us these things and has prepared us in these areas and, at the same time, we want to work in fellowship with the body. We are not competitive, but want to try to meet a need that we have seen going unmet for years. As I talked with the fellows in Bolivia, they were wondering if it would work out for me to work under the auspices of New Tribes Mission as God has shown us. On the other hand, they were in favor of the training program; they see the need and are perplexed to give other alternatives. So if you brothers have other ways that God has told you to train and develop leadership, I am open for counsel. I just want to see this need met.

There are many things unsaid here; it would take a book to say it all. But our plans are to return to Bolivia next summer, either under the auspices of New Tribes if this can be worked out, or apart from them but one in spirit and fellowship."

During the time home, we were invited by a pastor and his wife to attend a Christmas dinner for the whole church. We were to be the speakers on the subject of "Christmas Time in Bolivia." In Bolivia, Christmas is not the big holiday that it is in the States. To many it is just another day. However, to the Christians, it has real meaning apart from gifts, trees, and feasts: the fact that Emmanuel, God with us, came to earth and gave his life for our sins.

When Dino finished talking, the preacher's wife turned to us and asked, "Dino and Elaine, what can we do to help you two?" Elaine answered our heart cry by saying, "We just want someone to love us. We just want to be accepted and be able to fellowship with Christians here at home."

With tears in her eyes, the dear old lady said, "Surely we can do that." This was someone from the denomination that had rejected us for fourteen years, and we could hardly believe our ears. True to their word, the old couple invited us to a minister's retreat a few weeks later, and Brother Ruby stood and introduced us. He told the crowd that we were God's servants and that we would bless any meeting at which we were invited to speak. I think at least fifteen different ministers asked us to speak at their churches, and we found warm fellowship every place we went.

To make a long story short, we decided to go back independently of New Tribes, but still working in fellowship with the mission.

Again Dino writes:

As we considered returning to Bolivia and getting our base set up, we were challenged with putting our retirement home on the altar in order to have money to get the center going. After getting the okay from my family, we put it up for sale and used the proceeds to get things going at Horeb. There was really no need in asking God for funds when we had an asset that would cover it.

We have a wonderful promise from our Lord Jesus in *Matthew 19:29: And every one that hath forsaken houses, or brethren, or sisters, or father, or mother, or wife, or children, or lands, for my name's sake, shall receive an hundredfold, and shall inherit everlasting life.*

We had already purchased the land for the base and were hoping to be self-supporting, which meant we needed income to support the school and take care of the sick. One preacher told me that I couldn't expect help unless I explained what our needs were.

I did ask the little Brethren church in Salkum, Washington, where we attended, to pray with us about taking a tractor down to truck garden. I never dreamed that they would turn the prayer request into a reality. They bought us a Kubota tractor, which came with several pieces of equipment: a bucket, brush cutter, disc plow, and a rototiller.

We shipped it to Bolivia, and it was waiting in customs when we arrived. Sadly, it waited in customs for over six months.

I'm writing this in 2016, and the Kubota tractor is still running and being used in Bolivia.

Dino and son, Ben, using the Kubota tractor to make a barrel oven and cook stove.

Please see Appendix (C) for further info by Wayne Gill on why Horeb was needed.

PART TWO

Galatians 6:9
And let us not be weary in well doing:
for in due season we shall reap, if we faint not.

"Horeb" 1979
San Borja Farm and Christian Training Center

This begins the second part of our work in Bolivia. It is totally amazing!

Dino and I, our youngest son, Ben, and Dino's brother, Frank Kempf, returned to Bolivia in 1979. We had 220 acres of land and were hoping to be a self-supporting training center. We were convinced that this was what God wanted us to do. At the same time, Dino was feeling pretty battle-weary and felt that he did not fit what his image of a missionary should be. He felt he should not even call himself one, so when we arrived back in San Borja, he told the people he was not a missionary. The people corrected him, "You are a missionary!" Maybe he did not see himself as a missionary, but the people did.

Dino and Elaine's 220 acres.

Chapter 22

Plans Were Made to Be Changed

1979:

When Dino had gone to Bolivia to talk to the New Tribes Mission leaders and share our plans with the group there, the economy in Bolivia was stable, and the plan was feasible. So it wasn't a bad idea and it could have worked, but there was a big problem, not only for us, but for the whole country. Bolivia was battling inflation. The Wall Street Journal stated that the inflation rate in Bolivia was 116,000%. This meant that prices changed by the hour. It was impossible to know just what food, tools, or even a sack of cement would cost.

We had a Kubota tractor in customs in La Paz. Customs wanted $8,000 to get it out, plus storage. Since the sale of our house in Washington was not all cash, there was only around $2,000 available that could be used to bail out the tractor. We talked it over and decided that we would have to do something to support ourselves while we waited to get the tractor out of customs.

Elaine asked Dino to make an oven from a barrel. She said, "We will bake bread to sell."

Dino replied that there were a hundred small bakeries that we would be competing with, but we never once entertained the idea of giving up. We believed God would bless our endeavor. We were in a third-world country where the average worker earned around $500 a year.

Dino and his brother, Frank, made the oven, and we baked up a batch of bread. All the other bakeries sold bread which looked like hamburger buns, but we made loaves. We used butter and milk, and it was quality bread. We also made sweet bread and donuts. So Dino, along with Frank and Ben, took a huge pan full of our breads and hit the streets, shouting out our products. In less than two hours they sold it all. They were invited into all kinds of homes and sometimes, if the people did not have money, they would barter for eggs, chickens, or other items. We lived fine during those months.

The people were puzzled. What was that "rich" gringo doing out on the streets peddling bread? God proved to us that we could make a living in a third-world country, even one suffering from severe inflation. He would take care of us wherever we lived.

Dino liberates the tractor

I went back to La Paz to try again at getting our tractor out of customs. I hired a lawyer, but he wasn't able to do anything. He said that I had to pay what they asked. I met a missionary from Wycliffe; he was their business manager and over coffee I told him about customs and our problem getting our tractor out.

He said, "Dino, come with me to my office. I have a little booklet that tells how an immigrant can get into Bolivia the first time and get all of his farming equipment out of customs free of charge."

I took the booklet to my lawyer and he said, "No, you have to pay the $8,000." I went back to customs and found a little man with glasses and asked him if he could make me an immigrant. I told him I would pay him $400 if he would. I know at this point you are raising your eyebrows, but that is the way things are sometimes done down there. The man started working on it, and, in a couple of hours, I had the tractor and equipment out of customs, and I was a select immigrant!

We loaded the tractor and our other equipment onto a cargo plane and flew our cargo to San Borja to begin farming.

Our Kubota tractor being unloaded from a DC3 cargo plane.

We planted our crops, but the plants were yellow and sickly. Something was wrong; the blackeyed pea's leaves were white instead of green. The soil had no strength. We had met the Wilsons, a young missionary family in La Paz, and Jon Wilson was an agronomist; he offered to come down to help us. He tested the soil and told us what it lacked. We ordered the fertilizer and micro-nutrients he recommended, applied them to our crops, and in a short time they looked beautiful.

Chapter 23

Chaos in the Country and Rain

The Death Road

In April of 1982, Dino traveled to La Paz to transfer the title of a 1960 Jeep pickup truck the Lord had given us. We had to have it completely overhauled and fixed up as it was quite tired, but it had a good body and tires, and it would have cost about $5,000 if we had to buy another one, so we felt very fortunate to be able to fix this one.

After waiting for a month and a half for the pickup to be repaired, we finally got a telegram that it was ready. Dino flew to La Paz and prepared for the three-hundred mile journey through the Andes Mountains on what is known as 'The Death Road' which goes from La Paz to the Amazon region of Bolivia. It is legendary for its extreme danger. One estimate was that two to three hundred travelers were killed yearly along the road.

It should have been the best time of year to travel. June through September was the dry time of year; the problem was that it had rained almost continually since the beginning of June. It was now the first week of July, and the miles of the road still had deep, muddy ruts.

When Dino reached the village of Palos Blancos, he was only eighty miles from home but was told that the road was impassable. For eight days he stayed in a hotel waiting for the weather to clear. The rain had stopped for two days, and Dino decided to continue on with three men who had wanted a ride to San Borja.

The muddy road from Palos Blancos to San Borja.

A couple miles out of the village, they hit deep mud, and for sixty miles they fought ruts which often high-centered them. They chopped trees to fill the ruts and dug out yards and yards of road center. After four days, they made it through and overtook trucks that had been two weeks on the road. So seventeen days after he left to bring back the pickup, he arrived home. It was such a blessing for us to have the pickup.

February, 1983:

Bolivia was under a new government. Talk against Americans was getting stronger, and both television and radio were filled with pro-communist propaganda. The country was in such a financial crisis that everything (except wages) was five times higher than the previous year. The dollar exchange rate had risen from 25 pesos per dollar to over 400 pesos per dollar, so everything imported was unbelievably expensive. The communists were saying that it was all the fault of the Americans.

At one point, a group of men who were part of a drug cartel and armed with machine guns took over San Borja. They arrived in four small planes and assaulted and robbed another plane, which was carrying money to the bank in San Borja. Then they went to the bank and robbed it. (Two days later they came back and returned the money.)

Our daughter, Lori, was coming in on a cargo plane from Santa Cruz, so we went out to the airport to meet her. When the plane landed, the armed cartel men surrounded the plane and pointed their guns at the passengers as they came off the plane. As our daughter Lori stepped out the door and saw the guns pointed at her, she started to turn around and step back inside the plane. The lady behind her took hold of her arm and laughed. She said, "Don't worry; it is just Roberto. You'll be okay." Lori got off the plane, we got into our pickup, and went back home. Evidently Roberto needed some cash. Shortly after this, the Bolivian government sent eighty armed soldiers to San Borja until things calmed down.

June, 1983:

In the Bolivian news, the Americans were openly criticized, while Cuba and Russia were praised. The cocaine business continued to thrive all around us. We were really out of contact with the United States. It had been weeks since there had been a mailbag put on the plane for San Borja. It was so disappointing to go to the post office and find out that La Paz had not sent the mail again.

August, 1983:

Dino writes:

"The rain won't stop! Back in March we planted our first gardens, planned our first buildings, and pressed toward opening our first school in June. The wet-season rains which usually end by March or April just kept coming. The rain continued through July. We needed dry weather to get lumber from the jungles to build with. We needed dry weather to plow the fields and to harvest the crops. The road to San Borja was closed for weeks, and planes couldn't come in because the dirt air strip was too wet and muddy to land on. Food supplies were very limited. Every time we planted vegetables, the rain killed them."

We had a good rice crop because rice likes water; however, when the rice was ripe for harvest, the weather was still rainy. Finally in desperation, we took hand scythes and, wading through water and mud, cut the rice and carried it in bundles to the barn.

We had to get more micro-nutrients to spray on the plants, but once we did, we were able to grow beautiful vegetables. We bought a trailer and hauled vegetables the three miles into San Borja. People were thrilled with them because they were fresh. Vegetables had begun to come to San Borja by truck, but were usually in bad shape by the time they arrived. We were able to make a good living for ourselves, but it was taking up all of our time.

Our plan was to have a center that was self-supporting. God was able to do this, but He must have had something else planned, so we kept on doing what we were doing until He showed us something different.

October, 1983:

Elaine took a pickup load of watermelons into town, and because they were so anxious to buy them, the people practically mobbed the truck.

The next day we all went to a meeting in town, and, as we started back, someone yelled that there were thieves in the watermelon patch. About twenty of us swarmed in, surrounded them, and caught them with bags of our watermelons. I loaded the thieves up and took them into the police, along with the evidence, which the police kept.

Frank Kempf and his watermelons

The town people really liked the watermelons from our farm at Horeb. They were a lot sweeter than the ones shipped in from elsewhere. Ours were grown on ground that everyone said was only good for grass. We were so thankful Jon Wilson had shown us our land could be productive with the right nutrients mixed into the soil. God has blessed the whole area.

One day we were sitting around discussing how we needed to get a part for the Kubota tractor, and Elaine said, "For the price of a ticket to the States, we should just go and get it there."

Then Dino answered, "Why don't you?" So Elaine ran and packed a suitcase.

Actually it was a really good time to go. Because of the exchange rate between dollars and pesos, a round trip ticket was under four hundred dollars. We might never get a bargain like that again, so it was best to take advantage of it.

Chapter 24

School Building and Classes Begin

Even with all the rain and crop failures, we were able to go ahead and raise the school buildings. God has His resources. We received help from the States and were able to go ahead with the buildings. At that time in Bolivia, a dollar went a long way. We built a classroom, a kitchen and dining room, and a ten-room dormitory.

The first school house.

Our first school building was built from funds from a small church in eastern Washington. When we stopped off there and had a meeting several years before, they asked if they could send us support. They said that since they were small they couldn't send great amounts, and their denomination had told them that if they couldn't send a certain amount to forget it, so they started sending money to us directly. This small church sent us $800 that built the first school building.

April, 1984:

A big step of faith

Elaine writes:

Harold and Nora Rainey came to Horeb for a visit and we talked it over and decided to set a date for the first school courses at Horeb to begin.

The students had advanced as far as the Chimane teachers were able to teach them, which was through the fourth grade. So our first course would be for the fifth grade. It actually wound up as first through fifth grades because some other Chimanes who wanted to learn came in from areas that had no schools.

We also needed to continue on upgrading the teacher's education course. It is no secret that none of us really knew what we were doing, but the Lord helped us and blessed the work.

Nora and I worked on the literacy part of the course, and then Nora and Elsie worked on the math part. Since math is my weak area, I didn't attempt that part.

Dino and Harold did the Bible teaching. Len and Elsie Gill, who were involved in the Chimane river ministry, would come to Horeb to help with the classes and teaching of the Bible. They also handled the oversight of the teachers in the village schools when they were ministering on the river. All of us were involved in the literacy and worked together as a team.

Dino's account of the beginning of classes at Horeb:

We finally got the first school underway. We sent notices to the people who wanted to study in the fifth grade to come to Horeb. We were told by the missionaries who worked among them that twenty or so students who were in this grade planned on coming. Their own Indian teachers were not able to train them further because they needed more preparation and training to teach the upper classes.

With much anticipation, we got ready to receive the students. The problem was that they would live and eat here, and we were not sure how we would handle all of it. The big day came and no students showed up. Four days later, one fellow came with his one-eyed wife, who was very yellow and weak, and a small boy covered with scabies. "We came to study," he said with a big smile. He gave us hope that several more would be coming, so we started classes with him.

Our one student worked hard in his classes. He studied with real interest, and we went ahead as though there were thirty people in class. At night we sang, and I gave a Bible lesson. Elaine suggested we write a newsletter saying they are coming in to the school one by one. Anyway, the school was launched, and we were on our way. The people kept saying more students would be coming, but they were still harvesting their rice and other crops. The Lord knows. We launched out by faith to see what the Lord would do in supplying for this school, and so far He had only sent one student.

A few days later, our first student's brother showed up with his wife and a sister who was about thirteen years old. Then Manuel Carej came. He had been teaching, but realized that he wasn't qualified. He brought his wife and three kids, plus a girl to help his wife who was near to giving birth to their fourth child any day now. So our little school consisted of three men and three women, whom Elaine taught in the afternoon.

Someday we would no doubt look back and smile at this feeble start, but for now we were happy it was small.

We put down ten rules for the school. The most important rule was "No Drinking Here." This whole tribe is alcoholic, so this was a big order. The missionaries who are trying to teach the Indians in their own villages had no control over the drinking because they were in their own homes, but here we can control it. We also told them they will get a ration of food, but if relatives show up, they will have to share with them. We were already seeing grandmothers and brothers popping in to eat, so we had to deal with that, too.

The sick little boy who had came in with scabies and a cough was now in serious condition. We had to give him three shots of antibiotic. His mother was pale, had chills, and extreme stomach pains. The whole school group came down with the flu. The third family that arrived had a woman due to have a baby any day. I decided that babies should be born with a doctor attending rather than here with no professional to attend. We tried for three days to get our sick ones to town, but our truck just would not run. We would get someone to fix one thing, and something else would go wrong. Finally, on the fourth day, after a push, the truck started and we chugged to town.

The doctor told us the pregnant lady was close to having her baby and to leave her there as they knew we were having transportation problems. We left her, her husband, and their four children at the hospital. The next morning she still had not had her baby. Then the woman's mother arrived at Horeb, found out her daughter was at the hospital, and was furious. She went to the hospital and told her daughter to get out of bed. She couldn't have a baby lying down because she would die. So Dino, who was there at the time, came and got me to see what I could do.

When I got there, the woman was out of bed trying to have the baby in the usual Chimane way. The doctor came in and asked us to tell him when she was ready. I told him I didn't think they were going to let anyone help them. Sure enough, they went into a little room and the woman delivered the baby on a dirty floor, and then her mother came and told everyone it was born.

I ran and told the doctor, and he came running. The woman was hemorrhaging, and they almost lost her. Her mother had pressed on her stomach and then pulled the baby out. It was interesting that she was content to let the doctor take care of her daughter once the baby was born.

First group of students in Horeb; Harold Rainey in the back and Elefredo Zabalas, superintendent of the Chimane bilingual schools, on the far right.

By the time the men reached fifth grade, they were usually already married and had children. So if they were to continue their schooling, we needed to provide the means so that the whole family could be here. This eliminated a lot of moral problems, too. It was also obvious that a man could not be out hunting and working and going to school. As the men advanced, the wives advanced along with them. Even though they were still only in the fifth grade class, just being in another environment was an advancement. So we told them to come with their wives and children.

The men kept away from drinking while here and each night prayed that they would not go back to it. One night they were especially touched when an Indian preacher came by for a visit. They told him, "We don't want to just be good when the missionaries are around; we want to live for God daily." Two fellows said they were going to preach to their own people. One of the wives indicated her desire to follow the Lord in salvation.

During the first school course at Horeb we had a visitor, Maria Sidiroff, a lady from New Jersey, whom Dino had met in the post office in La Paz. She was a specialist in pottery and archeology, and spent a month with us. The Chimanes called her the "Waterpot Lady". She held classes on how to make pottery. We had a good time, and the students were enthusiastic about the process of making clay pots.

The ladies made about thirty flower pots, and we made an oven and baked them. Most of them turned out well. A few broke, but we were pleased with our first try. Some of the women said they would come back with their husbands to the next school classes and make water pots. They showed real ability, but, surprisingly though, the men took to it better than the women.

October 1984:

We started another two-month course. It was a good group of twenty-eight fellows. There were meetings every night with key Bible verses to learn. Spiritual interest was high. Their prayers were, "Lord, help us to be strong when we return to our villages to teach our people God's Word and help us not to fall into drinking traps." We were very pleased to see their growth as Christians in wanting to live what they believed.

A severe type of flu swept the camp, and some of the children were near death. The Chimane people often flee from sickness, and if there was a death, they might all leave. We had sick people other than students; some came to us in the last stages of TB wanting help.

They also needed a place to stay while receiving medication or treatment. We were usually filled to capacity, so they sometimes stayed in a shelter near our home. Some stayed with relatives who were students here.

One morning before dawn a student came to us crying that his young son had died. Dino asked him what he wanted to do, and he said, "We will go home and bury him, and I will return to study Sunday."

When Dino went over to see the boy, he found that he was actually still alive, so he ran to get the trusty truck and rush him to the doctor, but it would not start. The starter was shot, along with the points and the carburetor, and we didn't have the parts to fix it. We sent one of the men to town for the ambulance but before the ambulance arrived, the people left with the sick boy headed to their village in the jungle. Dino caught up to them on a bicycle and talked them into returning as the ambulance had arrived by this time.

The boy's parents said, "we have no money. We will be ashamed before the Bolivians. We will have nothing to eat at the hospital."

"You won't have to stay there," Dino told them. "But we must get your son to the doctor."

"If you go, we will go," they said. So we got him to the doctor, got medicine, and when they left Horeb, the boy was fine.

We also had seven weddings

The parents rarely wanted their daughters to marry, so the boys felt obligated to steal a girl if they were to have a wife. Recently, one of our strong preachers eloped with a girl he loved because the parents told him he could not have her. He came back two weeks later with her, and they accepted him. "I did wrong," he told us. "But now I have talked to the parents and it is ok. Now I can preach again."

The Chimanes marry according to tribal customs, but the Bolivian government says that only the civil ceremony is legal. Some years ago, the government named a Chimane as a notary public who could conduct legal marriages. As the Chimanes were so widely scattered, they took advantage of the opportunity to marry when the notary public was available.

Dino's brother, Frank, married a really sweet Christian Bolivian lady named Soledad who was from San Borja and is already busy teaching knitting to the women and doing medical work at Horeb.

Frank and Soledad wed.

Chapter 25

Quonset Huts and Volunteers

We already needed more housing here at Horeb. The sick people that were coming needed someplace to stay while they were being treated, and we lacked housing for the students. We discussed the need with our mentor, Pastor Ron Rice of the Presbyterian Church in Centralia, Washington, and he suggested a Quonset hut that was made of Ferro cement.

The mortar provides the mass, and the steel rods and wire mesh imparts tensile strength and durability to the material. An ingenious missionary from Africa came up with the idea.

One of the church leaders, Nick Pearce, had made a Quonset hut as a model behind their church. He then came down to Bolivia to lead a team of young people who had volunteered for a summer work group that would make several of these Quonset huts, which are still being used today.

When Nick came down, he flew into Santa Cruz. While waiting for a flight to San Borja, the airports went on strike leaving Nick stranded. So he had to wait several days for a flight. When the strike was finally settled, one of the mission leaders called me on our two-way radio and said, "Dino, I have good news and bad news. The good news is that the planes are finally flying. The bad news is that Nick was not on the flight. He is returning tonight to the States."

I said, "No way! He has the plans for making the Quonset huts, and the team of twenty workers are due to arrive soon." I called Nick, who confirmed that he was scheduled to return to the States that night. Nick said, "I prayed about it and feel the Lord would have me return to the States."

"Nick, I prayed about it, and I feel that the Lord wants you to stay."

He replied, "I really want to, but it looks impossible." That was a green light for me. Nick's presence was the key to the entire project. I knew the Lord was leading me to go get him.

I said, "Stay where you are. I will come and get you." I caught a ride on a small plane and flew out to Santa Cruz and met up with him. We boarded a flight to La Paz, the capitol of Bolivia, and from there we would take another flight into San Borja near our base in Horeb.

We had to stay overnight in La Paz. Our hotel was near the university, and the students were rioting. We made the mistake of being out on the street returning from dinner when the police came and threw tear gas at the rioters. The tear gas quickly spread down the street onto us, and our eyes were burning. We ran as fast as we could back to the hotel.

The following day, we were able to make our flight and arrived in time for the young people who were coming to help with the project. They were one of the Summit teams who volunteer for three-week trips to various New Tribes Mission locations in order to help missionaries who are working with unreached tribal people groups.

We are so thankful for the many people that volunteered to come help us. The Hard Hats for Christ group also came to help. Between the Summit group and the Hard Hats for Christ group, fourteen Quonset huts were made. We have used them for classrooms, a medical clinic, housing for sick people, and for the students. The Quonset huts turned out beautifully, but we could not have done it without Nick.

Finished Quonset hut.

We even used half of one for a kitchen for Elaine, adding another wood stove with a barrel oven. One of the huts we used for years as a clinic until the government built a clinic for the Chimanes. They worked well for our classes as we could use one wall for a blackboard.

Quonset hut classroom.

Another Summit group of young people volunteered for a project to build a much-needed four-room school building. Before they arrived, God sent two men from the Church of God in Centralia, Washington, who were able to get things ready for them. Harold Knopper was able to plan things, teach how to lay bricks, and lay out the framing for the roof before he left.

Volunteers

Three members of the group of young people that came down to build the school stayed behind to help us with the six-week course. They were Ernie Jones from New Jersey, Steve Hall from Washington, and Linda Grothe, who was a nurse from Wisconsin.

New Tribes Summit group in front of building they finished on their last day.

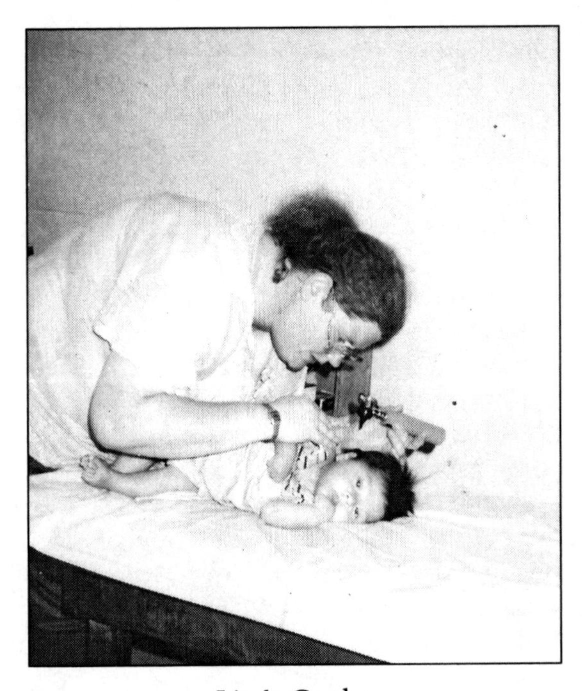

Linda Grothe.

Linda wrote the following account that touched all of our lives:

I would like to share with you an experience I had this summer that changed my life. I pray that this memory will be one that will never fade. I pray the lessons I learned that night in July will come to mind any time I am called on by God to step out in obedience to His call to spread the gospel to all nations.

We had just barely gotten settled into our huts here at Horeb when word came that another Chimane child had arrived at the gate looking for help. This was not anything unusual; it seemed someone new arrived every day. Some with TB, some with whooping cough, some with other physical complaints and injuries, all turning to the missionaries for help. But this little girl was different. I guessed her age to be eight or nine, but it was difficult to tell because she was so sick when she got here. I doubt she weighed more than forty pounds. Just a frail little body with every rib clearly visible, with sunken cheeks and hollow eyes. I will never forget those eyes. Deep brown eyes that pleaded for help. But the help that those dark eyes asked for, I was afraid would be too late in coming.

I was told that the girl's father had died of TB. There were no other children in the family, just this one. She had been taken to the local hospital the day that she arrived, but the doctor sent her back to us with orders to give fluids and vitamins intraveneously. She had had one bottle of fluids, and now it was time to administer another one. We could only pray that it would give her more strength. As it was, she was far too weak for the strong TB medications to be started, so we started the fluids and headed back to our cluster of huts for our evening meal.

We had just finished eating when someone arrived at the door asking me to come back. Something was wrong with the intravenous. So leaving my dishes, I followed them back to the hut where I had left Elisa and her mother. Four or five people stood at the doorway looking at the low platform bed. They spoke to one another in their Chimane language as I stepped inside. Elisa's mother spoke quickly, waving her hand over the place where I had placed the intravenous needle into Elisa's wrist. The missionaries, interpreting for me, said she wanted it taken out. "Put it in tomorrow," she said, while others continued to speak in the background. "They say she is dying." I told her I was not taking out the I.V. needle. I tried to explain that this would help to make Elisa stronger.

But as I sat on that bed talking to this Chimane widow through the missionaries, I saw Elisa's pattern of breathing change. I knew then that these people were right; Elisa was dying. So I took out the I.V. and watched as the widowed Chimane mother rocked her dying child.

She had one last request. Would we please take them home? I left the hut and walked through the dusky night feeling more helpless than I had ever felt. Elisa's mom wrapped her in a ragged cloth and carried her to the roadside to wait for the truck to take them home. While there, beside the dirt road, as darkness fell on this small cluster of huts in central Bolivia, Elisa died.

Two of the other Summit team members asked to go with Bruce Johnson, one of the missionaries here at Horeb, when he took Elisa and her mom back to the jungle, so they climbed into the truck's cab with Bruce. The Chimane people had a fear of riding inside of cars, so there, in the back of the open pickup sat a childless Chimane widow, a limp lifeless body cradled in her arms.

The trip was only twenty miles, but over the rough dirt road, it took over an hour to reach the jungle's edge. After they stopped, the Chimane woman remained silent as she carried her daughter's lifeless body into the darkness. Then the saddest realization of all hit. This woman has not yet come to understand the meaning of Christ's death for her and His resurrection. She walked away that night in spiritual darkness. No husband, no child, and saddest of all, no hope. No hope of eternal life with a loving God. For this Chimane family, the gospel came too late.

Please, Jesus, may I never forget that night in Bolivia when I sat by helplessly and watched Elisa pass into a Christless eternity. May I never forget your call to go forth into all the world spreading the good news of Jesus to all tongues and tribes. And may I come to you Lord at the end of my days having done as you commanded to your honor and glory. In Jesus name, Amen ."

Ernie Jones.

Ernie, after having returned to New Hampshire for a short time, came back and helped us for a year while the Gills and Johnsons were in the States. He was busy from early in the morning until late at night fixing electrical gadgets, motors, etc. When ever we asked him to do something, his cheerful reply was always, "You got it!" We wonder how we ever got along without him.

We continued to move ahead by faith. Sometimes I felt like the optimist who fell off a twelve-story building. About ten floors down, he said, "Well, so far it's going well." I'm glad to know the Lord is there to catch us.

The group of students in the foreground are Chimane teachers and the future leaders of the Chimane government. In the background is the brick building with the jatata-leaf roof that the young volunteers completed before they left.

The students would study half a day, and in the afternoons we had a work detail. We planted a good pasture grass on the property and found it more beneficial to raise cattle than to truck farm, and it was less work. We raised beef and still kept some vegetable gardens to feed the students and the sick. During the six-week courses, we would have anywhere from 100 to 150 people to feed, counting the sick people.

No one ever went hungry. We used gill nets and harvested fish from the many waterholes around the area. Bananas and rice were not expensive. We had plenty of milk from the cows to give the sick people and for our own use. We had a cream separator from the States that we used to make butter to sell.

Chapter 26

Unstable Again, School Continues, Medical Care

August 1984:

Those were good years because, after years of preparation, we were finally seeing fruit from our labor. Each year we would open more schools for the Chimanes, and the Bolivian government paid the teachers' salaries.

It was a really unstable time for Bolivia: the nation was paralyzed by a general strike, the President was kidnapped and then released after being held for ten hours, Communism was growing bolder, cocaine was still the number one export, air and land travel was grounded as no fuel was being sold, roads were blocked, food was difficult to buy, but through all this, God continued to bless us and the Chimane people.

September 1984:

Last school term, several of the men got excited about sharing their faith. They said that they were going to do it when they returned to their villages. Recently one student returned with large bruises on his chest. He was preaching to a group, and a drunk jumped on him, beat him up, and even pulled a knife on him.

Another student came in with great fear because he had preached against sin, and a witch doctor threatened to put a curse on him.

Some of the other students were able to share their faith without persecution.

This school term the students started coming in two days before school began, and we had a group of twenty-five men in the classes. The main class we have this term is the fifth grade, but five students were beginners who studied in the afternoon. Some were single, and some had families. We housed them, fed them, and treated their illnesses.

Most of the students were not Christians but had come with a real interest to know God. However, there were several Christians among them that were a great help to us in teaching these students about God. We sang with them every night. At times it was hard to get them to stop singing and to go to bed.

For the following year, this group would need to advance higher, as there would be new students coming in. At that time, there were ten primary Indian schools that taught up to the third grade. Our job was to take the students on up and to train the teachers so that they could teach higher grades. It was a big job, and the only help we had from the Bolivian government so far was to pay the teachers.

Medical Care

We didn't realize what a problem the medical care would be; as stated earlier, tuberculosis was rampant among the Chimanes.

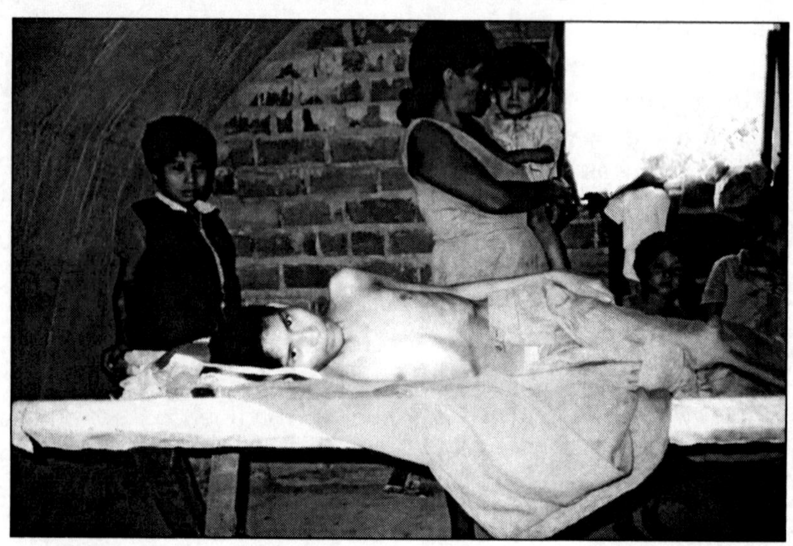

Rocky with TB.

When Rocky came to us needing treatment for tuberculosis, he was at death's door. We were doubtful that we could help him, but we started him on a series of medications and, along with the milk and food from the farm, he got better. He was able to hear the Word of God and became a believer in Christ.

Finally he was well enough to go back home. He lived several days travel down river from us in an area we had never visited.

This is a picture of Rocky when he came back to visit us.
We didn't even recognize him until he smiled.

We were overflowing with students, but sick people poured in just when we were busy with classes. Two women were hospitalized, which meant that some of our staff must be with them day and night. One died, and we buried her here, as they had come a great distance.

A stingray stung one boy while he was fishing; the pain was terrible. One man who suffered from a hernia for eighteen years was operated on in San Borja and stayed with us while recovering. The whole area where he lived opened up to us to share the Gospel, and several of his sons attended our school courses.

The medical services we provided at Horeb opened a lot of areas to us. The Chimanes believed that sickness was caused by witchcraft, and the fear of witchcraft had prevented them from trusting Chimanes from other villages. With students from the different villages coming to Horeb, all of this began to change.

One remarkable Chimane woman was treated at our clinic. I don't remember what her illness was, but she was with us for a few weeks. Not only did she get her health back, but she saw the Chimane School in action. She was very observant and went to the meetings and listened to the singing. All of this was new to her. She told everyone that came to Horeb what was happening there and as she traveled back to her home village, she told all the people about us. We lovingly called her "The Newspaper," not because she was so talkative, but because she was so good at reporting the truth about what she saw going on at Horeb. I am sure she would have been a great news reporter if she had had the opportunity.

"The "Newspaper" and our co-worker, Len Gill, at Horeb.

Chapter 27

Go Home, Return Refreshed, Work Continues, So Does Inflation

October 1984:

We felt we could make it, but realized that we would have problems because of the out-of-control inflation.

As the work moved ahead, we realized that we couldn't run a school, prepare Bible classes, and reach out to other villages with the Gospel, while trying to earn a living at the same time.

We had sold our home in the States and, through a small inheritance, had built up a small herd of cattle. The economy was suffering due to inflation, so in November, we returned to the States. We needed to present the Training Center in Horeb and its purpose and potential to Christians who were looking for a way to serve God and would like to have a part in the ministry to the Chimanes.

We could struggle on and live down here, but to be free to use the talents God had given us and to have a continual, effective ministry, we needed more help. We had almost exhausted our own resources but neither regretted nor were we ashamed that we had used our lives and goods for God, knowing that we will be rewarded in glory.

Students like Emilio made it all worthwhile; he was the first student to come to a course and had attended all of the courses. The other day he came and asked us for a blackboard and books to start a school in his area. He was doing this on his own because the children in his area wanted to learn. He also told us that the local witch doctor, who had given him such a hard time when he tried to preach to his people, had become a Christian and was now for the Gospel.

May 1985:

We were back in Bolivia, renewed and greatly strengthened. Several churches had taken on the task of helping us, and with that help we were able to move forward. We bought a Toyota pick-up and a diesel-powered generator for lighting. Up to this time we had been using 12 volt lights powered by our tractor battery. Helmer Glaas, an electrician and plumber, volunteered to come down from the States and put in the needed plumbing and lights. Now we could have lights at night, and we even had an indoor bathroom and shower that were gravity fed from our standing water tanks. Things were definitely looking brighter.

Economically Bolivia was still suffering; the exchange rate was one million Bolivian pesos to one United States dollar. The Bolivian schools hadn't operated for five months, and the Bolivian government was paying such a low wage that some of our Chimane teachers were quitting. This was very hard for us as we thought of the time and effort spent in developing these teachers who were now only receiving about fifteen dollars a month and needed more than that to live on.

If the teachers quit, the students' education and momentum of God's Word spreading would be greatly slowed. To subsidize their wages would set a precedent that would be hard to change. Most Chimane parents lacked interest in their children's education and could not be counted on to help the teachers financially. As a temporary solution, we gave the teachers more time off to work their farms so they could feed their families. We prayed that the situation would get better. And over time it did.

December 1985:

When we started our literacy program, we had very little of the Bible translated. As these fellows excelled in learning, we encouraged them to be teachers. Since they didn't have God's Word in their language, they were not the Christian leaders that we hoped them to be; however, they were slowly coming along and were teaching songs and what knowledge they had of God's Word to the students. As a result, a number of the students had become strong Christians.

January 1986:

We were encouraged; there was an awakening and awareness of God in two areas. One was from a jungle area about twenty-five miles north of us as the crow flies. Around forty Chimanes came to Horeb from this area. They looked like a hunting party dressed in the long native costumes and carrying bows and arrows. "We came for you to teach us about God!" they exclaimed.

It was nearly midnight when they were finally ready to go to bed. We had spent hours showing them a video series, which was in the Chimane language, singing, and explaining the Bible from creation through the gospel of Luke before they would let us stop. Some of them stayed two days more. "When are you coming to our village to teach us more?" they inquired. God's word was spreading amongst the villages.

Twenty miles to the south of us, another group of new believers were meeting regularly. "Please come and teach us," they begged. Two fellows there were showing real interest in trying to lead the meetings and teach.

February 1986:

Our co-worker, Harold Rainey, had a mild heart attack while shopping in town. He was 74 years old, and the doctor told him he needed to return to Canada. We really missed the Raineys, not only as co-workers, but as dear friends. They had shared much of the work while they were here.

August 1986:

It took Harold and Nora six months to actually leave as they had tasks they wanted to finish. With them leaving, we were really short-handed. It looked like we would have a group of thirty or so for our next course, and some of the students would be bringing their families. Picture yourself with fifty or so Indians twenty-four hours a day for six weeks. They were all young and full of energy. We were over-the-hill and exhausted, but God strengthened us for the task and what a joy it was to teach them and see them grow in the Lord. We thanked the Lord for the privilege of being here and having a part in turning these people from darkness to light, from false idols to the true God, Jesus Christ.

October 1986:

They came in waves, and we soon had around fifty-five students, plus their wives and children. For the first time, we had several women in the classes. One young girl had to be turned away because, with all the young boys here, it could be a problem. We can only solve this problem in the future by having a separate dorm for girls and dorm parents to care for them.

Christian Chimane men baptizing a Chimane woman.

We had several men students, who were advanced, helping teach the lower classes and helping with the meetings. Many of the students came from a long distance to attend the courses and wanted to be baptized before going back to their homes. So the Chimane Christian leaders and the students, their wives and children would gather together and have a baptismal service.

Our literacy program and schools are the heart of the momentum we have going; they are our first concern, and that is where we keep our focus. So whatever else is happening, we will make the effort to keep having classes.

Chapter 28

Threats, Exploitation, and Violence

January 1987:

Dino shares:

The Chimanes by nature were a very timid and fearful people. Their only defense has been to flee. The river merchants knew this and took full advantage of their fear of witchcraft and weapons. The merchants would often take the Chimanes' canoes and either sell or abandon them. On one occasion, I happened to be in a Chimane village, unseen by the river merchants who stormed in, shouting and firing their guns into the air. The terrified Chimanes fled, and the traders began chasing down the Chimanes' chickens and taking them to their large raft, which was already loaded with over a hundred chickens and several hogs that they had stolen from villages upriver. I stepped out of the jungle and asked them why they were doing that. They replied that the Indians owed them for trade goods.

I said, "I don't believe that, but even so, taking their chickens by force is no way to settle a debt." They only scoffed at me because they knew there was no law within miles, and I couldn't take them on by myself.

I remember a time when I was at a Chimane village, and they were roofing a hut. All at once, a shrill whistle sounded. The Chimanes perked up their ears. A few more whistles sounded, and one of the Chimanes whispered, "It's Michi coming."

The Indians took off into the jungle, and when Michi arrived, none of them were around. Michi always brought at least one, and sometimes two, five-gallon cans of cane alcohol. It was his favorite trade item with the Chimanes. Michi was one of his own best customers with the alcohol. He was drunk most of the time when he was among the villagers. He carried a pistol and, when he was drunk, often fired it in the air. What I marveled at was how the Chimanes had worked out signals with their whistling that would let each other know who was coming.

On one of Michi's trips upriver, he pulled onto the shore and went in to see an old drinking buddy, Pedro. He invited him to join him upriver at a drinking party where he, Michi, planned to spend the night. At that time, we were living among these Chimanes, and Pedro, a Bolivian national, had been working for me. I had invited Pedro to a Bible study in the evening and he said he would come; however, his desire to drink with Michi was far greater.

I later learned that in his drunkenness, Michi began to fire his pistol. Pedro, stone drunk, opened his shirt and said, "Don't waste bullets. If you are a man, shoot me." Michi pulled the trigger on the rusty old gun, and it didn't fire the first time, but on the second attempt, it fired and sent a bullet into Pedro's heart, killing him instantly. The following morning they brought the stiff corpse downriver and unloaded it at our house. We had just had a table made from an old mahogany canoe, which was long and narrow, so the body was laid out on our new table. We prepared him for burial for that same day because in the tropics bodies begin to decompose quickly and stink in a few hours. Michi was very sorry that it had happened.

On another of his trips, Michi was drinking and decided he wanted to sleep with the wife of a little Chimane man who didn't weigh over a hundred pounds. Michi grabbed the girl and began dragging her down to the beach with him where he had his mosquito net set up. The Chimanes' houses were close enough that they could hear her cries of anguish and pain as Michi brutalized her. The Chimanes sat in frozen silence, afraid to do anything about it. The next morning when Michi and his gang pulled out to continue their trip upriver, the girl was roughly shoved aside and abandoned. She went back to the village that she was from and never lived with her husband again.

Not all Chimanes are as timid as little Jose and his family. Another river merchant who was known for his brutality was Napoleon. He would go into a Chimane village, begin shooting his gun, and start grabbing chickens, rice, or whatever suited his fancy. One night while drunk, he climbed into the mosquito net where a Chimane man was lying beside his wife. He booted the man out and began to abuse her. The Chimane could not stand for this to happen, so he took his bow, shot Napoleon with an arrow, and finished him off with a knife. He dragged the body off into the jungle and hid it. But, some of Napoleon's crew went to town and told about it. Several family members and friends of the family (other river merchants), formed a mob and stormed the village where Napoleon was killed. Fortunately, most all of the Chimanes had fled, but they burned all of the houses and took everything they could find.

By that time his son, Fidelio, had made many trips with his father and now began his own trips. He always went well armed and didn't hesitate to rob, kill, and abuse the Chimanes. When he was coming upriver, the alarm was sounded, and he found empty houses to plunder. Fidelio had a hatred for the Chimanes that never waned. The Chimanes must always watch their backs or Fidelio might find them.

We had denounced these kinds of actions before, but we received very little encouragement that justice would be upheld by the law; nevertheless, God had heard their cry and moved on our hearts to at last cry out against this injustice.

Chapter 29

River Merchants' Abuses

February 1987:

Len and Elsie Gill's launch.

Len and Elsie Gill were our co-workers who had a launch and had for years traveled the Maniqui River, visiting and teaching in the Chimane communities along the way. They had many encounters with the river merchants. One of the encounters occurred while Len was checking the school at a village called Maraca. A couple of the Chimanes that lived in the area came to him to place a complaint against one of the river merchants named Fidelio. He tried to rape one of the Chimane women while her husband was out hunting. He threatened to kill her husband if he didn't get his way with her.

Len was trying to keep a low profile, but the people called him, saying, "Fidelio is here, and he is angry."

When Len got to the house where they were gathered, Fidelio was in a dispute over a basket of dry chocolate seeds. He was taking it without paying, saying he would pay later. Len greeted him, and Fidelio glared at him angrily. Len just looked him straight back; then Fidelio started accusing Len of being angry.

He started a long conversation, denouncing Len as a foreigner, etc; the outcome was he was still going to take the chocolate without paying for it. At that moment a Chimane arrived out of breath saying that the chocolate was in payment for a machete to another river merchant, so Fidelio left it.

Even though Fidelio gave up on the chocolate, he was still upset about Len, a foreigner, standing up for the Chimanes. Len asked the Chimane teacher, Felix, to show Fidelio the document that the Chief of Police of San Borja had given Felix recognizing him as the legal authority of the area. Fidelio's brother was also there and started to read the document. He realized that the document was real, but Fidelio still tried to claim that the document didn't apply to him. Fidelio did become more rational and even friendly after Len invited him to the launch for a cup of coffee and some bread and cheese.

Later, the Chimanes said that before Fidelio left the area he became angry with a Chimane man and began kicking him. He dragged him to the beach and started pushing his head under the water. Fidelio put him in a canoe and took him down river. Witnesses were not sure if the man was still alive.

There is a large group of Chimanes who are fed up with drunks, rapists, and those who come to rob with guns. They are asking for it to stop.

While we were at Maraca, some Chimanes arrived on their way downriver with a letter for Dino from Juan, the teacher from Yocumo. Juan was very concerned for a young man named Papi. A river merchant named Choco was angry with Papi. He said that Papi had a debt with him. Choco beat him up, using the butt of his revolver to strike him on the head, and made him work without pay. This river merchant had more than two acres of coca, from which cocaine is made, planted at the village of Ocuña.

"This man is really bad. We don't want him coming here. We don't want him around. You need to tell the police about this, Dino."

Papi's story:

My name is Papi. I have a wife and a small son. To me the jungle is home. I know the names of the different trees and when a bird sings, I can tell you what its name is.

My dad taught me all I know about hunting and farming. We could live well here in the forest, but the river merchants won't leave us alone. We want to live our own lives and do what we enjoy doing, but the merchants come and make us work for them.

The one I hate the most is Choco. He is a big bully. When I hear that he is coming, I go into the jungles and hide. Choco came to where we lived along the river because he was looking for workers.

We were at my dad's place drinking some home brew when Choco came along. He offered us alcohol. He got mad when we refused to drink it. We know his trap. He will give us a drink, and then we will want it. We should have taken off to the woods, but he caught us by surprise. I got a bottle of alcohol from him and got drunk.

The next day I felt terrible. Choco said, "You owe me. Get your bed and come with me."

"I don't feel good, I protested."

"Get your bed right now," he ordered.

I know this man. He works us for days with no pay and hardly gives us food to eat. I knew it would be bad, so I said, "No! I will work and weave jatata leaves to pay you with."

Choco really got mad. One of the other merchants grabbed me and held me, and Choco grabbed his revolver by the barrel and started to beat me in the back of the head. My dad and brothers stood frozen and watched. I passed out, but when I came to, Choco was still there.

"Get your bed, boy," he ordered. "If you try to run away, I will hunt you down and kill you."

The back of my head was a mess. The skin was broken and chunks of flesh had been torn out, but I had to go. We poled his canoe for several days upriver and arrived at the place where his workers were cutting mahogany boards with a power saw. My job was to carry these boards out to the river where they could be put on a raft and taken to town to sell. The boards were real thick and real heavy. Each day I wondered if I would die from being so tired. I wanted to run away in the night, but I knew that I would have to live far away from my parents and my village because if I returned there, this devil would kill me like a dog.

Finally I had had enough. I didn't even care if Choco killed me. I was going to escape. He wasn't there anyway. He had gone down-river with a raft-load of lumber, so I plotted my escape. I waited until late at night, and, when I was sure his guards were asleep, I slipped off into the jungle. No one shouted, so I kept going. I slept a few hours under a big tree, and when I woke up, it was day time.

My body was tired and ached from the hard work, but I knew that I had to get home. That evening I arrived home, and I was happy to see my wife again and little Manuel. My dad and mom were really glad to see me too. When I told them that I had run away, I could see the fear in their eyes. Just then we saw flashlights coming fast up the path from the river.

We heard Choco, and I fled to the forest. "Where is that lazy Papi?" he thundered. "I'm going to kill him! He owes me money."

"He's not here," my dad lied.

"Where is he?" Choco screamed. He knocked my dad down with the butt of his rifle and started kicking our kettles and our dogs. Mom told me this later because I didn't hear him. I was running as fast as I could go.

There was a house boat out on the river, and I swam out to the boat and asked for help.

Leonardo, (Len Gill was called *Leonardo* in Spanish) reached down and helped me onto the boat. Choco had followed me to the river and onto the boat. Len told Choco to leave me alone. Choco was really mad at Leonardo, but he left.

Leonardo wanted me to go to town and tell the police, but I wouldn't go. I am afraid of the police. They might get mad at me.

About four moons after this happened, I was in San Borja, and Dino told me that I needed to tell the police about Choco. I was afraid, but I went. The police chief looked at the back of my head and there was no hair there. It was covered with scars from the pistol whipping Choco had given me.

The police arrested Choco and took him to jail and charged him a fine. Then they let him go. I didn't get anything for the days I worked for him.

Sometimes at night I have nightmares and wake up screaming. I think that Choco is beating me. I am always afraid he will grab me again, and I watch every canoe that comes upriver. If it is his canoe, I'm gone to the woods. I am afraid he will cast a spell on me and cause me to get sick and die. I hope that he gets sick and dies so he won't bother us anymore. I hope when Manuel grows up things will be different, and he won't have to be bullied by these bad people.

Len Gill and Dino finally take a stand against the river merchants

Dino writes:

There was no law along the river. I did not choose the role I was put into, to be a protector of the Chimane people; however, I was challenged by the police chief of the town of San Borja to catch the perpetrators, take them to him, and he would punish them. Actually the police only extracted a fine and let them go, but it did make the river merchants more cautious.

It was a lot different from the States. The police didn't actually have a vehicle, so we were told to bring in the offenders, and they would deal with them. So when the offending merchants arrived in port, I took the police in our pickup, and we brought the merchants to the police station. We got a statement in writing that two of the worst offenders were never to return among the Chimanes. We hoped this would cause the other merchants to take notice that the police were getting serious; the police had already given the authorization for our seventeen teachers to report abuses in the future.

Chapter 30

Law Enforcement

One night, a pickup stopped at the gate at our base in Horeb, dumped off a Chimane, and sped away. I went out to see him and saw blood was coming out his mouth. I took him to the hospital three miles away, but at two o'clock in the morning, he died in my arms. He had been kicked to death.

We buried him on our property where we had already started a cemetery, but we never did learn who he was as no relatives ever contacted us.

There was an older priest in town and a very friendly nun who came out to visit us a few days later. In our conversation together, I told them about the incident. They were greatly disturbed by it. That evening during mass, the priest lashed out at the parishioners, "How can such a barbaric thing like this go on in our town and the police do nothing about it?"

One of the parishioners carried these words to the chief of police. The man became enraged, and said, "No one told me about it. Who told the priest about the incident?" The reply was "Dino, the gringo missionary."

The chief of police ordered me to the police station, and when I arrived, he glared at me and asked, "Why didn't you report this occurrence to me? The priest has the entire town in an uproar about it. How do I know that you weren't part of the problem?" he probed.

'Sir, with all due respect," I countered, "I have lived here among these people for many years and have denounced abuses on many occasions, but have never seen justice done, not even in one case. That's why I didn't report this one. What's the use?" I challenged.

"Listen, Mister. Not all law officers are alike. If you will bring the complaints here to me, I will see that justice is done," he retorted.

"Chief, I accept that challenge. You will be hearing from me," I promised. I left the police station still somewhat doubtful, but determined to try.

When I heard that Choco, the bad merchant had come downriver and was now in port and in possession of some stolen jatata leaves, I went to the chief and told him about Choco. The chief said, "I don't have any transportation. Bring him here."

I asked for a policeman to accompany me, and he sent two along. They arrested Choco without incident, put him in cuffs, tied his feet, threw him in my pickup, and we were off to the police station. You can guess what happened next. The chief exacted a big fine from him and let him go. I had made one more enemy.

This was repeated time after time. The chief of police's way of bringing justice was to exact fines for his own pocketbook. There was no justice or recompense for the victims, and each time I was involved with my white Toyota pickup in bringing in the offenders, I was making dangerous enemies.

The Chimanes caught on quickly, and almost daily they were at our house denouncing some thug. But, by this time some of the river merchants were beginning to get wary and afraid to abuse.

A Killer named Daniel

On one occasion a group of Chimanes came to our house crying, "Dino, a killer has moved into our village, and we are all afraid." I found out that this man was an Indian who had married into this Chimane tribe. He was armed and dangerous and had already killed four people. I took the people to the police station to voice their complaint. The Captain asked them if there was a way into their village by road. They told him that there was a logging road that led to their village, but the killer lived in the jungles a mile or so away. This was about the only village that had a road into it because a logging company needed one to reach the sawmill they had built there.

The chief said, "Bring him in, and we will punish him."

I said, "Give me a policeman to accompany me, and I will go there tonight."

He said, "No, come here around four in the morning, and I will give you a man to help you."

I rather doubted if I would find anyone awake at that hour, but, sure enough, there was a policeman waiting for me. I never carried a gun or knife, not even a club, because I always sensed that God was not only directing me but also protecting me.

We drove up the rough logging road and, to our surprise, a number of people were outside their leaf lean-tos with their little lights that consisted of a piece of rag rolled up and stuck into a bottle of kerosene.

"He's down there in a lean-to about a half a mile away," someone whispered.

"Someone will have to go with us and show us the place," I said.

"I will take you near, but then I will hide so that he can't see me," an old man offered.

"Okay, let's go." I ordered.

When we neared the lean-to, our guide pointed out where he was sleeping and then faded into the jungle. The leaf shelter was very small with no walls, just a roof. We could just make out his form as he slept inside a thick mosquito net.

We eased closer and grabbed his legs. He put up quite a struggle, but the officer and I subdued him and got a pair of handcuffs on him.

He asked, "Why are you doing this?"

"Because you are a killer," I answered.

He said, "My name is not Daniel."

I said, "Don't lie. We know who you are." By the time we got back to town, it was daylight, and the jail was stirring with movement.

This man, Daniel, had killed four people–the most recent one over a machete of all things.

After they locked him inside, the chief asked, "Who is going to feed this man? Since we don't furnish food for the prisoners, if no one feeds him, I will have to let him go."

I was shocked but told him that I would see that he got fed. He didn't have a change of clothes, so I also had to buy him some. And, it gets worse.

The day after he was put in jail, his wife came to our house with all of her children and stated, "Dino, you have put my husband in jail; now we have nothing to eat. You will have to take care of us."

"You live among your relatives," I told her. "They are the ones who fear your husband and asked for help. Let them feed you."

I asked the police chief when the man would be sent to prison. He said, "The prison is in Trinidad, an hour's flight from here. If you want him to go there, you will have to pay for the plane trip."

After a month, I went to the lady who prepared the food for Daniel and told her I wanted to pay her for another month. She started crying and said, "When my son took the food last night, the jailers opened the door, and the killer walked away. Please don't tell the chief that I told you this, or they will punish us."

"I won't," I promised.

The next morning I went to the police station and asked about Daniel. "He climbed over the wall and escaped last night," the chief lied. "If you find him, bring him back," he ordered. Several months went by, and I heard nothing about the whereabouts of Daniel.

Then one day a Chimane from a village called Napoles came to Horeb and reported that his son and another man had an argument over a woman, and his son had been killed.

I went to spend some time with them in their sorrow, and, although I didn't know it at the time, I was later told that Daniel, the killer, had heard that I was at the wake and came looking for me with his army carbine. They said that I had only been gone around fifteen minutes when he arrived.

How I thank the Lord for His angels and His arm of protection. I never heard anything about Daniel again.

Len, Catalina, and Elsie Gill.

Len and Elsie Gill, our co-workers, had been threatened as they were witnesses to many various abuses against the Chimanes. We felt as lambs among wolves, but we knew God had us there among the Chimane people doing His work, and He was protecting us.

Many of the merchants are killers, and now a great fear for them is that their ′coca,′ from which cocaine is made, might be found out by the authorities.

Yet, there is momentum, a moving of God's Spirit among the Chimanes, and they will someday be free from bondage and fear. God Himself is going before us and helping us.

Recently we settled a matter by casting lots like they did in the Bible. A young woman claimed that one of the Chimane teachers had raped her, and he claimed that he hadn't.

Which one was telling the truth? I finally cut two sticks, one long and one short and prayed that God would cause the lying one to draw the short stick. The woman drew the short stick, and after a while the truth came out that she and the teacher had consensual relations together, and when her husband found out, he beat her. It made her angry that she was beaten and nothing happened to him, so she claimed the teacher tried to rape her to get even with him.

In April of 1987, Dino wrote in a newsletter: "In the last letter we talked about the river merchants who were abusing the Chimanes. The police gave us a written guarantee that two of the worst offenders would not be able to return to the areas where the Chimanes live. The latest news is that these merchants paid no attention to the law and are up among the Chimanes, well armed, and very angry with the Indians for denouncing them."

One big problem we realized was that the Chimanes had no visible form of government. They lived in small family clan groups, scattered over an area of hundreds of square miles. They were no match for the Bolivian river merchants who abused and exploited them.

Now there is a new threat: as colonization is moving into the area, hundreds of new families are settling here, and the Bolivian government is talking about moving the Indians off their land and putting them all on a reservation. If this goes into effect, it would be a disaster for the Chimanes.

Meanwhile the school courses at Horeb continued on.

Chapter 31

Under Attack!

August 1987:

While we were living and working with the Chimanes in the steaming tropics, trying our best to help them, the anthropologists decided that missionaries shouldn't be allowed to work with the tribal people.

Suddenly several leading newspapers, along with radio and television stations, began to blast the mission organizations that worked with the tribal people. They published an open letter for public opinion with the purpose of removing the missionaries who were working with the various tribes, accusing them of ethnocide by mistreating, exploiting, and even killing tribal people.

A newsaper in Santa Cruz, Bolivia, dated August 30, 1987 published an article titled, "*Anthropologists Request the Expulsion of Two Evangelical Missions*" and a newspaper in La Paz, Bolivia, dated August 29, 1987, stated, "Around sixty Bolivian anthropologists and investigators met together and signed pronouncements, urging the expulsion of two Evangelical missions..."

When you are some of the people working with a tribal group, you take that personally, especially when they were petitioning the Bolivian government for immediate deportation and the ring-leader was the Bolivian Head of Indian Affairs!

See Appendix (D) for more information on the articles from the Bolivian Newspapers.

Under investigation

A commission led by an army colonel was formed, and Dick Wyma, the Director of New Tribes Mission, was ordered to take them via their airplane to visit the tribes where the missionaries were working to investigate the charges against us.

Our work among the Chimanes at Horeb was the first place they visited. From here they flew into the other tribal areas.

It was quite alarming for Elaine and me as jeeps and motorcycles came racing into our yard. They contained the mayor, judge, ex-governor, and several other important leaders of San Borja. Someone had said that we were being attacked so the leaders of the town of San Borja came out to Horeb, walked up to the Commission, asked who they were, and let the commission know that they were behind our work.

They said, "We are the authorities here. How dare you come here and attack these missionaries? When you come here, you are to come to us first and present your business." The colonel said, "We aren't attacking them; we are just visiting to see how things are."

He then asked if our students knew the National Anthem. At that, our bare-footed Chimane students stood at attention. They didn't just sing it; they belted it out. One thing we had done from the beginning was to pattern our schools after the Bolivian schools; we had a Bolivian National as our director, we respected all of the patriotic holidays and hired a local music teacher to teach the Bolivian patriotic songs. The Bolivians are very patriotic, and we believed this was needed.

Students standing and singing the Bolivian National Anthem.

The colonel saluted, and the town leaders clapped along with the Commission. When the Commission saw what we were doing with the Chimanes and how the town backed us, it changed everything. We didn't realize until that moment that the town leaders knew what we were doing or even cared. We were so thankful for the town leaders who came and defended us, and we were grateful that we had followed the Bolivian culture to honor their National Anthem, other patriotic Bolivian songs, and their holidays.

From then on, when we had occasion to travel to the capital city of La Paz, the head of Indian affairs would send a driver to the airport to pick us up in a limousine and take us out for a meal.

The Commission continued its inspection among other tribes, but there was no more talk about the missionaries being kicked out of the tribes. Hallelujah!

See Appendix (E) for a retraction from the same newspaper dated October 6th, 1987, "Evangelical Missions Complete an Effective Labor Amongst the Tribes Living in the Amazon."

Chapter 32

The Water-Pot Lady Writes a Letter

Earlier in our story we told how Maria Sidiroff (The Water-Pot Lady) came and helped us with one of the courses. Dino was in La Paz at the post office when she heard him speaking in English to a friend. She told him that she was in Bolivia to study the different methods of making clay water pots. She was very disappointed because the people where she planned to go were demanding too much money for her to study with them. She has made many trips with archaeologists, and the study of ancient pottery has had an important part in understanding a people's ancient culture. Her son who was traveling with her had been bitten by a dog and had to go back to the States. Dino told her about our work with the Chimanes and that if she wanted to, she could come down and visit us and that some of the women were well known in the area for being the best at making water pots. A Chimane woman, Santa, was so well known that everyone called her husband "Gregorio Cantaro" which translated is "Gregorio Water Pot."

A few days after Dino came back to San Borja, Maria arrived at our house on a motorcycle taxi driven by a little old man whom we called "Suicide" because he had so many accidents. She was so happy when I greeted her at our door. With just an invitation from a stranger whom she had met in La Paz, she had flown on an airplane over the Andes Mountains into a town in the tropical lowlands of Bolivia, rode on a motorcycle which took her through the town of San Borja out through the grasslands of the Beni. You can imagine how relieved she was to meet the man's wife and be assured that she was welcome at Horeb. Since we were having classes, she could be a part of trying to preserve the art of making water pots with them. She spent a few weeks with us and the Chimanes.

We thank you, Maria, for the time and effort you took to write this letter in our defense.

November 24, 1987
Dr. Pedro Plaza Martinez
Director del Instituto Nacional de Antropolgia
La Paz, Bolivia

Dear Dr. Plaza'

I have recently received a letter from missionaries of my acquaintance in San Borja expressing their fears concerning efforts of some Bolivian anthropologists to have them expelled from the country. As a Roman Catholic of fourteen years of education in American convent schools, I arrived in April, 1984, totally unprepared for what I encountered at the San Borja Farm and Christian Training School directed by Dino and Elaine Kempf. They are Evangelical Missionaries who have worked among the Chimane people for over thirty years who invited me to San Borja to conduct a study of pottery making.

Since Evangelicals focus their religious beliefs upon individual interpretation of the Bible, an important part of their activity, after contacting a group, is to gain knowledge of the spoken language. Most often this language is known only to a small group of isolated people who can neither read nor write in that tongue.

Dino Kempf lived among the Chimanes to learn their spoken language and works to encourage literacy, and a sense of pride in Chimane culture, among the students at the San Borja Farm and Christian Training School.

However, thoughtful people cannot ignore material needs in favor of only spiritual and cultural values. As you know, a school for adult Chimane males must care for the families of the students. The Kempfs provide spiritual guidance as well as food, shelter, practical farming instruction, and health care for the men and their families while they participate in the program.

During my stay in 1984, I observed that the day was divided into three parts. Classes were held in the mornings for the students, and after a mid-day break, everyone worked at farming tasks. Several evenings a week the Kempfs served refreshments in their home to accompany religious instruction. In many different ways during each day, I observed Dino and Elaine demonstrate profound concern for each individual at the school. A practical solution to the problem of obtaining food, advice on personal conflicts, appreciation of Chimane culture, understanding of Bolivian government regulations, or immediate health care were some of the daily services they performed for the Chimane people. All these activities were conducted with the utmost dedication by the Kempfs, who have chosen to leave their family and friends in America to make a lifetime commitment to the Chimanes.

I travelled to San Borja to conduct a study of pottery making among the Chimanes, a tradition that is in jeopardy. The Kempfs hoped that through my research, a revival of Chimane pottery making could be instigated at their school among the families who accompanied the students. However, the two women identified as potters were unable to accept me as a student. Maria Wamayo, a San Ignacio potter living in San Borja, did agree to instruct me in her method. Sra. Wamayo utilized a production technology that she learned from her mother. Her technique involved the use of a kiln, which is a method not employed by traditional Chimane potters who prefer open-pit firing of pottery.

I am disappointed to have lost the opportunity to record the Chimane pottery making tradition and hope to accomplish this goal on another visit to San Borja. My studies with Sra. Wamayo form an important chapter in a book I am writing on traditional pottery technology. When published, I will deliver to you the ten copies of the book that your department requested.

Intimate daily contact with the work of Dino and Elaine Kempf for the one month provided me with an opportunity to evaluate the important work they are doing among the Chimanes. News of recent attacks on their integrity by some officials of the Bolivian government has encouraged me to write to you. As a student of Margaret Mead at Columbia University, I became aware of the importance of advocates among people in the midst of rapid culture change. Mead often referred to her role among the people of New Guinea as such an advisor, and I observed the Kempfs utilizing a similar approach in their work among the Chimanes. Professor Mead's commitment rested upon a scholarly foundation, and the Kempfs' source of strength is their religious conviction.

The results of their work are similar: an abiding respect for the individuals involved the native culture, and the nation as a whole. I respectfully hope that these comments can offer to your department a point of view that will assist in your relations with the San Borja Farm and Christian Training School. My religious background is quite different from Evangelical Missionaries, but I was able to appreciate the importance of their unique contribution.

Respectfully submitted,
Maria-Louise Sidoroff

Chapter 33

Help Arrives, School, and Progress

Old Blue, the Power Wagon, Jan and Bruce Johnson, Kara, and Talitha. Their daughter, Vanessa, was at Tambo, the school that our children attended.

In 1987, help did arrive in the form of Bruce and Jan Johnson as they began their journey in Chimane Land. They were such a vital part of the work, and God had some amazing plans for them, much more than we could ask or think. You will read about it later on in this book.

It is good to have some younger people coming into the work as the rest of us are getting older.

Girls Come to School

Our current Bible course had ended; sixteen students, most of them new, made a decision for Christ. I remember telling a young fellow who came in late that we couldn't take him because we were full. "But I want to learn God's Word," he pleaded.

When the term ended, he was one of those who stepped forward to receive the gift of salvation in Christ. What if I had refused him from attending the class? Four girls came for the course without husbands. This was a first for us as we were afraid to launch out on this for fear of problems. One girl's grandmother offered to watch the girls, so we agreed that they could come. Three of them did great, but one ran away, taking Manuco, a male student with her.

When the girl's father tracked them down, he asked Manuco, "Do you love my daughter?" He answered, "I'm not sure." The father didn't like that answer and socked him on the jaw. Again the father asked him if he loved his daughter. Again Manuco answered doubtfully, so the father socked him a few more times and asked again, "Do you love my daughter?" This time Manuco answered, "Yes, I'm beginning to love her." They have been married for years now.

December 1988:

The next course was the six-week bilingual-teachers course. We had to cut expenses in order to have this course, so we shortened it to four weeks by having extra classes in the afternoon instead of work detail. That way we would still be able to get all the needed hours in. It was an exhausting schedule for the staff here at Horeb, but we made it work.

We had thirty-five Chimane teachers, plus their wives and children. All together there were probably eighty people. Every house was filled, so we were really thankful for the four new Quonset huts that were built by the Hard Hats for Christ volunteers.

Some of these teachers had been teaching for years and were leaders in their communities. They weren't happy about having to come in for advanced training and that we had asked them to help pay for some of the food they were eating. Some of them were here with their wives and several children. To add to the confusion, we also had eight men from two other tribes come in.

The cooks wanted to quit because the teachers had such a bad attitude and complained about the food. There was plenty of well-prepared food, and nothing to complain about; however, two cooks got mad and took off. One Sunday several students left without permission and went fishing. We don't force religion, but we have a rule that they are to be at all classes and meetings and that they must get permission before they leave the property.

One of the fellows who had gone fishing got stung by a stingray. We tried the new method of shocking with DC current at the stinger wound area, and it helped.

I knew I had to do something about the truancy so I told each one who had left without permission that he had to peel an entire bag of rice. Rice had to be peeled by hand with a pestle. Some balked and said, "We will go home first."

"If that is what you want, hit the road," I told them. "If you can't obey the rules here, then we won't have you."

Each bag had the name of the perpertrator on it, and they could peel it when they had time. It was tense for a couple of days, and then they came with big smiles and blistered hands. "We finished our punishment," they boasted, and finally they said, "We are ashamed for our actions." So everyone weathered that storm with all the teachers and families and staff remaining.

Chapter 34

Battle over No-Man's Land

A summary of 1988:

Elaine writes:

For us, the Kempfs in Bolivia, it has been a battle on behalf of the Chimane tribe. In our entire thirty years in Bolivia we had never had a battle like this. The Chimanes were having all kinds of problems.

Things had changed drastically; roads had opened up the country. The timber companies had moved right into the forests where the Chimanes have always lived and hunted, and the areas where civilization hadn´t yet reached were getting smaller. Homesteaders were moving in by the thousands.

Cheating the Indians had been a way of life for many. Without leadership and without organization, the land where the Chimanes lived had always been considered up for grabs. The Chimanes had never worried too much as there was always somewhere else to live.

Now there was someone to help them. Dino was at Horeb, so he could speak for them and they could stay here when they came to San Borja. They started coming to Horeb and asking Dino to go to the police with them to report the abuses to the land judge or the town authorities. Dino was the one person that could help them, and they trusted him.

The people in San Borja had always liked Dino, but now because of helping the Chimanes, he had made a lot of enemies. They blamed him and said, "It didn't use to be this way. It was Dino that has caused the Chimanes to stand up for themselves."

Another thing that the Chimane people did that really made the river merchants angry with Dino was if the people didn't want to sell something to the merchants, they would lie and say, "We can't sell that; it belongs to Dino." So it would look to the merchants that Dino owned most of the pigs, chickens, and products along the river. That wasn't true, but the people were afraid of the merchants and didn't know what else to say.

As abuses happened, the teachers started writing letters. The witnesses fearfully presented themselves in town, and Dino went with them to try to find help as most of them didn't speak Spanish. At that point, we ran up against crooked officials who would take no action.

Groups from various Chimane communities were coming to our house saying that they had made the trails and wanted to measure the land. They had brought bananas, yuca, etc. to pay for the measuring. What was complicated was that one part was under Colonization, another in the Reserve Land, and another should be measured by the Land Reform group, but no one knew where the line was between the Reserve Land, Colonization, and the part of Land Reform.

Sixteen years ago, Dino helped the Chimanes measure seven communities with the help of the Brigada Mobil surveyors for the Land Reform law. We had the number of those documents, and the plans were in La Paz. The sad part was that after sixteen years, the titles had not been issued; they were still languishing in the Land Reform office. Dino had made numerous trips to the Land Reform office, and they always assured him that they lacked very little in order to be issued.

One of these was the Community of Fatima where there were twelve Chimane families living. Simon and Cruelia, who were river merchants who traveled up and down the river and traded for products, harassed and tried to take advantage of the Chimanes. The Chimane people feared them as Cruelia knew about the Chimanes' fear of witchcraft and would threaten them and tell them that she would put a curse on them.

They saw this place and used the pretext that they wanted a small piece of land to plant tomatoes on. That was the beginning. After that they went to the Judge of Work, and solicited a parcel of land 150 meters wide by 2,500 meters long in the Community of Fatima. The Judge of Work doesn't actually have the authority to give the right of ownership to others. That was the work of the Land Judge.

After this, they made another document using Cruelia's name, with the same date as the one before, which showed that her land bordered the land of her husband. They left out Leoncio Tayo and the original owners of the community of Fatima that lived there and had already applied for a title to the land.

It was very plain that they did it with the intention of taking it from a group of indigenous people who couldn't defend themselves. When they began to clear the land inside of his property, Leoncio realized that they were taking away his land.

When the Chimanes told us about it, Dino went with them and talked to the Land Judge. He told Dino to take someone and get the land measured to be sure that it is the same land as the Chimanes' papers said.

He took the Land Judge and the surveyor and proved that the former plans of the Indians' land were accurate. Then Cruelia and Simon came up with another plan. They hoped to shut Dino up by denouncing him, and then they could take the land from the Chimanes because they wouldn't have anyone to stand up for them.

The river merchants had a harmful letter aired on both radio and television against us. The river merchants, the very people that had been guilty of most of the abuse among the Chimanes, accused us of causing problems among the Indians where none had ever existed. They accused us of forbidding the Indians to work for them, of bribing the police, and many other things that were not true. It is amazing that the people who had been fighting to get some help for the Chimanes were the ones being given a bad name. An investigation against us was started.

The river merchants of San Borja had written a letter that contained a series of accusations that were both false and harmful and also claiming that they had letters from the civic committee, the judge, and various institutions.

We sent a letter to Judge Lidia Moscoso in San Borja requesting her as Judge of Instruction to show us what to do concerning the demeaning letter against us. She replied stating, "No one in this office, particularly me, has supported what the merchants are claiming." The Mayor of San Borja and the other institutions also answered in kind.

Orlando Del Rios, the President of the Civic Committee, wrote us stating, "By no means has the act of having our stamp on the said letter signifies that my authority is in agreement with the said accusations and is without merit because it does not correspond to the truth.

a) On the contrary, such acts signify a shameful action on the part of the river merchants and their respective leaders by mocking the authorities.
b) Also we have complaints against some of the members of the association for taking possession of land that belongs to the Chimanes.
c) It has been proven that some of them have robbed the Chimanes.
d) Lastly, a member of the River Merchant Association obligated a Chimane to work for him at the point of his shotgun. When the Chimane took the shotgun away from him and broke it, he returned with a twenty-two and made him obey.

This cannot be called living in peace. The people will have to respond to the judge for their actions."

Chapter 35

River Merchants and Human Rights

The River Merchants didn't just denounce us in San Borja; they filed a complaint against Dino with the Human Rights Organization in La Paz. The River Merchants claimed that the missionaries were interfering with their right to use the Chimanes to earn a living.

We didn't know about it until Dino and some Chimanes went to Trinidad and a lady from the biological station told him that there was a Letter of Accusation against him. It was sent from La Paz to the office of Human Rights in Trinidad requesting an investigation.

They went to the office of the Human Rights group and talked to a representative about the investigation. He said that they were a small institute mainly working with the indigenous groups in the Moxos Province, and they knew very little about the Chimanes in the Ballivian Province. They wanted to help the indigenous people, but when it comes right down to it, the Indians would have to help themselves. He said he respects the Evangelicals and Catholics, but both are damaging the culture, and we should leave the Indians alone and not teach the Bible. The Human Rights people in Trinidad don't seem to realize that by denying the tribes the opportunity to hear God's Word, they deny them the right to choose.

The conversation was low key, both parties agreeing to disagree. What we did agree on was the fact that the Indians were being exploited because of their alcoholism and fear of witchcraft. For the most part, the anthropologists will be a year or two among the

Indians, and the missionary will spend many years among them. The changes that are happening cannot all be blamed on missionaries.

January 3, 1989:
Chimane Rights and Human Rights

Elaine reports:

We sent all of the information we had gathered to Dick Wyma, the Director of New Tribes Mission in Bolivia, so he could present it in person to the Human Rights Organization in La Paz.

Dick went to La Paz and presented the documents, and also showed the backing we had from the local authorities.

Dick told us that the lady he visited at the Human Rights Organization was a bit reserved–not really commenting much on the case, simply saying that they would be investigating the matter.

Dick explained, "She said it would be best if we help the Chimanes represent their own case to the local authorities. I explained to her that you are only taking part because the Chimanes do not speak Spanish and are afraid of being deceived by the local authorities. She listened, but still felt that you should be in the background and use your ability in the language to instruct the bilingual teachers and others of how to work through the government authorities. I told her of the cases of injustice that you have seen and, of course, she has heard much of the story having spent time with you in Trinidad.

She feels, Dino, that in spite of your earnest desire to help in these cases, it is best you take a low profile and try to work through the Chimane leaders and have them go to the local authorities."

Dick felt it would be important to have a letter which we could present to the office in La Paz clearing him with the Human Rights people.

Chapter 36

Stone Axes

Then the river merchants tried another trick. They accused us of having prehistoric bones and stone axes in our possession. They circulated a story stating that we had a special plane that would fly in from the states and remove these artifacts, and they were asking for an investigation. They were always trying to come up with ways to divert us from defending the Chimanes.

We didn't realize that there could be trouble with the stone axes. Every once in a while, as we walked along the beaches of the Maniqui River, we would find a stone ax or sometimes prehistoric bones. The Indians' explanation about the bones was, "They were animals too big to get into the Ark."

There were other small rivers where the Indians would find stone axes and would bring them to us. The Chimanes had no use for them, and they were something of interest, so we would trade something for them and bring them back with us to our house. It wasn't illegal to have them; it was only illegal to remove them from the country.

I had around sixty of these stone axes that, according to the curators of the museum in La Paz, dated back a thousand years. They said that they were pre-Inca and were from the Arawak civilization. The bones were from various extinct animals.

One day when I was at the San Borja airport, I met three men from a museum in La Paz; one was the Director of Archeology in Bolivia, who came to San Borja to look at some ruins.

They had come to view some graves from the Inca civilization which had been unearthed, but by the time they arrived, the pottery and other artifacts had already been sold on the black market to European countries. I told them that I had a lot of artifacts that I would be willing to donate if they would carefully list each item and sign a paper that stated what they had received. They agreed and came out to our house at Horeb and collected the artifacts. They signed their names and what their positions in the museum were and departed.

The day that the river merchants accosted me with their accusations, I handed the president of the Civic Committee the signed paper, and he read it aloud.

There was a crooked lawyer that these merchants had brought along, and he sighed, "The Gringo bested us again."

The river merchants were determined to get rid of Dino. One of the merchants had a sister who worked in a government office in La Paz. He had her take a letter to a member of the Bolivian Cabinet denouncing Dino and wanting him deported. This cabinet member was reading the letter, when in walked her nephew who was from San Borja. She asked him about the accusations in the letter. "That is one big lie," he declared. "I know the missionaries, and I also know how the river merchants abuse the Chimanes." The letter was shredded and thrown in the waste basket.

Chapter 37

Agreement between Chimanes and River Merchants

Elaine continues:

The problems continued to worsen. The river merchants continued to spread lies about us over the television and radio. Finally the town leaders of San Borja stepped in and called another meeting of the river merchants. The judge, the civic committee, the mayor, and the Catholic priest were present. There were around eighty of the river merchants there; several Chimanes; Fidel Honor, the pastor of our local church; Dino; and me.

The president of the Civic Committee presided, and the merchants stated their grievances against Dino and requested that Dino Kempf and Leonard Gill be deported from the country.

The Civic Committee president responded, "Everyone has the right to request deportation, but the laws give the accused the right to defend themselves. The fact is that we are not here for that. That would be judicial in our opinion. Previously we announced that this meeting will be for reconciliation, and we are going to leave what happened in the past, in the past, and decide how we can work from here on.

"We are looking for a beginning. We are not a tribunal, we are friends. The case has gone through the entire town; everyone is talking about abuse to the Chimanes. This also includes the Human Rights Committees in Trinidad and in La Paz.

"The problem is that there are some that we should bring to trial. All of Bolivia is going to know how we solve the problem. Lay aside the hatred and animosity, and we will settle it. We wash the dirty rags here."

Lidia Moscoso, the judge stated, "We want to settle this here and now. There is no place for discussion. Look for solutions between you and Dino and the Chimanes. The Chimanes are arriving at a new status in civilization. Before the Chimanes did not know there is diversity with human rights, and it is so with the other tribal groups too. This tribunal has no authority for judicial accusation. Let's make an act that the river merchants will follow."

Then the Chimanes presented the paper that they had written, and Dino was asked to speak.

Dino said, "In the first place, I didn't come prepared for a debate. It isn't my problem.

The Chimanes have now demanded their rights. The problem is that the abuses do not occur here in San Borja. Who is going to be in charge of leading a commission to investigate? The Chimanes want recognition of the Chimane people who have been put in charge and when an incident occurs in their area, they want assurance that the authorities in town will back the authority of the Chimanes.

There was a case of a shotgun that the Chimanes took away from an abuser. There was a young Chimane who was given a paper naming him as the one in charge, and they laughed at him because the paper wasn't worth anything. We need an agreement of mutual respect.

In the case of abuses, it will be difficult to investigate because of the distances involved. Who will investigate it?

Another thing is the defamation of my character. In the past, I requested a letter with the official seal of the authorities and a public clarification but never received it."

The president of the Civic Committee said, "We need an agreement. To me it seems if we leave without an agreement, we are going to forget what has happened here today.

We also have to write to Human Rights that no previous problems exist that we have not settled."

After a number of meetings, our lawyer wrote up a satisfactory agreement, which everyone signed.

Then our lawyer turned to the merchants and said, "We still need one more thing; a letter must be written clearing up all the lies you have aired about Dino."

"We thought it was all over," they exclaimed.

"No! You have made false accusations against him that must be cleared up," she stated.

So they wrote a letter saying that they made accusations against Dino that were not true and they take back all they had said. Hopefully the struggle with the merchants has finally come to a close and we didn't even get shot at.

See Appendix (F) The River Merchants Apologize Document

One of the things that was agreed on is that each Chimane community will have the authority to appoint their own officials to represent them and keep the peace.

Also, the river merchants sent a letter to Human Rights in La Paz withdrawing all their charges against us.

The result was quite a good, binding contract between the Chimanes and the merchants that travel the river. With the backing of the town authorities, the Chimanes appointed men to enforce the law in every Chimane settlement along the river. There would also be a stiff fine if the merchants were proven guilty of abusing the Chimanes.

I will say that the president of the Civic Committee did a good job of arbitrating between us. He told the Chimanes that they would always be abused so long as they were not organized. They had for centuries lived in small, clan groups, scattered over a vast area of the lowland jungles, very isolated one from another.

He turned to the group of Chimanes and said, "You have no organization, no visible government, and you need that. I will give you ninety days to get organized, select your president, and those people who will be under him. The town lawyer and the judge will help you with the legalities."

What a wise move that was on the part of the president of the Civic Committee. United, the Chimanes could do a lot, as you will see.

If you asked Dino, "What in the world is a missionary doing getting mixed up in all of this?" His answer would be, "God is urging us to help free these oppressed people. If we didn't sense His direction and the moving of His Spirit within us, we would not dare to venture into these areas. They have been in bondage for centuries. In bondage to fear, drunkeness, witchcraft, and oppression. Now, they are turning to God, and God, in turn, is helping them. There is much resistance to letting them go, but God will bring them out."

Chapter 38

The Tsimane' (Chimane) Government

January 1989:

The Chimanes were given ninety days to form a government. How do you help a tribe that has never had a government to organize one?

The Civic Committee told us that Judge Lidia Moscoso and the lawyer, Mari Luz Denis, would help them.

The young Chimane School Teachers were the core group. They and their students that had come to Horeb were the only ones in the whole tribe with the capability of going ahead. They had no concept of government. Remember, up until the time the Chimane people had started coming to Horeb, the individual groups of Chimanes did not mix together. They were very afraid of witchcraft. The thing that united them was their language. They had no leaders or laws. We certainly had no training of how to form a government.

There were believers in Christ among them; they had been taught the Chronological Lessons and knew that God had brought the Israelites out of Egypt, how they crossed the Red Sea and entered the Promised Land, and they believed it. So we prayed and God helped us figure it out.

How does the government work in the United States? You have cities, counties, states, and federal government. We have little groups of Chimanes scattered upriver and downriver, so we decided those were our cities, and they chose local leaders to represent them.

The groups of villages in a designated area along the river would be the equivalent of the counties, with the villages choosing someone to represent their county.

The states would be made up of the county groups with the counties choosing a representative from upriver and downriver. These would make up the members of the Tsimane' Tribal Council and then the Secretary and President would be chosen to represent the leadership of the tribe.

The judge and lawyer wrote up the papers. We drew pictures representing the river areas. The Chimanes got busy; this was something that the people wanted.

They wanted to be called *Tsimane'*. "That is our word." they declared. So their official name is *Tsimane'*. They also included the Spanish word (Chimane) so that there would be no doubt.

On March 3, 1989, the people sent in their delegates to vote. They and the authorities of San Borja gathered at Horeb to officially recognize the act of forming the government and chose their leaders. Since most of them didn't know how to write, each candidate was represented by a color, and the people proudly went in and put their colored vote in the box. This is how they formed their government. They now had someone to officially represent the tribe and could legally sign papers. The Tsimane' were now officially recognized by the Bolivian Government.

Official Tsimane' Seal.

THE CONSEJO TSIMANE'(CHIMANE) was formed on the 3rd of March, 1989, which consists of the following:

Gran Jefe: (The Chief):	Valerio Roca Muiva
Secretary (teller/advisor)	Jorge Añez Claros
Consejo member Number 1.	Francisco Mosua Yujo
Consejo member Number 2.	German Cayti Lero
Consejo member Number 3.	Adrian Roca Moye
Alternate 1.	Oscar Roca Moye.
Alternate 2.	Lorenzo Maito Nosa
Alternate 3.	Benjamin Cayuba Claros

It should have been impossible, but our God is the God of the impossible, and the Tsimane' government was formed.

See Appendix (G) for more information on how the Authority Structure was set up for the Chimanes. Pains were also taken to give Chimane names to the different positions.

See Appendix (H) for more information on the Threats, Exploitation, and Violence

PART 3

Chapter 39

The New Tsimane' Government

April, 1989:

The responsibility of the Tsimane´ government was on the shoulders of some very young men. They were from the first generation of the young men who had learned to read on the literacy trips we made on the Maniqui River and from the children who were taught by the Chimane teachers.

Valerio Roca, the chief, was probably in his mid-twenties when he was elected. The chief was responsible for handling matters affecting the tribe as a whole.

Jorge Añez was elected to the high position of tribal secretary to represent the tribe before the national authorities. He was only nineteen-years old, and he would be representing a people who had never had any type of formal government. Soon this young man, who had not spoken Spanish previously, was dealing with national officials trying to resolve problems between the Bolivian nationals and his people. He would be meeting with Bolivian government officials and traveling to foreign countries, including the United States, for meetings related to tribal affairs.

Jorge Añez, Tribal Secretary.

Soon after the Chimanes had organized, Mauricio Hauser, the owner of the sawmill at Fatima, told Dino about a meeting in Trinidad regarding the request of an area in the rain forest for the tribal groups. Dino mentioned it to the Chimanes, who had not heard anything about it. The Chimanes sent Jorge, who had a limited knowledge of Spanish, and asked Dino to accompany him as his interpreter to the meeting.

At the meeting there were a number of tribal groups represented. These groups had organized together and had requested that an area in the rain forest be granted to them for their territory. They had several powerful organizations backing and helping them.

There was a lot of discussion at the meeting, including comments from a German anthropologist who spoke out against Dino saying that religion was doing damage to the Indians.

Jorge stood during the meeting and said, "We Chimanes are so thankful for Jesus Christ and the Word of God. It is changing our lives. Before we were a tribe of drunkards, but now we are changed. We Chimanes are teaching God's Word to our people, and it is changing their lives. We are so glad for God's Word."

As the discussion continued, Dino and Jorge realized that the area being requested by the other tribal group was the area where the Chimanes currently lived. It was in an area of the rain forest that the government had told the Chimanes they should petition for themselves, including in the petition the entire area where they lived, fished and hunted in order to be able to continue their customs and way of life.

The advisors to the other Indian groups insisted that the territory be given as a multi-ethnic area, but Jorge said, "No! We have different customs, culture and language. We have lived apart for centuries. The other tribal groups live in villages, and they have leaders. Chimanes live scattered. When a member of another tribal group arrives at the house of one from their tribe, he is welcomed; he has his meal assured. When a Chimane arrives somewhere else, he is not received like that; only with his own people. It will be like what happened to our people who lived along the upper Beni River. Colonization gave parcels of land to the indigenous groups from the highlands to relocate, and also to our people who lived there. Now those people are the owners of everything, and our people became their servants.

The other tribal groups will dominate the Chimanes if this area becomes multi-ethnic, and the Chimanes will become tired of being their servants and will leave. Then they will become nomads, because they are a timid, passive people, and their only defense is to flee."

That was the beginning of a number of trips to Trinidad and La Paz. The Civic Committee of San Borja intervened for the Chimanes to represent themselves as they were not being included in the meetings and talks about the territory in which the Chimanes had lived for generations. This was the land that the other tribal groups were asking the government for.

The Census

Commissions were formed, and various teams went throughout the area of the rain forest designated for the tribal groups. They recorded the exact number of inhabitants of each community, the places where they hunted, and the distance they went in order to hunt and fish. A Chimane person was included as interpreter and guide in each commission, in order that they would relate better to the people and so the people would not be embarrassed or shy. Each Chimane was sent with their own notebooks to keep records.

A strange occurrence happened among the census teams, though. When a team neared where a group of the most primitive Chimanes were living, the team would turn around and go back. They never got to where those Chimanes were living and, therefore, did not include them in the census.

The Chimane guides that accompanied the teams had written down in their notes, "It lacked an hour before arriving where our relatives live, but the members of the team said they were tired. They said that the canoes could not go any further upriver and there was not a good trail. We wanted to go ahead, but they would not, so they went back without completing the survey. Also the census team that traveled along the Maniqui River never got into that area so these Chimanes were not added to the census."

Consequently, the Chimanes that went with the census teams and who knew how to fill out the interviews formed their own group at their own expense and got the required data.

June, 1989:

Dino and I were asked to accompany Jorge Añez and Chief Valerio to La Paz as their interpreters. Our work was to review the maps, marking the places and settlements of the people that lived in each place. We also marked the places that the Chimanes needed and generally occupied for gathering, hunting, and fishing, as well as what distances they traveled and what work the people of the Chimane communities did.

For the meetings we always arrived on time to begin our work, but the others always arrived late. There was an urgent need for the government to see the finished results and hopefully sign off on it. We were fearful of the upcoming national elections and what would happen when the government was changed. The new Bolivian officials might not have the same interests in dealing with the indigenous peoples.

Wood-Mizer

While we were in La Paz, we were notified that the Wood-Mizer Company had heard about our work and had donated one of their sawmills. It was being shipped to us in Bolivia. We were told to check at the World Vision office in La Paz, so we went to the office where we were told that the sawmill was already in customs. They were checking on the best way to get it since customs wanted to charge $4,300 to release it.

Chuck with sawmill.

Someone said that we could get it out for a minimum amount of dollars except that it lacked a document from the United States stating that the sawmill was for the use of the Chimane Bilingual School. We soon got the needed document, and the sawmill was delivered. Two men from Centralia, Washington, volunteered to come and train some of the Chimanes to operate the mill, which would give both the school and the Chimanes an opportunity to be self-supporting. This was truly a miracle of God's perfect timing.

We Are not Nomads

While we were in the city of La Paz, an article came out in the newspaper stating that the Chimanes were only some eighty families of nomads. In opposition, we informed the newspaper that the data was false; the Chimanes are not nomads. They have schools, and they live in communities, both of which indicate that they are not nomads. The next day the newspapers published the clarification that we had given them.

Jorge did his best to keep the Chimane people advised on what was happening by sending out newsletters asking that the people who could read share it with others. He explained to them what was happening and urged them to pray to God so that He would hear and grant their petition for ownership of the disputed land.

Chapter 40

Dispute over Chimane Land

November, 1989:

Jorge Añez and Elifredo Zabalas, the director of the bilingual school teachers, went to an assembly in Trinidad where they were told that the president of Bolivia would be coming to sign the paper that would grant the territory that was promised to the tribal groups. However, the other tribal groups, in spite of Jorge's objection to their action, sent a telegram to the government refusing to accept any part of the offer. Once that telegram was in the hands of the government, the president's signature would not be binding. Jorge told them that the Chimanes were in danger of being without a territory. He told the other tribal groups a number of times before they sent the telegram that there was not any way that the Chimanes would refuse what the government was offering. The Tsimane' Council wanted the government to go ahead and grant the part of the tribal area where the Chimanes live along the Maniqui River. Since it was clearly marked out on the plan for the land grants that the government had presented, it would not be difficult to grant that part to the Chimanes.

Jorge recognized that there was nothing that favored the Chimanes and apart from that, the other tribal groups were planning to declare a state of siege if the government did not agree with their demands. The Chimanes would not go along with this.

Jorge returned to San Borja and told us what had happened. The Tsimane' Council sent a telegram to La Paz expressing their agreement to the proposal of the land that the government was granting to them. Also, they did not want a misunderstanding with the other tribal groups. The tribal groups have their own needs and the Chimanes have theirs.

This telegram arrived after the one sent by the other tribal groups. Consequently, nothing was done at that time, so the struggle continued.

In answer to the telegram, the Chimanes were told to go to Trinidad as the Bolivian president, Jaime Paz Zamora, was going to be there. Since all of the Chimane teachers were at our teachers' training school in Horeb, they all went to Trinidad for the November 18th meeting.

Chimane bilingual teachers, including Elifredo Zabalas, the director of the Bilingual Schools.

The president of Bolivia arrived in Trinidad the same afternoon as the teachers. That night there was a parade around the main plaza where the president gave a speech in which he said, "All the land titles have been signed." But the petition for the disputed territories was not signed because of the telegram that the other tribal groups sent.

The next morning the other tribal groups and the Chimane teachers had a meeting with the representative of the government.

Again the other tribal groups said that they did not want the land divided; they wanted all of the area that the government had originally offered, which included the area offered to the Chimanes. They also wanted all of the timber companies to leave these areas.

Jorge told them that the Chimanes would not refuse what the government had offered to them; they were happy to accept. One of the men from the other Indian group answered Jorge in a rude way; it seems he was bothered by what Jorge was stating, but Jorge only told them the truth. "No one was telling the Chimanes what to do. We have people counseling us, but nothing more. We are free, and we have liberty to do things in our own way without excessive demands, and we support the government's offer to us, the Chimanes."

The government representative reassured the Indians that the petitions before the government concerning the territory would not be hard to consolidate. But to the Chimanes it was a very complicated issue. There were timber concessions and cattle ranches in the area. Along with that, there was a tax of eleven percent levied for the towns, San Borja included, and the towns had been happy because they could build roads, schools, and other necessary things with the tax money.

May, 1990:

The Battle for the Land Continues

A representative of the other tribal groups came to San Borja and spoke with the Chimanes at Horeb. She informed them that the other tribal groups had decided to accept the land that the government was offering them. She explained that it is better than to risk not having anything. She asked the Chimanes if they were in agreement to receive the territory that the government was offering them.

They told her, "We are ready to accept the territory now."

"Good," she said. "If the government does not keep its word, are you ready to join the march?"

"We are ready," the Chimanes told her.

After this, the leaders of the other tribal groups appointed two Chimanes that lived in the other tribal groups' area to be the representatives of the Chimane people. They had them write their names and where they lived. Then this information was included in a document they made up and sent to Trinidad. It stated that if the government did not grant the area to them, they were going to march to

La Paz and demand it. The Chimanes were deceived by these Indian leaders in a very underhanded way.

For the next two years the Chimanes were pretty much ignored; they were not advised about meetings nor were they given any money to help with travel expenses to Trinidad and La Paz. Any time the Chimanes tried to work with the other tribal groups, they were not treated as equals or respected.

Arson at Arenales

In June of 1990, the Chimanes who had lived for years in a settlement called Arenales, which was along the road from San Borja to La Paz, accused a family of colonists of setting fires to some of their houses to chase them away. The colonists wanted to take over the land that these Chimanes were living on.

According to the Chimanes, the problem started when they accused one of the colonists of stealing a block of salt from a Bolivian rancher. The thief was chastised and fined. Because they told on him, he was resentful against them, and soon a bag of clothing hanging in the house of a Chimane was burned. Then another sack of clothing was set on fire in another house. As is their custom, the Chimanes store their new clothing in a bag they hang from the rafters.

Some months afterwards, a house was completely burned down. Their clothing, bedding, kettles, rice, machetes were all burned. A Chimane woman saw two young men and a woman near the house that had burned. She testified against them before the police in San Borja. The police had Dino take two policemen and bring back the perpetrators. They, of course, denied the charges. They said that the Chimane woman that had accused them was crazy, and they denied being in the area where the house burned down. The police arrested one of the young men, but he insisted that it was the "crazy" woman who set the house on fire, and they let the young man go.

Still another house was set on fire, and the owner lost everything. No one saw who did it, but the same people remained under suspicion.

Since they had no vehicle, Dino went and got the police again. When we arrived, there were about a hundred angry Chimanes gathered. Even though they are generally peaceful and timid, they were at the boiling point and were ready to take action against the colonists.

One Chimane came with a shovel and a knife. We could hardly keep him from attacking a young colonist who was thought to be their leader.

Besides setting the house on fire, the three colonists who had been accused had grabbed the woman who testified against them, tied her legs so she could not run, and then beat her. None of the three denied this after being hauled back to the police station. We requested an investigation about the case to avoid another confrontation with them, but nothing was done by the police and the harassment continued.

Is it possible that these indigenous Chimane people, because they are poor, will not be protected by the law? If it was a rich person who had been wronged, I think there would have been an investigation right away, but five times perpetrators had set fire to the Chimanes' houses with the intention of forcing them to leave, and nothing had been done.

More complaints against Simon and Cruelia

We were continually getting letters from the Chimane teachers reporting abuses along the river, asking us to tell the police. Simon and Cruelia were some of the worst. The people were afraid of Cruelia; they thought she was a witch, so she took advantage of this and threatened them. Simon would get drunk, get in fights, and shoot his gun; he would even shoot at the Chimane children. One report said that Cruelia had held a Chimane while Simon beat him. When Simon shot an ox that belonged to one of the men in a Chimane community, we took Simon and Cruelia to the police. The witnesses testified against them, and we showed the police the agreement that the Chimanes had made with the river merchants where the abuser had to pay a fine of five hundred pesos. The chief of police refused to charge them; he said that instead they were going to have Cruelia and Simon sign a guarantee that if it happened again, they would have to pay a fine of two thousand pesos.

After that, there were many more complaints against them. Simon entered another house where the Chimanes were drinking strong chicha. He sat and drank with them until he was drunk, and then began to challenge them to fight, but no one was brave enough to accept the challenge. He got his .22 rifle and fired four times, shooting at a pair of pants hanging from a rafter. He was there quite some time challenging the men to fight.

After resting awhile, he got angry again and reached for his rifle, but one of the Chimane women grabbed it and ran to his canoe at the river. She put the rifle in the canoe, the other people brought Simon and put him in the canoe, and they sent the drunken merchant down the river.

Rumors abound

All kinds of rumors and lies went around. One of the river merchants started a story saying two helicopters from Horeb dropped poison in the river. There was another rumor that they were going to send in two hundred helicopters and carry the Chimanes off. If the Chimanes would not get in the helicopters, they would shoot them. The Chimanes were so scared that they ran off, leaving behind their chickens, pigs, and all their belongings. Another merchant told them that all of their young men would be forced in the army and that scared them, too.

Chapter 41

To March or Not to March

August 1990:

The other tribal people met together and decided that if the government did not give them their land by August 2, the "Day of the Indian," they would march in protest to La Paz with their bows and arrows. This meant a week's walk for the Chimanes at a pace of forty miles per day.

The Chimanes were supposed to get their land on August 2nd, and just like the previous two times, the other tribes refused. What the government wanted to offer was really fair, but the other Indian groups were being used by political agitators to cause trouble for the government. Those groups wanted to have all the Indians march to La Paz in protest against the government.

The Chimanes wrote two letters that explained their position but could not find a way to send them safely to La Paz. Then a Bolivian senator came to San Borja for a funeral, so they were able to talk to him. He was very happy with the news that the Chimanes wanted to settle peacefully, as the whole town was upset that the Chimanes might march against the government. He called the Minister of Agriculture, who was responsible for the decision on the land, and had the Chimanes talk to him. The Minister promised they would have their land even if the other groups turned theirs down. The Chimanes were the only group asking for land where they already lived.

By August 10th, we still had no official word. Then another phone call came, saying that the government would sign the papers. We heard that a commission from the other Indian tribes was coming to try to convince the Chimanes to join the protest march to La Paz. The Chimanes sent a telegram requesting that the government advise them of their decision before August 15, 1990. They needed to know if the land donation was certain by that date so that they would not commit themselves to join the march against the government.

On Saturday, August 11th, a commission came over from Trinidad to get the Chimanes to change their minds and join the march. The commission really intimidated the Chimanes, but they held firm. August 12th, we waited–no word; August 13th–no word. Finally, on the 14th, a telegram arrived saying that the government had accepted and that the Chimanes were being given almost one million acres of land. The head of Indian Affairs would arrive on Saturday to arrange things for the Minister to come and give the Indians their land, probably on the twentieth.

Saturday the 18th arrived, and we received a telegram saying that on the next day at 8 a.m., the Tsimane' Council was to meet with a government commission to work out the details to bring the Minister of Agriculture, and possibly the President of Bolivia, down to give the land to the Chimanes.

Sunday morning it was raining, and no one arrived. In the afternoon, Dino called La Paz and was told that they had not lied: the Chimanes were getting the land, but the weather was bad, and, the commission could not get to San Borja.

Also on Sunday, the students arrived for school, so we had one group waiting for the land, another group for school, and also a group of sick people.

On Monday it rained all day, so again no one arrived. The deadline of the marchers arriving was getting close, too. Maybe a thousand Indians from other tribes would be arriving here on their march to La Paz and would try to convince the Chimanes to march with them. They had convinced one member of the Tsimane' Tribal Council to go along with the other Indian group, and he was trying to get the Chimanes to join in the march. The Tsimane' Tribal Council dismissed him because he had turned against the best interest of the tribe.

Despite the rain, Dino got called to go to San Borja. It turned out that the Chimanes at La Cruz had finally become fed up with people taking their trees from them. A few weeks before, they had poured out some wood-cutter's gasoline and burned the logs that the thieves had cut down.

Some of the river merchants in town wanted the Chimanes put in jail and forced to sign a paper giving the merchants permission to cut wood in their area. The Chimanes would not do it. Dino was accused of swaying them, but he did not know a thing about it. It turned out to be the Chimanes and Dino against the river merchants again.

Dino finally told them in Spanish "*Me levanto las manos!*" ("I'm lifting my hands!"), meaning he was not going to be involved. The Director of Indian Affairs was coming, and he could settle it. The river merchants kept telling Dino that he could not "lift his hands" and leave the Chimanes on their own. The Chimanes got a kick out of it and told them that they would wait, too; they were tired of people taking their trees, and if the authorities wanted to put them in jail, they would have to put the entire community in jail because the women had helped. It was a community project.

The town was upset that the Chimanes had burned two trees. Dino told them that it was not good, but not long ago, five Chimane homes had been burned to the ground, and no one said a word about that.

So now the marchers were arriving, demanding Indian rights; the government was arriving to give the Chimanes their right to the territory where they lived; and the other tribal groups were still trying to claim it as theirs.

It was the first week of school: students arrived, sick people arrived, and the river merchants aired another bunch of lies about us on the radio and television:

"We were inciting the Indians."

"Should a 'Gringo' have so much influence over a tribe?"

"We were getting rich, and the Chimanes were getting poorer."

"Someone with a good heart should be running the schools for the Indians."

The commission arrived with three representatives of the other tribal groups. They went on to La Paz and said that they would be back on Friday to drive the Chimanes to where the other Indians were and that the Chimanes would receive their land there. This turned out to be a lie.

On Tuesday, August 21, the call was put out for all the Chimanes to come to Horeb to receive their land, and on Thursday a thousand Chimanes arrived.

Also on Thursday, a group of forty Indians from the other group arrived at Horeb after walking twelve days through the jungle to join the march to La Paz. We took them in and explained to them that the

Chimanes were not joining the march because the government was quite fairly giving the Chimanes their designated land. They told the Indian marchers they did respect the others' right to march if they wanted the mahogany trees in the other areas of land but not on the designated Chimane land. All would be well if each group respected each other.

It was hard to believe a group of a thousand Chimanes were sleeping in our yard and cooking on little fires. Women and children were all getting along well; there were no arguments or loud voices. In the early morning, we woke up to hear them laughing and talking. They are such a gentle people and so gentle with their children. There was also no drunkenness.

The San Borja town officials helped. The young fellows organized the food distribution and anything else that needed to be done. The town sent trucks out to pick them up and sent food for them while they waited.

Part of the Thousand Chimanes Waiting at Horeb.

By Friday no one arrived, and no word was received until evening. The Chimanes had promised to march into San Borja and thank the government for giving them their land. So on Friday afternoon men, women, and children lined up and marched, holding up the signs that they had made, and carrying gifts of mats with bows and arrows on them to be presented as gifts.

One thing the Chimanes were determined to do was support Dino. One sign said, "The Gringo Stays." They also made speeches at the town square. San Borja had never seen anything like it.

The march was well organized, and the Chimanes were happy to have done it. On the way home, one of the women said she was tired, and one of the men answered, "It is a good tired." It was amazing how the women entered in. Never in the history of the Chimane tribe had they gathered together like this. It also proved their government was truly working.

When we got back to our house, it was already dark. Some leaders from the other march had come to demand a list of everyone and berated them for marching because the leaders had not given them permission. There was a big discussion. The Chimane leaders told them, "The leaders could tell the other tribal groups what to do if the people agreed, but the Chimanes had their own group and their own government, and they didn't recognize the other group's authority to tell them whether they could or could not accept their own land."

Friday night we were told that the Bolivian Minister of Agriculture was coming the next afternoon, and everyone needed to stay here until he arrived; however, on Saturday morning, we heard that the president was taking the week end off, that the other tribal groups had rejected all negotiations, and that they were going to keep marching to La Paz.

About that time some people were feeling doubtful; however, we told them to wait as the government had promised to come. About then, a town official arrived to say that the commission would be here at 4 p.m., but that they were still meeting to work out all the details so the Chimanes could have their land. That brought a loud round of applause. They were also told that right after the meeting, trucks would take them home, but, as it would already be dark, we were concerned about the people leaving at that hour. They told us that they did not want to go until the next morning; instead, they wanted to have a meeting to thank God for their land as they knew it was He who had done the impossible for them.

At 2 p.m., Dino went to town and found out that the plane would arrive in half an hour. He drove back in low gear as the truck was running very poorly. Ernie grabbed the Old Blue Power Wagon, and he loaded up the Chimane tribal leaders. They went with banners flying, arriving at the airport just as the Minister stepped off the plane. He was so happy that they were there to meet him. They loaded them all into Old Blue with the Chimane leaders and brought them to Horeb, along with newspaper men, including some from the New York Times, and their television cameras. We were all tearing around to get ready because in Bolivia things usually don't start on time, let alone an hour early.

People in Horeb line up along road to La Paz.

The Chimanes were lined up along the road waiting for the Commission to give them their territory. This is the same road through Horeb on which the Indian protesters traveled on their march to La Paz.

The river merchants came and tried to force their way in to talk to the Minister. The Chimanes formed a solid line of people and forced the merchants back, finally pushing them out and locking the gate behind them. For a while it appeared there would be a fight, as the river merchants had severely abused the Chimanes in the past. The merchants were in the midst of a group of a thousand Chimanes, but the town officials and a number of high government officials were here, so there was no trouble.

It was a wonderful meeting with the Minister of Agriculture, Mauro Bertero, greeting the Chimanes in a few words of their own language. They clapped and were so happy. He presented them with the paper that gave them the right to their own territory. Praise God!

After the meeting, the Chimanes presented all the officials with gifts of bows and arrows and almost every artifact we had on hand at the house. Then outside of the gate they formed a solid line of bodies on both sides of the path all the way to the truck with room to walk between. There was much hand shaking, clapping, and laughing. Just before the Minister got on the truck, he knelt down and talked to a very shy little Chimane girl, and she kissed him on the cheek. It was really sweet.

Chief Valerio Roca and Minister of Agriculture Mauro Bertero.

That night we had an awesome meeting. The people rejoiced and talked until midnight about how they were to behave, what they were going to do, and how they would not in their own strength try to fight people. They recognized that God had helped them. It was a miracle that this previously unorganized tribe could organize and with the help of a foreign missionary that they called *Chaitidye' Dino* which means "relative" (a very high compliment) in Chimane, ask the government for land and get it. They prayed, and they thanked God. It was so exciting to see their love and gratitude to the Lord!

On Saturday, we asked a doctor to come out because we had a number of sick people. The doctor spent hours treating the sick. We had been given a microscope for the clinic, and on that Saturday afternoon, Rosauro, our medical worker, was able to diagnose one little twelve-year-old girl with tuberculosis, so she was able to get the early treatment critical to a cure.

Activities started very early Sunday because Chimanes are early risers. The trucks finally arrived, and everyone got on their way.

Chapter 42

The River Merchants' Threats

Flatbed truck loaded with Chimanes going back home.

August 1990:

Monday we went back to teaching school. A woman came from town that had been in meetings with the river merchants and overheard that they had made plans to attack us and take us hostage. Their plan was to create an incident, take Dino prisoner, haul him to Trinidad, and make false charges against him.

We were not sure of the woman's motive for telling us this, but Dino had already been threatened publicly on radio and television. A list of false charges had been made, along with the threat that if the local authorities didn't remove Dino from San Borja, the river merchants would take action and do it themselves.

After hearing what the woman had to say, the missionaries at Horeb talked things over. We were concerned that the leaders of the march would provoke an incident with the Chimanes and us so that we could be blamed for interfering in the march.

The marchers would be coming on the road to La Paz which passes right through Horeb. We decided that Dino should go where Wayne and Ruth Gill lived at the village of La Cruz along the Maniqui River and get Wayne's thoughts on what was to be done.

So after lunch, Ernie took Chuck, the logger, and Dino up the road in Old Blue as far as he could, and from there they walked to La Cruz.

We called the Chimane leaders together to tell them what we knew and asked them what they thought.

They felt that Dino should stay at La Cruz, and that it would be better if the rest of the Americans also came to La Cruz until the march was over. They would send the Chimane women and children out to the river just in case of problems, and the men would stay at Horeb.

That night after dark Ernie made another trip in Old Blue out to the river with the Chimane women and children. We sent food and a cooking kettle along.

Maurice Olsen, the dentist who had come to work on the Chimane's teeth during the school course, Frank, and I (Elaine) decided to go to La Cruz. Soledad decided to go into town and stay with her mother. We would leave at 3 a.m. That would give Ernie time to get back with the truck, and he could walk to La Cruz with a Chimane for a guide. The Chimanes kept patrolling the place during the night and checking in town and at the river to see if anything was happening.

Jorge Añez had quietly infiltrated where the merchants were meeting and listened to their plans. They had gone out and talked to the marchers. They wanted them to cause an incident at the house as they went by, but the marchers refused to do it.

At 3 a.m., those of us still remaining at Horeb left in Old Blue for La Cruz. We arrived at the river at 4 a.m., but had to wait two hours for it to get light enough to see. I was so glad one of the Indian teachers had come with us; he went across the river and made the arrangements for the canoes. We tied two small canoes together and floated down river. While it was still dark, we waited on a sandy strip of beach that extended out into the water. I did not realize how close I was to the edge when suddenly it crumbled off, and I was up to my armpits in water. I was glad I had something dry to change into because before we arrived at La Cruz, a cold south wind had started to blow.

It took about three hours to get to La Cruz, and it started raining just as we pulled up on the beach. As I climbed the bank, I was stung by a bunch of black fuzzy bees. By that time it was raining hard. We were close to Wayne Gill's house, so we just went sliding along in the rain. I grabbed a stick to help me along as I had injured my ankle a few months earlier and had my foot in a cast for a while. This was the farthest I had walked since I took the cast off.

Frank and I were last when we came to the famous log crossing on the way to La Cruz. The others went ahead on another trail as they didn't want to cross the log.

The log crossing.

We always used the log to cross the creek, but I knew that my weak foot would not allow it, so I decided the only way I was going to get across that slick, uphill log was by sitting and scooting across. In all, it took about a half hour to arrive at Wayne's house.

Nevertheless, we all arrived safely. Dino and Wayne had been waiting with the tractor at another place for us, so we had to send one of the Chimanes to tell them that we had arrived. Wayne had also gotten stung by a wasp. We both took an antihistamine, and that, along with my lack of sleep the night before, put me out for the day.

The mission plane came in that same day, and Dino flew to Cochabamba. From there he went to La Paz to try and get some guarantees that this nonsense would be settled down.

Really, it all boiled down to this: the Chimanes had their land, and the river merchants did not like it, so they wanted to strike back at Dino as a blow to the Chimanes.

Back in Horeb the other tribal groups marched through without incident. There were only three Chimanes among them; they had come from a different area that had no contact with our group. By this time, they were tired and hungry and wanted to flee. I think that they probably did so.

After the marchers went by, the Chimanes infiltrated the town and gathered information about the actions of the merchants. The river merchants wanted to have a demonstration; consequently, they sent messages out over the radio for days, but they couldn't get the people together to demonstrate against us.

The Chimanes were keeping an eye on things, and all was calm at Horeb. This was our first time as refugees, even if it was for less than a week. We were all okay and, once again, God faithfully took care of us. Praise Him!

Chapter 43

The Battle Continues On

Elaine Continues:

We finished another week of school. All the women and children had come back. I had floated in a canoe with them downriver to get here before school started. We had five more students than before we had left, and all were eager to study.

Still, the battle continued with more attacks on the radio against Dino. All the accusations were lies, such as we were shipping out planeloads of treasures from Bolivia and inciting the Indians.

The river merchants were pressuring the police to investigate an incident pertaining to the Chimanes burning some downed trees. After investigating the complaint, the police chief of San Borja called in the group of Chimanes from La Cruz. The Chimanes had been so angry about the merchants cutting down their trees that they burned them. That had caused an up roar in town because the merchants said the Chimanes burned 16,000 board feet of lumber. Chuck, the logger, went to La Cruz and measured the logs himself. He calculated that it was about 2,000 board feet that burned, and there were still a lot of good logs left. The Chimanes did not lie about the burning because they said the logs belonged to them. The merchants tried to get the Chimanes to say that Dino told them to burn the logs, but they would not comply.

The chief of police needed someone to be incarcerated for trial so the Chimane teacher, Dionicio, volunteered. The Chimanes did no wrong in burning the logs; they did not agree that anyone had the right to go on their land and cut down their trees. The Chimanes were told they only owned the standing trees, but once the trees were cut down, whoever cut the trees down owned them.

Dino returned Monday in the mission plane and said that the government was preparing a letter. They told him anyone that had worked over thirty years with an Indian tribe deserved the backing of the government, so we just waited for the river merchants' next move.

In the meantime, school went on. The Chimanes took over more of the work and were no longer so timid about facing problems. All of this increased their faith and ours.

September 1990:

The Case against the Chimanes

Things calmed down fairly well. The river merchants brought a lawyer over from Trinidad, hoping to do something bad against us and to do what they could to keep Dionicio, the Chimane school teacher, in jail. The lawyer talked to the judge, but she told him that they had no proof of anything against us; however, we had plenty of proof of libel and other things against them. The lawyer left, and since then we have not heard anything more against us.

But the wood-burning case against the Chimanes got bad. We sent a telegram to La Paz asking for help from the government. The government said not to worry because they were very pleased with our work, and they were working on things there, so we should have more patience.

In the meantime, we had to settle with the merchants or Dionicio would go to prison. The Chimanes finally promised to give the pirates, who stole the wood from them, 11,000 board feet of wood for the 2,000 feet that they had burned. The judge told them it was the only way to get the charges dropped against them.

A senator came to San Borja to celebrate his father's birthday. He talked to the Chimanes and wrote a letter denouncing the theft of their wood and the jailing of Dionicio, and the senator took it to Trinidad for them. I doubted that we had heard the end of the case, but since we did not know when help would arrive, we were satisfied that it was at last settled and the Indians involved were no longer being hunted.

During all of this, we lost a week's teaching time which the students wanted to make up. They were very interested in learning.

A Visit with Two Men from Israel

Two very interesting Jewish fellows from Israel who were touring South America came by. The Chimanes wanted the young men to write and translate in Hebrew for them.

Then the Jewish men wanted to know some Chimane words. We told them that, "you is me and me is you" in Chimane." They said that was as confusing as Hebrew. In Hebrew, she is he, he is who, and who is me. They went with one of the Chimanes to experience what life was like among the Indians.

Chapter 44

Land Grants Designated

September 29, 1990:

The marchers went back to their homes, and the newspapers were full of what the government had awarded the Indians. The government established a multi-ethnic area for the tribal groups, including the Chimanes, and even sent two timber companies out. In addition to that, the Tsimane' were given their own territory of a million acres.

The Chimanes were now owners of land in the multi-ethnic area set aside by the Bolivian government. The Chimanes had a plan showing the territories designated for them and for the other tribal groups, but the boundaries were not indicated. The government said that there was no money to measure the land, but Dino told them that the Chimanes would help. The government just had to get them a surveyor, and they would do the rest.

We were also trying hard to keep the Chimanes from a confrontation that would end in someone being killed over the timber issue. We needed a lot of prayer and wisdom in knowing how to help the Indians to proceed at this point. They had no capital, no skills at running power saws and sawmills, and they needed to know a lot of things fast. The Indians were told that all of the timber left in their area after the first of the year would belong to them.

The number of "power-saw people" reached epidemic proportions since everyone wanted to get in and take timber off of the land given to the Chimanes. When the area had been under contract to the big timber companies, they were big enough and tough enough to keep the pirates out. Now that the government had given this land to the Indians, who were known to be backward and timid, a tree slaughter was underway.

The Chimanes wanted this territory because it was where they had been living for generations. A lot of other people wanted the land, not because they wanted to live there, but because the mahogany was worth a lot of money. If the Chimanes wanted their land, they were going to have to face a lot of strong opposition. The other tribal groups had also been given land in the multi-ethnic area, but it was still undecided how to fairly divide the area and protect the primitive Chimane communities who lived there and had never been touched by civilization. They had powerful backing from a number of groups who each had their own reasons and purposes for wanting control of the territory.

In the eyes of man, the Chimanes were in a very weak position, but the efforts of many people praying and the knowledge that God is all powerful made the difference that others may not realize. The Chimanes had advanced a long way.

The timber companies had given the Chimanes money for permission to retrieve the cut logs that were left. With this money the Chimanes were able to be more active.

The government continued to reassure them that they were not forgotten and that they would make no settlement without the Chimanes present and their needs considered.

We were hoping that once this land issue was resolved, the Chimanes could settle their differences with the other tribal groups and go on from there. It was a matter of respecting each others' rights.

The other tribal groups even went to the extreme of accusing us of opposing them because we were Protestants and they were Catholics. They brought in the hierarchy of the Church to help them, and at that time, since there was no division between Church and State in Bolivia, the Catholics wielded great power in the government.

Because of their large support base, the other tribal groups felt that the Chimanes did not have a chance against them. A group from San Borja was formed to support the Chimanes. This group felt that the Chimanes would win because they had a genuine right to the area. This group included a judge, two lawyers, and presidents of several organizations in town, as well as a Catholic priest and the town's mayor.

The group was very beneficial to the Chimanes. When muscle was needed, the mayor, or someone like him, would get on the phone and tell the government what was going to happen if they didn't get down here to see to things; for example, all logging roads would be blocked. At one point the mayor told the government officials in La Paz that if they did not get down here, he would load up the Chimanes and take them to La Paz so everyone would know that they were getting a bad deal.

The town of San Borja was also concerned about the taxes from the sale of the mahogany. They wanted their share. The timber companies preferred to deal with the Chimanes because their claim was just and they were more reasonable to deal with.

Chapter 45

Three Thousand Chimanes Gathered

June 14, 1991:

The Minister of Agriculture, who was in charge of Indian affairs and forestry, notified us that he planned to come to Horeb in one week. They sent money to help feed the people because they wanted a thousand or more Chimanes to be present as visible proof that they did actually exist.

Minister Mauro Bertero and Chimane man with mat and small bow and arrows.

The Chimanes made a gift to him of a mat containing a minature bow and arrows. The arrows that they use for hunting would be a lot bigger. A set of Chimane arrows would consist of a bleeder arrow for large game, another for smaller game, an arrow for fish, and an arrow with a flat tip for birds. They depend on their skill with bow and arrows to feed their families. They also gave him some of their carrying bags, which have a unique weave; they do not have a cross-thread, and it always has a diamond-shape design.

The big day arrived. The minister, the archbishop, another priest from La Paz, a congressman, plus both newspaper and TV people came. Over three thousand Chimanes came, and that count did not include children under five years of age. The town officials and the Catholic priest from San Borja, who had represented the town organization that had formed to defend the Chimanes, also came.

The Chimanes presented the minister with gifts of their weaving, bows and arrows, and even the Chimane typical dress which he put on. They played their flutes and drums and did their typical dance, and he joined in.

The night before, we were up until midnight with a lawyer and two men from the forestry program preparing the written speeches that would be read by the Chimanes. We also prepared a legal document which we wanted the minister to sign if need be.

The document outlined two points: One, that the government would recognize the Tsimane´ Council as the only government of the Chimane Tribe, to which the government agreed; Two, the Chimanes would require a meeting here in San Borja to discuss how to fairly divide the multi-ethnic area to protect the primitive Chimane communities.

July 1991:

The Wood-Mizer Mill

The government temporarily put a halt to all logging operations. The one exception to this was the tribal groups in the area. We wrote a letter to the Wood-Mizer company, who had donated the sawmill, explaining that we needed to turn the sawmill over to the Chimanes. The government had told everyone else to cease and desist. Thousands of mahogany trees had been felled and only the best cuts taken out. There was a lot of lumber they could harvest from the limbs and logs remaining that would be a big help to their economy.

We quickly received a letter from the Wood-Mizer company saying, "We are pleased to see that the action you have taken is in the best interest of your Indian friends. We understand fully your problem with owning the sawmill, and we approve of your decision."

August 1991:

The Beginning of the Radio Ministry

We hosted a week-long course for fifteen students to learn to make and present radio programs. We hoped to put the good knowledge gained from this course into practice. Although the owner of the local radio station was not friendly with Christians and his equipment was small and weak and didn't reach the larger segment of the tribe, this was a start. We hoped that we could do a lot more in reaching these Indians by radio in the near future.

If it wasn't for that Gringo:

There was really a good spirit here in Horeb and such a willingness to work together. The Chimanes were learning to take responsibility, although there was so much to learn all at once, and it was pretty overwhelming for them at times. We had to be sensitive on how to help them without doing it for them.

Because of the nature of our work, Dino and I had been pretty much in the "line of fire" all these past months. Actually, God had been working in powerful ways for the Chimanes. People who didn't know God would say, "If it wasn't for that 'Gringo,' the Chimanes wouldn't be doing all these things." But we knew that it was all God's doing, and we gave Him the glory.

Frank and Soledad Kempf.

Frank and Soledad Kempf

Frank and Soledad were very dedicated to the work among the Chimanes. Frank did the farming and drove many of those needing treatment to and from the clinic, as well as taking food to those in the hospital in San Borja. He was a real encouragement to Dino and me, as was Soledad who tirelessly devoted herself to the clinic here in Horeb.

Frank Kempf writes:

"Soledad and I have been very busy with the sick people in the little clinic. There is lot of TB and whooping cough. In the last two months, two Indians have died, but eleven or twelve have returned home after receiving treatment.

We have a good start on our farm project. The bananas help to feed our milk cows. The pineapple and banana crop has been good this year. Our corn crop was small, but we managed to feed the chickens and ducks for six months without buying extra feed. We now have fifty chickens and one hundred twenty ducks. We have disposed of all of our grown ducks, except for a few layers and a flock of babies. Our goal is to place ducks, chickens, and milk goats with the Chimanes.

We are pleased that the Lord has blessed us abundantly. Please pray He will continue to bless our school and farm.

My brother, Dino, continues to work very hard to help save the Indians' land and timber, which a lot of profiteering people would like to take. We marvel each day at how great our Lord is and how He takes care of His own. It pleases us to serve Him and to be a part of the work here.

Elaine Continues:

Soledad had been practically carrying the clinic work by herself; Dino and I were tied up with other things; however, Soledad had done a good job, and Ernie had been right there to help wherever we needed him.

When Ernie left in September, we had a going-away meeting for him with the Chimanes and the staff. We sang a few of the favorite Chimane hymns and some hymns in Spanish. Different ones spoke, and Dino translated some in English, some in Spanish, and some in Chimane. It was a really good time and very meaningful for all of us. There were many tears as Ernie left the team; we knew we would miss him.

Len and Elsie Gill returned to La Cruz, and Bruce and Jan Johnson came back a few days later. It was so good to have our co-workers back."

Chapter 46

Dino, You Are Unwelcome Here!

December 1, 1991:

Some of the prominent Chimanes were unable to attend an international conference for indigenous leaders, so I was chosen by the Chimanes to accompany one of them. Sixteen different countries were represented.

When I saw a sign written in big red letters "Reject all foreign missionaries from working with tribal people," I knew it might get uncomfortable, but I was totally unprepared for what came next. A man unknown to me jumped up and made an accusation, "There is a foreign missionary here with the New Tribes Mission. His name is Dino Kempf. Brothers, he is a man who took dogs into the forest to capture and kill the Yuqui Indians. This is the man who for years has taken gold from Indian land and has become rich exploiting them."

Then another known agitator took the microphone, added to the accusations, and demanded that New Tribes Mission be expelled from Bolivia. People were gnashing their teeth, and I wondered if they would tear me apart. Then the moderator said, "Dino Kempf, leave this assembly immediately because for us you are unwelcome here." I left immediately on a truck. Jesus said that when this happens, we are to rejoice. *Matt 5:11-12 Blessed are ye, when men shall revile you, and persecute you, and shall say all manner of evil against you falsely, for my sake.***12** *Rejoice, and be exceeding glad: for great is your reward in heaven…* We are to jump for joy because our reward will be great in heaven. We witnessed God's Word fulfilled before our eyes, and we do thank Him for counting us worthy to suffer shame for His sake.

Early 1992:

Politics

The two major political parties in San Borja were A.D.N. and M.N.R., somewhat like our Republicans and Democrats. Up until this time, the A.D.N. had been in power and had been very helpful to the Chimanes, but now that was about to change.

Bolivia had a very interesting voting system. There were no primaries and any number of parties could run for office, meaning the votes would be split up between everyone that ran. Then the losers could give their votes to any party they chose, so it turned out the losers were the ones that elected the president or mayor or whoever was running.

The elections were held in December 1991, for the town officials, including the mayor of San Borja. Although the A.D.N. lost by twelve votes, it was still undecided who would be the mayor of San Borja because there was not a majority.

The senator from San Borja was with the A.D.N. party. He was angry at Felipe Hauser, the owner of a big timber company in San Borja, because the workers at his sawmill were not residents of San Borja. They had come from another area of Bolivia and had been contracted to work at the sawmill. They had voted for the opposing party, the M.N.R.

The senator went on local television and vowed to get Hauser's Timber Company out of the area and to give the concession to the local people, which included the ranchers and river merchants. With that promise, the local people grabbed their power saws and started an uncontrolled cutting of mahogany trees. This really upset the Chimanes. The standing mahogany trees were owned by the Chimanes, but the felled trees were owned by those who cut them down.

The Bolivian government passed a law to not give any new timber concessions until 1995. There was a clause that allowed the right for the Chimanes and other tribal people to go into a "joint venture" with someone who had capital and equipment. There were a lot of people wanting to make a deal with the Chimanes but, instead of the 50/50 deal that the venture called for, they offered to give the Indians 30% of the net profit while they took 70%.

Fifty of the Chimane school teachers and community leaders came to Horeb. As they talked, they decided against any deal. "No more slavery," they shouted. "We want to log our own timber."

When this statement was read in a gathering which included the local ranchers and river merchants, they were furious and stormed out of the meeting. They said, "We'll take the timber, one way or another."

They were trying to force an agreement that day as they feared that the M.N.R. party would soon be in power and would block the agreement.

The following day, thirty men with power saws, heavily armed with automatic rifles, crossed the river and went by motorcycle deep into Chimane territory. They ran off the two policemen positioned by the timber company working in that area and began to cut trees.

As you might guess, Dino was accused of being the one who would not let the Chimanes sign away their timber. The Chimanes had made their own decision, but he was the scapegoat.

One of the Chimane community leaders came in to denounce the cutting of trees in his community and complained that they had threatened to kill him if he didn´t let them cut the trees. We sent a fax to Human Rights and went to the police. That afternoon, three armed men came to the Tsimane' Council office, wanting them to retract the fax and say the man was lying. They took Chimane Chief Valerio with them and forced him to sign a retraction.

When the results of the election were decided, the A.D.N. won. They installed the mayor, and that very afternoon the town authorities called the Tsimane' Tribal Council in and told them to sign the timber contract by the end of March or else.

The Chimanes looked to us for support, but the big dilemma for us was that we were so tired that our nerves were shot because of the pressure of what was happening. We were torn in half. We wanted so badly to get away from it all; we needed a rest from being hated and threatened and insulted. On the other hand, so much was happening, and our presence was so vital, that we hardly saw how we could leave.

About this time, Dino started having some dizzy spells. The doctor from San Borja diagnosed it as an inner ear problem, and said he had to be in bed for a few days. A few months later, a MRI showed that Dino had suffered a stroke.

Chapter 47

Making Plans to Leave Bolivia

March, 1992:

On March 6th the Chimane-elected leaders met together with the Tsimane Council for their yearly meeting. This year the Chimanes would be able to handle issues and problems before them as they had been progressing very well at governing themselves.

We were making plans to leave Bolivia, but we were very concerned about what could happen to the property at Horeb if we were not there. The title to the land was in our name, and we were afraid other people might move in and take over the land or confiscate it when we left. We had to return home as Dino's declining health was becoming quite serious.

John Beuchner, who was a Peace Corp volunteer and a lawyer, drew up a document that stated a designated portion of the land, buildings, school, and other assets at Horeb were for the Chimanes only. This, we believed, was a safeguard to protect the Chimanes.

We made sure that the authorities in the town of San Borja would follow the agreement. They were actually impressed that we would write a document that put in safeguards and established ownership to the Chimanes. It also established what part of the land belonged to the Chimanes. The lawyer and the judge helped by instructing them on how to legalize the documents.

Dino's summation:

We could give you details of many more trials, problems, achievements, and victories, but our story is getting too long, and it still is not finished.

A lot has changed since two petite single ladies arrived in San Borja. That was in the early 1950s when there were not even roads into the area. People had to fly in and land on a dirt strip. From there the girls loaded up their supplies on an oxcart and headed to the river where they found someone to take them in a canoe up the Maniqui River. June Ferrel and Gladys Callaway lived with a Chimane family for a year studying the language and customs of the Chimanes. Wanda started a work in the village of San Borja that continues today.

The Chimanes have a custom that when a girl gets married, the pair lives with her parents in her village. Putting this into practice, Gladys married Gene Callaway, a single missionary, and took him to the tribe. Several years later, June did the same with another single missionary, Ken Ferrel.

In the years the Callaways were working in the field, Gene became fluent in the language, compiled a dictionary, made a grammar book, and started to translate the Bible. Having the language in writing was a big help to us who came later.

Elaine and I came into the Chimane work in 1957. Several years later Harold Rainey, a Canadian missionary who had already worked with two other tribes in Bolivia, came into the work. Once again the Lord used love to recruit another worker for the Chimane tribe. While on furlough, Harold met the one woman for whom he had been looking for over fifty years, Nora, a school teacher from Canada, and brought her back to the work. What a great old couple. They gave themselves to the work in an unreserved way until Harold's health failed at age 75, and they tearfully went back to Canada to continue with us in prayer.

Len and Elsie Gill, another couple who had worked a term in another tribe, came into the work. Len was the one about whom it had been said that he could not learn the language, but he did. Years of driving determination allowed him to learn and teach Chimane with clarity. He and Elsie were troopers. Their boat trips among the Chimane people were invaluable in the teaching of literacy and the Bible. They always took with them a young Chimane who wanted to teach, and by the time the trip was over, that young man would be preaching with authority and power.

Frank Kempf, my brother, came down years ago for a visit after retiring from a lumber company, and he stayed on to help us. Another person was brought into the work when Soledad, a Bolivian lady, became his wife. Since her arrival, she has been a dedicated worker in our medical clinic.

Wayne and Ruth Gill came into the work after being in the Trinitario work and translating the New Testament into that language. Because of their work, the Chimanes have the Word of God in their language in an accurate translation that speaks to their hearts. This talented couple has been invaluable to the growth of the Chimane church. We have many books to work with besides the Bible, such as health books, Spanish books, math books, etc., that allow us to teach the Chimanes in their native language.

Because of the Gills' dedication in producing the needed materials for the schools and the creation of the training center at Horeb, we were able to use literacy as a key to evangelizing the Chimane tribe. We reasoned that we could not develop church leaders unless we had God's Word written in the Chimane language.

Bruce and Jan Johnson came into the work in August, 1987. We were so grateful for their help while we were there, and they are still involved in the work after all these years.

From the beginning we faced strong opposition towards schools, and parents refused to send their children to study. We tried literacy classes in the villages for adults and children together. It took several years of living in leaf shacks, on beaches, and out of a dugout canoe before we finally got readers.

The Wycliffe Mission in Bolivia offered us a course for Indian school teachers. To begin with, Elaine and I accompanied two Chimanes to take the training. When we returned after three months, the two fellows, Dionicio and Luiz, set up schools in their communities and, because they were Chimanes, the parents sent their children.

We continued on from there even though the Wycliffe people left Bolivia in 1984. Wycliffe had an agreement with the government that the teachers who took the training would be certified. Even though the agreement was with Wycliffe, we continued to request the certificates, and the government continued to certify and pay the teachers.

A training center named Horeb was established. In addition to the schooling they received at Horeb, for the first time in their young lives, the Chimanes were freed from the tremendous pressure put on all to participate in the community drinking. The fellowship of other believers had a strong impact on their lives. One of the main reasons the students came to this course was that they wanted to learn more of God's Word. Many of the teachers and preachers have come out of this group.

In March of 1989, the Chimanes held their first elections and formed their first government. They had never had any form of visible government before this. They had lived in small family clans run by the older members of the clan. God, in His perfect timing, called us into the work and laid the schools on our hearts so that these people would be educated and able to defend themselves.

Their Eden was invaded a few years ago when big timber companies came in, making roads and removing the timber. Colonists from the highlands of Bolivia followed the roads and began taking the land where the Indians had always lived.

The Chimane leaders were the young ones who could read and write, and many were Christians. In 1990, the Bolivian government gave the Chimanes more than a million acres of land with its natural resources.

We count it a real privilege to have had a part in the job of teaching the Chimanes to teach others.

When we look upon those from the Chimane tribe dressed in white robes before God's throne, we will also gaze upon those faithful ones who prayed for the work for years as Jesus had taught all believers to do and their prayers moved the hand of God.

Over the years a host of helpers came to the work, some for a few weeks and some for months; they built schools and housing for the students, and they did plumbing, electrical, mechanical, and other needed work. Many individuals have stood with us for years. The Bible tells us:

John 4:36b "That both he that soweth and he that reapeth may rejoice together."

Horeb:

Deuteronomy 4:9-10 Only take heed to thyself, and keep thy soul diligently, lest thou forget the things which thine eyes have seen, and lest they depart from thy heart all the days of thy life: but teach them thy sons, and thy sons' sons; 10 Specially the day that thou stoodest before the LORD thy God in Horeb, when the LORD said unto me, Gather me the people together, and I will make them hear my words, that they may learn to fear me all the days that they shall live upon the earth, and that they may teach their children.

Horeb, San Borja in the late 1980s.

God gave us the vision of a center, and then He led us to a piece of land–two hundred twenty acres of bare grassland, surrounded by cattle ranches. The difference with this piece of land from the land around it was that God had chosen to bless it and use it to bless the Chimane people.

The day it was measured, the surveyor asked what the name of the land would be. One of our Bolivian friends said, "Horeb would be a good name." And that is what it was called.

"Horeb" was a name very significant to the people of Israel, and it is very significant to the Chimane people; it was the place where God revealed Himself to them.

What it became to the Chimanes was a place of blessing, where they found hope and help both for their physical and spiritual needs.

It was the one place in their world where they could come together without fear of witchcraft.

Horeb was a central meeting place never before seen in Chimane history. It was where the teachers were trained, and the Chimane children learned to read. At an early age, these children could read the translated Bible and come to Jesus Christ in saving faith. Today they are the leaders of the Chimane tribe. God's timing is always right. It took all those years for this generation to mature and be ready for what God had planned for them and us.

At Horeb the Chimanes united and formed a government, chose their leaders, and recognized that it was God Who did this for them. They gave thanks to Him for His blessings, and for them Horeb became the central part of Chimane Land.

June, 1992:

We leave Chimane Land
Elaine:

We had a tearful goodbye as we left Horeb. We flew out over the Andes Mountains in a small plane and attended the yearly missionary conference of New Tribes Mission at Tambo where our children had gone to school. Then we made the long overnight flight from Bolivia to Florida where we transferred to another flight, arriving in Kansas City around two in the afternoon. Our son, Ben, met us at the airport.

Dino was tired from the trip but that was not unusual; however, during the night he started vomiting and was in a bad way.

Since Dino was a Korean War veteran and there was a VA hospital not too far away, we decided to call and see if he could be seen there. We were told if he had his discharge papers and if it had the right number on it, he was eligible. I had brought a bunch of papers in my suitcase and among them were Dino's discharge papers, with the right number. Remember all those years ago when he was drafted and went to Korea? We didn't understand it back then, but now we do. They took excellent care of him and did multiple tests, including MRIs and CAT scans, which showed that he had had a stroke. It also showed that he had a previous stroke. We are thinking that when he was sick in January and they thought it was an inner ear infection, it was actually a mild stroke. When I think of all the traveling in the first six months of this year, all the days spent in La Paz in the high altitude, the airplane flights, the stress and strain, it is obvious that God was taking care of him through it all. We saw how God had gone before us and prepared us for this time.

Dino:

After arriving home, Elaine's mother gave us a house in Chehalis, Washington, for an inheritance. Because we were fluent in Spanish, we were able to earn a living as medical interpreters. God is so faithful.

We have experienced what the Bible talks about when it speaks of warfare. We have been on the front lines, and we have faced the enemy. The battle is still there, but we have come aside to heal our wounds and rest our souls, and hopefully return.

Chapter 48

The Work Continues but Not without Challenges

December, 1992:

The bilingual schools continue on in Chimane Land, but not without challenges. The bilingual teacher training session was held at Horeb. Bolivia officially supports bilingual education even to the extent of paying the bilingual teachers. However, on the local level the national school teachers see it as a threat to their control and jobs. This year a new school director in this area made an attempt to dismiss some Chimane teachers and replace them with national teachers who would teach exclusively in Spanish. The Lord used Len Gill and Serafin Henrich of the Horeb staff to thwart his intentions, but the battle continues on. The Chimanes have kept Tsimane' as their language, but some have learned Spanish which has helped them communicate with those outside.

The Promised Medical Clinic

As the Bolivian government had promised, the new medical clinic was built at Horeb, and they also supplied a doctor. Maria Rivero, a missionary nurse, was sent out by her church in Santa Cruz, Bolivia, to help in the clinic.

Horeb Medical Clinic.

January, 1993:

In the early days the only Chimane social life was drinking, but now the Chimanes were having a good time without getting drunk.

Bruce and Jan Johnson wrote:

On New Year's Day, we had a game day. We had wheelbarrow races, sack races, water balloon and egg tosses, bow and arrow shooting, and tug of war. The bow and arrow shooting was the highlight. We had them shoot small arrows at balloons on a board, and there was a prize behind each one. It was exciting to see them shoot, from the youngest all the way to the grandmother, Antonia.

Then the men had a contest shooting the big arrows into a target. That went real well, too. Then Bruce set up a water pail over a person's head. When they hit the target, the water emptied on the person's head. They really liked that one, too. It was a fun day, and everyone did a lot of laughing.

All the Chimane schools had a soccer ball, and soccer became an important part of their life. The Chimanes even had a champion soccer team, and the people of San Borja cheered them on. A few years ago, the government built them a big soccer stadium at Horeb.

Chapter 49

Chimane Politics, a Split in the Leadership

In March of 1993, the Chimanes had their elections. They elected Alejandro Cayuba as the chief of the Tsimane' Tribal Council and the former chief, Valerio Roca, would be going back to his village to teach school. The rest of the tribal council stayed the same for another year. The villages were well-represented. The tribal council made all of the arrangements for this and paid for all of the representatives' expenses.

Len and Elsie Gill give some of the details of the split in leadership:

The school teacher, Alejandro Cayuba, was voted in as the new chief of the tribe. They only allowed three names on the ballot: Valerio, Alejandro, and Juan Mayer. Juan received three votes, (he told his backers to vote for Alejandro), Valerio got eight votes, and Alejandro seventy-two votes.

Someone had been prompting the people on who to vote for, so they stopped the voting and started over again. Valerio refused to give up the office. His wife's relatives got real angry and left. Valerio called for another vote and got even less votes this time. He attempted to get the judge and the lawyer to side with him, but the only thing they could do was to say he could help Alejandro for a while.

About a week after the elections, Valerio went on television in San Borja and said the elections were a fraud and also said some bad things concerning Jorge Añez. The reporter afterwards asked some pointed questions about whether or not Valerio was in contact with the present Tsimane' council.

It is obvious that it is all political. A certain Bolivian man, who had been such a big help in the beginning when he was the president of the Civic Committee, was Valerio's big backer, and the old river merchants, who had continually caused trouble for the Chimanes, were using Valerio and his two brothers-in-law as pawns.

They have formed their own "Council," and Valerio was installed.

Things were in a panic here in Horeb, as someone told them that Valerio was coming by force to get the pickup truck and take over the center.

The newly elected Chief Alejandro and other key council men were in Cochabamba at a meeting. The Chimanes at Horeb hid the pickup in a grove of trees behind Len's house.

Later in the day, it was a blessing to see that Jorge Añez had returned earlier than expected, and he calmed everything down. He explained that the Tsimane' Council is independent from the government, and legally Valerio and his followers cannot control or remove it.

After that, the former mayor of San Borja spoke on television and said that an error had been made, and the troublemakers were generating divisions in the tribe. Instead of promoting unity of the tribe, they were going against the legally instituted leaders of the tribe.

Valerio and his followers had a meeting with the M.N.R. party people and, after the meeting, got the whole bunch drunk and took them home.

When they went by, Jorge Añez followed them in the Chimane's pickup and talked to the Chimanes. They had been sent home to convince the tribe to side with Valerio. Jorge talked to them directly and told them, among other things, that they never before had fought among themselves and that this was a trick of the Bolivian Nationals to divide them and to take pressure off of the Nationals.

If ever there seemed to be a clear division between those that want God's will and those that are against it, we have it now with the new "council" against the legally-instituted Tsimane' Council.

Jorge Añez announced that Valerio had sent a notice telling them to turn over all official papers to him. Jorge knew this was not legal and did not do it. He and others are going to Riberalta tomorrow to talk to Goni, the head of the M.N.R. political party about the situation. It ended up with Valerio being rejected by the Chimane people.

1994:

International Pressure to Change the Alphabet

A letter from Wayne Gill:

A group of the Chimane teachers, including Rosauro and Desi, went to the town of San Ignacio to attend some meetings about reforms in education. There was an international group putting pressure on the Indian tribes to use one alphabet for all the tribal groups. They were discussing making changes to the alphabets of the different tribal languages. Rosauro and Desi were against making any changes to the Chimane alphabet, even though all the other Chimane teachers were convinced to do so. They would be replacing many of the Chimane letters with a new orthography, which would mean that they would have to be taught to read all over again, and all the books would have to be replaced. The other teachers wouldn't listen to Rosauro and Desi.

I was obliquely invited to San Ignacio but knew how independent the Chimanes are and that I would just be a hindrance. I worried about it for days (that was not of the Lord), and the next day Jorge Añez asked Len to come out here to get me for a meeting with all the Chimane teachers.

The teachers asked for my input, and that was of the Lord! They had a chart of the new alphabet. After a few minutes of listening to them trying to explain the proposed changes, I asked permission to speak to them and took most of the hour explaining about the International Phonetic Alphabet, which the international group had followed in many of their choices. It can be used to write any language in the world, but it is not used for the final alphabet. For that you always should follow the national language.

I felt a little like the Apostle Paul defending myself as I told them how I had worked on languages all over South America and in Africa. I explained to them that the linguists could discuss it on the basis of the International Phonetic Alphabet. I showed that the "unification" of the alphabets was pointless as the Chimanes would never read Trinitario or Yura.

I showed how it would only benefit the linguists; it would not benefit the Chimanes at all. I asked Jorge how many readers there were, and he figured over a thousand. I asked if they would go back to school again, and everyone agreed that they would just stop reading instead.

Jorge immediately understood everything. I left, and they discussed it; the decision not to change was unanimous. Even Tomas, one of the first Chimane teachers, said in the meeting, "The Word of God is already written, and we can't change that."

The same afternoon, one of the teachers had a meeting here in La Cruz to present the new alphabet. Again, it was rejected. Adrian told me that the same thing about the Word of God was mentioned. One of the Chimanes was very outspoken about how that is not the way Chimane is written.

I am so thankful to the Lord for the way He did it. No big battle and no hold outs. He is so faithful, and to think of all the hours I wasted worrying about it!

I don't know what the next step is. The international group was supposed to return in a couple of weeks after presenting the new alphabet and obtaining the support of the tribe to change it. I don't know what will happen. I suggested that the Chimanes write a letter confirming the tribal decision not to accept the new alphabet. The one thing is that you cannot force anything against the will of tribal people, and that is a plus in this matter, but they will probably try some new way to get them to accept.

I remember how I worried about the Tsimane' Council being taken over by those evil men. Time after time, the battle was won only to have them attack again.

Horeb and the bilingual schools are the key battleground for the Chimane tribe. If they impede the teaching of literacy in Chimane to such an extent that the children do not learn to read, and if they are successful in purging all Christian influence (they call it western influence) from the schools, you can see what will happen.

Elaine writes:

I was sent a copy of the letter that the Chimanes sent to the group who wanted them to change their alphabet. I was so proud of them when I read what they had written in Spanish; they were students that had been in my Spanish classes. They stood firm even when they were told that they would not have help in getting other books printed if they didn't change their alphabet. They said, "No." And that means the same thing in both languages.

The following is translated from Spanish into English. I've entitled it:

"Thank You, but No Thank You."

To the responsible personnel of CIDOB, Santa Cruz

Distinguished Associate:

The goal of this letter is to greet you and wish you a lot of success in your daily labor. We are also appreciative of the sub-secretary of Ethnic Affairs who was here for a week to revise the alphabets.

We also sent some colleagues so that they could listen to the recommendations of the commission who came for this purpose. The interventions that were made in San Borja and San Ignacio were well understood by the Chimanes who participated.

When the commission returned, a meeting was called with the principal body of those in charge of education, the Great Tsimane' Council, the director of the Bilingual Nucleus Horeb, and the bilingual teachers. In this meeting the following was discussed:

We thanked the national and educational authorities who are prompting this labor to better the education in Bolivia.

The teachers would be facing the problem of changing the present alphabet that had been taught for thirty years. We will not change what we have previously taught and teach new signs and symbols that are unknown to us. That would mean starting completely over. We have more than thirty bilingual schools, Chimane-Spanish, with more than a thousand students in the primary level. In the next level, we will come close to having 1,500 students.

It is true that we do not have linguistic technicians, but we do have very good students that will continue to train themselves. We know that they depend on having the grammar and phonics in their own language with all the grammatical forms.

We have lots of printed material with our own syllables, and it is difficult to substitute or change what has already been written and edited.

The ethnic groups who do not yet have their own written language urgently need it, so it is all right for the ones in charge of revising the alphabets to do so for them, but the Chimane teachers already have their own methods and procedures for teaching their students in their own language along with their own phonics. In the schools and communities we teach in our own language, which is not a language that needs to be recovered. We do not need our alphabet or our writings to be changed.

With nothing more in particular, we thank you.

Chapter 50

Radio Ministry Starts Radio FM 105.5

A donation to buy radios for the Chimanes got Bruce Johnson started in the Radio Ministry

Bruce and Jan Johnson.

In 1991, we had a course at Horeb for training radio announcers and programmers. Adrian Roca was one of the students at the very beginning. He is very shy, but when he teaches or gets behind a microphone he is a powerful man of God. In 1993, we unofficially started broadcasting over the local radio station. We now have two Christian radio stations that broadcast God's Word daily. Many have heard the messages and come seeking to know more about God.

July 2004:

Horeb

Adrian Roca writes:

"This testimony is for you brothers who live across the sea. I am your brother, Adrian Roca Moye. I send this word for you. Even though I haven't seen you, we who believe in God are brothers together before God's face, because there is just one God, the One who lives in heaven and made this world and the heavens and everything we see.

Adrian Roca.

I continue working for God by making radio programs that teach God's Word so that our relatives (fellow tribal members) may continue hearing God's Word. I am very concerned for my own relatives, the Chimane people. I want them to really understand God's Word, so they will grow in God. I am also very concerned about those who are not yet believers, that they may also hear God's Word both by radio and in their meetings. Then if they repent, they can be saved. Therefore, I thank God for you because you have helped us by supplying the means to keep the Gospel on the radio."

Rosauro Plata is another of the men that lives at Horeb and is part of the team that is responsible for the radio station.

The following is a condensed version of a testimony written in Chimane by Rosauro Plata:

"One night eight years ago I came home after a church meeting. Suddenly a light shone up above, illuminating where I was. It was very bright, brighter than the sun. I was afraid; my heart stopped.

Afterward, I entered the house and said, 'Surely God's Spirit has appeared to me.' I had already accepted the Lord, but I wasn't strong. I was afraid when I preached. But then God chose me, and His Son gave me strength. He controlled me and gave me ideas how to tell God's Word.

Rosauro Plata, with his wife and two of his children.

When I saw the shining, I began to grow in the Lord. He chose me by His love and gave me the work of preaching. Because God had mercy on me, He sent to me His Spirit and gave me strength.

When I was young, I had no strength. I didn't know anything and had no wisdom because the devil and sin ruled me. But now Satan no longer rules me because I believe in Jesus Christ. It has been ten years now that I follow Him, and I continue preaching God's Word. I tell God's Word, more and more."

Wayne Gill writes:

From the beginning the Chimane people have never been taught to rely on or even to expect any type of subjective experience. They have been taught to rely on the Word as given in the Bible and not to depend on feelings.

Rosauro's life has been based on the Word. The Gospel of John in Chimane was sent down in our absence. When we arrived, I asked him if he had received a copy. He answered, "Yes, I've read it through three times." He remarked once, "God's Word is so sweet."

In the above testimony, you can recognize phrases right out of the Pauline epistles. The experience was not something Rosauro was seeking or expecting in any way. He has never preached this experience nor suggested that others seek something similar. I heard about it a few weeks ago when he casually mentioned it in a message, and I asked him to write it down for me. What did he see? I don't know. But it is a great encouragement to me that God is sovereign, and He can and obviously does put His hand on a person in a way I cannot understand.

Rosauro has to preach, for God's Word burns within him. He does not just get up and talk. He is gifted in using illustrations and in laying out Scripture systematically and clearly. A few days ago, I was visiting the Chimane training school and wanted to speak in the evening meeting. That was Rosauro's class, so he suggested I teach in the morning instead, although he later asked me to take five minutes in the evening so the women also could hear me.

The Chimanes are in charge of the radio and prepare the broadcasting and programing themselves.

These men broadcast Christian teaching several hours daily and take turns making trips to other villages to teach God's Word. The radio station here, FM 105.5, truly helps our brothers who live far away so that they can continue hearing God's Word.

Chimane radio crew: Sandalio, Adrian, and Rosauro.

God's Word printed in Chimane:

In October 1997, the completed New Testament and portions of the Old Testament were presented to the Chimane people. It is hard to imagine the amount of work it took for Wayne and the rest of the team to make this a reality. A good literacy program among the Chimanes resulted in excellent readers who are able to benefit from the Word of God in their language.

Jorge Añez, the Tsimane' Council leader who shared in the dedication of the Bible ceremony, said, "This Word is valuable to us. It is more valuable than the Bible in English or Spanish. The English Bible has no value for us. Neither does the Spanish Bible because we can only understand a little of those languages. But this Bible, written in Chimane, is very valuable to us."

The Chimane Scriptures

1:1 Tashche' jiquej itŝi'dyem' jedye', chat qui mu' Jen' jäm'tye ọij jac judyeya' mayedye'. 2 Jambi'dyem' jäm'

Genesis 1:1 in Chimane

Rosauro Plata said, "This is the work of many years… we need to take it and use it."

In a culture where appreciation is not usually shown, the Chimanes met together and praised God and thanked all those who had helped in the translation and made it all possible.

Wayne Gill died on June 7, 2006. Within the year, on April 25, 2007, Ruth Gill went to be with the Lord. After Wayne had died, Ruth always signed her letters, "Pressing on." Their legacy lives on.

Wayne and Ruth lived a life of service to God and to the Trinitario and Chimane people of Bolivia. Their dedication and hard work in translating the New Testament into two different languages and creating numerous other literacy materials left an awesome example to inspire future generations of missionaries.

Wayne and Ruth Gill Family.

Chapter 51

The Pioneers Meet Up Again!

July 2007:

We got a phone call that Dick Wyma, who was the Director of New Tribes Mission in Bolivia, was visiting his son who lived in Washington State. He wanted to get together with the retired missionaries who lived in the area, so we met at a restaurant in Olympia.

Dick Wyma and Dino.

June Ferrel.

Marge Day and Gladys Callaway.

These three women were among the group that day. Marge Day and Wanda Banman flew in the small plane that landed at the air-port of San Borja in 1950. Marge stayed a year with Wanda in San Borja and then left and worked in another tribal area for years. June Ferrel joined Wanda in 1951. A year later Wanda decided to stay in San Borja and work with the group of Spanish-speaking believers. In 1952, Gladys and June went to live among the Chimanes and learn their language. I'm so glad to have pictures of the pioneers that began the work in San Borja and the Chimanes. I regret that I don't have a picture of Wanda Banman.

Chapter 52

One Final Trip to Bolivia

August 2007

Elaine and Dino with one of the Chimane teachers, Miguel Hiza, and his family.

God blessed Elaine and me with one final trip to Bolivia. The biggest surprise was that my Chimane language turned on like a faucet, and I had no trouble speaking or understanding the language. We stayed with Len and Elsie Gill at Horeb. Daily the Chimane people, some walking many miles, came to see us.

When we arrived at the airport, there were a large number of Chimanes to greet us. It was so good to see them again after being gone for sixteen years.

Antonia

We were so glad to see Antonia. We have included part of her story in this book. She is a strong Christian, and she and her family have had a great influence on the work among the Chimanes.

Antonia and Dino.

Antonia probably was born in the 1930s when a high percentage of Chimane babies did not reach five years of age. Serious illness was thought to be caused by witchcraft, the rainbow, or other supernatural powers. But God had His hand on Antonia. When she was in her thirties, some foreigners came to her village attempting to learn her complicated language. As they learned, they spoke of an all-powerful God and His Son, Jesus, whom God sent to save the Chimane people. It was all very strange to her and extremely difficult for the older adults to grasp. But Antonia was interested, and, over a period of many years, she became convinced of the truth.

No one knows when she made the decision, but she does believe. The most impressive thing about Antonia, whose husband had been dead for many years, is the impact she has had on her family members.

The schools started by the missionaries did not exist when Antonia was growing up. She did not learn to read, but she learned to listen to the Word, and she learned to pray. She prayed for her extended family and has been a lighthouse to them.

It would be hard to overestimate her influence among the Chimane people, especially the women. Her grandson, Jorge Añez, accepted the Lord at an early age and became an exceptionally gifted teacher, both a school teacher and teacher of God's Word. He was one of the most important members of the Tsimane' Council.

Marina and Jorge Añez, Chief of the Tsimane' Tribal Council

The Tribal Council Declares a Holiday

The Chimanes said that they wanted to declare a "Dino Kempf Day" so they shut down the schools, killed two fatted calves and cow, and had a big fiesta.

I was thrilled at the way Jorge Añez, the chief, summed it up. He said, "We couldn't have done what we have done without the help of the missionaries. We are so grateful to them because we now have a clear vision. We know where we are going and how we are going to get there, and we are able to go on from here."

Dionicio, one of our first teachers, said with tears in his eyes, "If you hadn't come, we wouldn't know God."

This is a translation of the document presented to us. The original is framed and hanging on our wall.

DECLARATION of RECOGNITON

Mr. and Mrs. Bernard Dean Kempf and Elaine Keenan Kempf

IN CONSIDERATION: That the evangelical missionaries of North American nationality, Bernard Dean Kempf and his wife, Elaine Keenan Kempf, established themselves in San Borja in 1956, and in the year 1958, they came to the Chimanes with the finality of evangelizing the Chimanes, having excelled in the work of education and the formation and capacitating of Chimane bilingual teachers, creating educational units and consolidation of the Tsimane' writing with a definite alphabet, supporting a medical program and of defending the rights of the Chimane that have resulted in the formation of the Tsimane' government called the "Great Tsimane' Council" which is the maximum and only organization that legally represents the Indigenous Chimanes and the consolidation of the indigenous territories: The Indigenous Territory Chimane and Indigenous Territory Pilón Lajas.

THEREFORE: In merit and recognition of your outstanding and excellent work given in benefit to the Chimanes "The Great Tsimane' Council," in the use of its specific attributes confers the organic ordinance and its law, we declare the evangelical missionaries of North American nationality, Bernard Dean Kempf and his wife, Elaine Keenan Kempf, Teachers, Guides, Defenders, and Faithful to the indigenous Chimanes.

This document was given to us in the office of the Gran Consejo Tsimane' in the city of San Borja, Wednesday, the 19th day of September, 2007.

May God always help you in every way,
Yoshoropai Chätdye' Dino judyeya' Elena Chätidye'
(Thank you Relatives Dino and Elena)

Signed and sealed by the members of the Great Tsimane´ Council.

Back row: Lenna, James, Loren, Laura
Front row: Len and Elsie Gill, 50th, anniversary

Since then Len and Elsie Gill have retired and are back in the States living in Florida. Wayne and Ruth Gill are in Glory, along with Gene and Gladys Callaway, Harold and Nora Rainey, June Ferrel, and Dean's brother, Frank, who died and is buried in Bolivia. His wife, Soledad, is living close to us in Washington State.

Dan and Judy Burke, who had joined the Chimane work after we left, went to work in Mexico, and Bruce and Jan Johnson are back in the States, but the radio ministry continues on, and Bruce makes trips back and forth to help keep it going.

Chapter 53

The Test of Time

So the test of time has arrived. Will they continue on without the missionaries? The answer is, "Yes!" The work continues; Chimane teachers continue teaching the Chimane children, and even though the government says that no longer is religion to be taught in the schools, the Chimanes say, "We are Chimanes; we will teach what we believe."

The radio messages are still being broadcast with Chimanes preparing the programs and teaching the Word of God to the people scattered throughout the rain forest. The Chimane government is still functioning.

Dan and Judy Burke.

When the president of Bolivia asked what he could do for them, the President of the Tsimanes' said, "We want our missionaries back."

When Dan and Judy Burke went to visit the Chimanes, they were asked to come back to Bolivia to work with them again, so they moved back to Bolivia.

July 31, 2014

You can see by the jackets in the picture that the steaming tropics are not always steaming. When a south wind from the Antarctic blows in, there is a sudden drop in temperature, and it is cold.

Dan Burke meeting with the Chimane church elders.

Epilogue:

June, 2015

Bruce Johnson writes: "My last trip to Bolivia was to follow up on a new way of getting the teaching and audio out among the tribal people.

You probably realize cell phones are now in the hands of most tribal people. Many young people and older Chimanes have their own cell phones or borrow from someone who has one. Seeing how these devices are now readily available and other devices soon to follow like I-Pads and smart phones, we have begun to record the chronological teaching into video format for use on cell phones or flat-screen televisions.

These sessions are about ten-minutes long to start with and are put on a small memory card with a microchip that can be loaded on most electronic devices.

We are also working on redoing all the videos that we have used at Horeb for years on the Genesis Project, including the Jesus Film. All these films can then be reformatted for cell phones or other viewing devices.

I don't know how they can afford these devices as nothing has changed in their income. Somehow they get cell phones. The four Chimane fellows at the radio station are working on the project of the Audio Bible on microchip.

Adrian's son, Herman, is a huge help and does a great job teaching.

Adrian Roca and his son Herman.

Herman has graduated from high school and is fluent in Spanish. The lower grades of school are taught in Chimane, the upper grades are taught in Spanish, and the students are fluent in both Chimane and Spanish.

Soledad, Dino and I translated some discipleship lessons in the Spanish-spoken area of Bolivia where we lived using the local vocabulary. We sent it to Herman, and he translated it into Chimane for us.

Horeb is pretty much Chimane Land

The Chimanes have a huge indoor soccer court, a remodeled medical clinic, and, of course you know, they have 24/7 electricity. Lights are always on, and the radio station broadcasts day and night.

This report was written in 2015. Jorge Añez will be mayor of San Borja for another five years. Evo Morales, the president of Bolivia, has had at least three dinners in Len Gill's old house where Jorge Añez lives.

Dan and Judy Burke still visit communities and go to places like Ushve and Oromomo, which are so deep in the rain forest we could not reach them. The Word of God is getting spread by foot, airplane, radio, and now cell phones.

Every copy of the Chimane Bible that is in print is in the hands of the Chimane people, and Dan and Judy Burke are working on getting more printed. After all these years of teaching the people to read, we now need to provide Bibles for future generations so they may have their own copy of God's Word to read. Imagine what it would be like in our own country to be told, "There are no more Bibles in print, and we don't know when there will be."

Dino and Elaine at home in Washington State.

We are witnesses of the grace of God poured out on the Chimane people in God's time.

Dino finished his Journey
September 15, 2016

His heart was so tired that he went to sleep and his life ended and his spirit was set free.

Just before I left him that night, he looked at me and winked with a twinkle in his eye just like he did when we were young. I have that moment to remember. We had been married sixty-five years.

We had this book almost ready for publication, and Dino really wanted to see it in print, so our friend, Mike Neeley, and I finished the last bit that was needed.

Dino was in poor health for a number of years, but he never quit talking to people about the Lord. His last years were spent in Yelm, Washington, where he spent hours on the computer sharing his thoughts on his blog, "Dino's Devotions." He also continued working in the jail ministry. His friend, Jim Reynolds, would push him in his wheelchair with the tube from the oxygen tank in his nose to the church meeting room in the jail. He would sing with the prisoners and talk to them about our Lord Jesus Christ.

He wrote "The Butterfly Poem," and it is a good way to end the journey.

Elaine Kempf

The Butterfly Poem

Metamorphosis is a word that few can understand;
how butterflies evolve from worms that crawl upon the sand.
So different are the two of them that one would never know
the butterfly was once a worm 'cause it would never show.

A caterpillar has lots of legs; his body's long and hairy.
He's not too great to look upon; some say he's even scary.
A butterfly is beautiful to all both young and old,
but how he came to be this way is waiting to be told.

He hatched, he grew, and he did the things that all worms do;
too soon his body slowed, then quit 'cause he was surely through;
that is what we thought he was because a grey cocoon was spun,
held tightly by the webs of death; but new life had begun.

And metamorphosis, that word again, we can't quite understand;
for it's unseen to us what change comes o'er a seed, a worm, a man.
We cannot see with earthly eyes the change in man that's wrought;
but we can see the butterfly and lo… the answer that we sought.

Life on earth at best is short, beginning from a mother's womb;
growing, working, caring, laughter, ending at a lonely tomb.
But life beyond is in reverse; it's like us choosing winter first;
and life seems gone till warm spring comes and showy
flowers burst.

We feel peace, but sadness, too; no bitterness or blame.
We feel the loss, and loss it is; there is no better name;
and soon the same will be our lot, but joy will follow sorrow
when new life trades the place of old; 'twill be no sad tomorrow.

Our caterpillar minds on earth can't seem to understand
this metamorphosis process a loving God has planned;
but when quite like a butterfly we freely fly above...
the reason for the change we'll know... the answer is God's love.

In wisdom God has chosen to hide what lies beyond our sight,
but gives us clues along the way that shows the future's bright.
Reach out by faith, and trust in Him, the Comforter is nigh;
He will not fail, and should we doubt,

Behold the Butterfly.

Dino and Elaine Kempf

Post Script

One last note about our children who shared this journey with us; four of them have master degrees. Lori is a certified Spanish interpreter. Darrel was a pilot in the military. Dixie and Ben are both nurses. Randy works as a counselor with various indigenous tribal groups. He has authored two books, *Happiness Lost & Found* and *Thoughts of a Man*.

Appendix (A)

The James Washing Machine

James washing machines have been used by pioneer missionaries for years. Elaine had one in the 1950s, and Judy Burke was still using one when this picture was taken in 2007.

Judy Burke with James-brand washer

Appendix (B)

Themes of Chimane Culture

By Wayne Gill,
Latin American Consultant Coordinator,
New Tribes Mission.

Although anthropologists have written about the Chimane people, none have mentioned the hostile elements that make their world so dangerous to them. These are the most important things in their lives and yet are overlooked by anyone who superficially views their life.

They believe a rainbow can bewitch a person or place a foreign object in their body which can move around and cause pain. If it reaches the heart, the person will die. There are two defenses. The shaman can blow tobacco smoke and massage the area to remove the witchcraft, or it can be sucked out.

Marcelino, a Chimane boy of about eleven years of age, suddenly became ill. When they saw he was deteriorating, he was taken to the little hospital in San Borja. The doctors diagnosed his problem as meningitis and immediately began treatment with heavy doses of antibiotics. Because they had waited too long to seek help for the meningitis, the boy soon died.

For us there is no mystery about his death. For the Chimane, there is also no mystery. Only they look at it differently.

They believed the rainbow caused his death. It bewitched the boy. The rainbow is both a visible rainbow and a person that is usually invisible who is able to do harm to humans.

Appendix (C)

Reaching Scattered Alcoholics

by Wayne Gill
Latin American Consultant Coordinator
New Tribes Mission

Only those who have had exposure to alcoholism can begin to understand the power that this drug exerts over those under its influence. Some people are freed from its power almost immediately when they turn to Christ, but many continue to struggle with it for years. For most former alcoholics, the only solution is complete abstention from alcohol in any form. This makes planting a thriving church in a tribe that practices group drinking a very difficult matter. Let's look at some of the ramifications of church planting in such a society.

Drinking is not considered wrong in most of these societies. Though it causes many social and physical problems, the cultural hero or their god drinks, and this makes it acceptable for the people as well. Drinking usually starts with fun and laughter and all too often ends in fighting or even death. One of the nicest men where we live put out his brother's eye in a drunken fight. Suicide is common when under the influence of alcohol, and several people that we know of have died this way. Add the loss of material benefits by people who have so little and the health problems caused by it, and the cost of drinking is high. Yet they do not consider drinking as really bad. Often it is the way a boy proves he is a man. One of the most insidious things is that those who are drinking put extreme pressure to join on others who would choose not to drink.

While the people consider it acceptable, we missionaries consider it a terrible evil. It is such a visible sin; it is all too easy to put so much emphasis on the drinking problem that the tribal people see not drinking as a sign of a true believer. The danger is that the Gospel becomes a message of works: those that believe and do not drink are saved, and those who drink are not saved or have lost their salvation. Even where the Gospel has been clearly taught and the believers know that avoiding drinking has nothing to do with obtaining salvation, the drinking issue still seems to them to be a test of a true believer.

For years missionaries have preached the Gospel to the Chimane people. As a strategy was sought for reaching them, two barriers always came up: the problem of alcoholism and the fact they lived scattered throughout a large area. No one village was large enough to use as a base for a growing church. So we embarked on a different strategy.

Church planting efforts were continued at the largest settlement, La Cruz, but simultaneously a training center was established named Horeb. We had also hoped that the bilingual teachers, many who were Christians, would become the church planters out in the settlements. It soon became obvious this would not work. Some did attempt to preach the Gospel, but many did not. We decided it was more realistic to look at them as just teachers for making the tribe literate.

Horeb was set up as a school. Students would finish what the bilingual teachers could offer them in the settlements, and then, if interested in further study, they could come to Horeb. The courses were of short duration, six to eight weeks long. One problem of long-term training is that the tribal people are often not willing to return to the simple life they had before. We wanted to avoid this problem, so we set up the Horeb courses to be short enough so that the students would not be separated from their culture for long periods of time. The students received two hours a day of Bible taught chronologically. This has had a tremendous impact on their lives. In addition to the schooling they received at Horeb, there were other advantages. During the weeks they were at Horeb, for the first time in their young lives, the Chimane were freed from the tremendous pressure put on all to participate in drinking. Though we were not naïve enough to think that all are able to resist after returning home, it does allow them to live for a period of time without alcohol and to see that it is possible. The fellowship of other believers had a strong impact on their lives, too. I believe that few of the Chimane believers who are walking with the Lord would have been able to break away from the drinking without the time away from the pressure and especially without the teaching of the Word that they have received at Horeb. The primary interest of most of the students is the Word of God. We do not suggest to them that we are training preachers, yet after several sessions, those who are faithful men return to their communities and share what they have learned.

Appendix (D)

Article from Bolivian Newspaper

Riberalta, May 10th, 1987: (translated from Spanish)

A letter published here in Bolivia against missionaries working in the tribes, mainly Wycliffe, New Tribes Mission, and the Swiss Mission.

"This is an open letter for public opinion and is designed and written with the purpose of removing the missionaries who are working in the various tribes located in the tropical Amazon areas in Bolivia, South America.

The participants, who are members of various Bolivian institutions in the IV Gathering of Solidarity with the Indigenous groups living in the Orient and Amazon regions of Bolivia, have come together in the city of Riberalta, Beni, to declare and denounce before the public opinion both national and international the intrusion of fundamental religious missions who have entered the indigenous communities, who are destroying the beliefs and culture of the people who live in the Bolivian Amazon. We give the following information and request the following:

Since 1955 when the Summer Institute of Linguistics, known as the Wycliffe Bible Translators, began their work in Bolivia they have caused a gradual ethnocide… ""We request the immediate expulsion of the New Tribes mission and the Evangelical Swiss mission… the government should organize a work commission, to go to the mentioned areas of the mentioned peoples groups… there should be norms for this work and the promotion of an investigation of all the institutes that work in the areas of the indigenous people referred to."

Appendix (E)

The following is a retraction from the same newspaper that printed the immediate expulsion of the New Tribes and Swiss mission from Bolivia dated October, 6, 1987 after the inspection was made.

EVANGELICAL MISSIONS COMPLETE AN EFFECTIVE LABOR AMONG THE TRIBES LIVING IN THE AMAZON

La Paz, the 5th of October, 1987: The New Tribes Mission and the Evangelical Swiss Mission are doing an effective work among the indigenous tribes who live in the Amazon, according to the information given by the inter-institutional inspection among the indigenous groups visited. This information was given to the Minister of Relationships to the Exterior, Guillermo Bedregal.

This commission, which is made up of representatives of the university, Ministry of Education, and the National Museum of Ethnography and Folklore, made an inspection trip the 9th of September to Riberalta for the purpose of determining the veracity of the grave denouncements by the political authorities of Beni over the charge of ethnocide and culture change among the tribes living in the Amazon, on the part of the religious sects afore mentioned.

According to the information given, both religious organizations are developing programs that are a benefit to the ethnic groups visited and are relatively completing the things that they promised to do... The commission recommended that they not have their agreements rescinded between them and the government and the evangelical missions but rather be reactivated, taking into account the following various decisive aspects, among which they should have in mind...

Appendix (F)

River Merchants Apologize

The following document written in Spanish and translated into English is the apology to Dino regarding accusations made against him…

A letter dated 15th of October, 1988, was sent to the local institutes, and broadcast, over the radio station "Radio Ballivian" and the television station "Borjana de Television" against the foreign citizen Sr. Dino Kempf.

It is right to clarify that all the concepts and accusations were senseless, expressed in the present letter against Sr. Kempf, and were the result of a moment of tactlessness and confusion, far from the truth.

At this date, having satisfactorily resolved in concordance of a definite agreement and in the presence of the local authorities, we amicably remove all of the charges against the person of Mr. Dino Kempf.

In accord to what has been expressed and desiring a peaceful coexistence, we greet you very sincerely.

Signed and sealed by The River Merchants: President, Secretary of Conflicts, and Secretary of Finances. San Borja 20th of January, 1989.

Habiendo sido difundida una carta en fecha 15/de Oct/1988, dirigida a las diferentes Instituciones locales y leída por los medios de difusión: Radio – emisora "Ballivian" y Canal tres "Borjana de Televisión, contra del ciudadano extranjero Sr. Dino Kempf.

Cabe aclarar que todos los conceptos y acusaciones sin sentido, vertidas en la presente carta contra el Sr. Kempf fueron el resultado de un momento de ligereza y ofuscación alejadas de la verdad.

A la fecha habiendo arreglado satisfactoriamente mediante acuerdo de transacción definitivo y en presencia de autoridades locales levantamos en forma amigable todos los cargos contra su persona del Sr. Dino Kempf.

Por todo lo expuesto, y deseando una pacífica convivencia, saludamos muy atentamente.

Appendix (G)

Chimane Authority Structure

A hierarchical structure was set up for the Chimane tribe. Pains were also taken to give Chimane names for the different positions to help make it less foreign to them.

1. The Guards *(jutactyi'* "sent ones"): There are two or three guards in each village. They are to support the town leaders.
2. The Town Leaders *(ji'cäts yu'tacsity,* "puts them correct, even"): There is one leader in each community. He is to settle the disputes and deal with minor crimes within the community. A major crime is referred to higher authorities.
3. The Zone Leaders *(muju'cha' ' cojcacsity* "greater caretakers") are to handle problems that the town leaders are unable to deal with or problems affecting the zone in contrast to a problem affecting one community. The Chimane communities along the Maniqui river and others in this area have been divided into eight zones *(cojcadye'* "caring for places"), each with a zone leader.
4. The Council (*tashche' bu'yity* "first positioned ones") is composed of three members and the President of the Council *(muju'cha' bu'yity ayo'* "greatest positioned chief.") They are to handle matters too difficult for the other leaders and matters affecting the tribe as a whole.
5. The Tribal Secretary, *(ji'chiqueyacsity* "teller, adviser) is to represent the tribe before the national authorities.

This will be a learning experience for the Chimane people. We have no illusions that this will solve all problems, but it is a start towards seeing them take responsibility for their own problems. This seems far from preaching the Gospel, but without a stable community, there can be no stable church.

Appendix (H)

Threats, Exploitation and Violence

Elaine writes:

In 2004, I made a trip to Bolivia to help in one of the teachers' training courses. While I was there, the Tsimane' Consejo presented me with an 856-page book to take to Dino. We translated the note that was written on the inside page and was signed and stamped with the Tsimane' seal.

"This book we give to you, Relative Dino and Mrs. Elena. We are truly thankful for the great help you gave us. We will not forget you. We will always be thankful to you and be thinking of you.

I, Jorge Añez, President of the Great Tsimane' Council, along with the names of the other members of the Council. Blessings on you, Relatives. We also pray to God for you.

San Borja, the 17th of September, 2004."

I translated the pages pertaining to the "Tsimane' Council" that are included in the book, and Dino was even mentioned in the account. Enciclopedia Beniana, Hugo Aguirre Ortiz, Trinidad – Beni-Bolivia, 2004 pg. 301

The Chimanes, in conjunction with the Mosetenes, make up an isolated social-linguistic group. The main marked difference between them is that the Catholic Church only was able to establish in 1804, a work among the Moseteno, but was unable to do the same with the Chimane along the Río Maniqui and surrounding areas.

It is very complicated to establish the ethnic history of the Chimanes, particularly in the colonial times. All who occupied this territory near the Andes were known as Chunchus. One of the first concrete references with the Chimanes comes from Father Armentia who indicates in 1905, that the Uchumanos or Chumanos, also called Ucumanos, are the actual Chimane race and language Mosetene …

In 1693, it is known, that the Jesuits established their Sixth Mission by the name of San Francisco de Borja, for the Churumane Indians, who resisted it being established, and that it resulted in the death of one of the priests, in this way demonstrating their opposition and resistance to civilization. Only in the decade of the 1950's was the Church able to establish a mission that still exists this day located in the region of Cara Cara, and then moved up the Maniqui River, with the name of Misión Fátima under the responsibility of the Congregación Redentorista. This effort was still not able to achieve the same intensity accomplished, also in the 1950's, by the evangelical group of New Tribes Mission represented by Dino Kempf.

New Tribes Mission was able to develop in two strategic areas. The first one in the Community of La Cruz along the Maniqui River, and the second three kilometers from San Borja identified as Horeb. The importance that the Chimanes themselves give to this Evangelical Mission is created from the objective experience in regards to the following facts:

a. For the first schools created by this Mission, the pastors learned the Chimane language and trained more than fifteen bilingual teachers, who work in the schools that were formed.
b. The most dramatic history of the life of the Chimane is the permanent threats, exploitation, and violence on the part of the river merchants (comerciantes) that enter the zone; they even eliminated a number of Chimanes without the local authorities doing anything about it. The ones that cared enough and committed themselves to the defense of this ethnic group were the missionaries of the Evangelical Mission, even achieving the imprisonment of a number of comerciantes. For this reason, the Chimanes were drawn to the mission in search of help.
c. Until the decade of the 1980s, the Chimanes lacked political organization or central authority which would be dedicated to their own internal problems and would also represent them in the local and national political context. That is why in 1989, with the help of the Evangelical Mission, the Gran Consejo Tsimane' was formed. This account was obtained from the "Centro de Investigación, Preservación y Promoción Cultural Tsimane."

Appendix (I)

Volunteers

Besides representing our mission in the United States, Dale and Edna Hamilton made a number of trips to Bolivia to help us. We will always be grateful for their years of service.

Edna and Dale Hamilton in the Vamti.

The Vamti was developed by a group that called themselves "A Cup of Cold Water." It was a little utility car for the farmers to use. They used the chassis of a VW car and powered it with a 15-horsepower Briggs & Stratton engine. On the back of the Vamti is a power takeoff where we would install different attachments, including a meat grinder for grinding different meats.

Several teams from the United States have formed and gone to Bolivia to build schools, housing, and install plumbing. Six men and one amazing woman with Hard Hats for Christ came and worked on the Quonset hut projects.

Greta Nelson of Longview, Washington, part of the Hard Hat team.

Gene and Eileen Gross, Lenna and Loren Gill, and Mark Morarie were part of the work at Horeb, as well as a number of New Tribes missionaries who came from time to time to help during the courses.

Barbara Symons and Becky Wallace came in 1987. Becky is a nurse and was on hand to help with any medical problems. Barbara helped with the office work, cooking, and taking care of the newly acquired goats. We want to thank the churches in Winlock and Centralia, Washington, for sponsoring these two very capable helpers. They have faced heat, bugs, and sickness, as well as being jammed in a house that is "Grand Central Station" for the Chimane Indians, and they were still cheerful.

Dorrie Wallace, a nurse, called us from California and told us that the Holy Spirit had told her to come down and help us in Bolivia, so we said, "If the Holy Spirit told you to, then come on down." She was a real blessing. She fit right in, and the people loved having her here.

We now have a good water well here. Harold and Jack, our Washington well drillers, really had a time of it, though. We were working with old equipment and hit sand that kept caving in and causing the bit to stick. Near the end of their stay, a casing was put in place, and we finally had an abundance of clear, good-tasting water.

We are grateful for Jack from Olympia, Washington, who brought us some lab equipment for our medical clinic so that we could do blood, stool, and urine tests here.

Vern and Mary Albright were busy repairing equipment that was long overdue for it. Mary was also a big help to Elaine, who had her foot in a cast while they were here.

We thank God for the San Borja Farm and Christian Training Center Board; it was such a vital part of the work. We thank the two treasurers of the board, Mary Albright and Greta Nelson, for their many years of service and dedication to keeping track of and reporting the state of the finances to the board. We greatly appreciate the board's faithfulness.

We would like to give a very special thank you to Pastor Ron Rice. Words fail us in being able to say what a tremendous encouragement he has been through the years. From the time he and his wife, Sharon, became involved in the work, they provided the momentum that was needed to move forward.

Truly, we give praise and thanks to God for each and every one of you that has been a part of reaching the Tsimane'.

I recently read a caption that said, "Few people are successful unless a lot of other people want them to be." Thank you so much for your prayers and financial help. And thank you to those who have come to Bolivia to allow the Chimane Indians the privilege of hearing the Good News of salvation.

CPSIA information can be obtained
at www.ICGtesting.com
Printed in the USA
FFOW02n1128070618
47081692-49482FF